Acting Locally

Concepts and Models

for Service-Learning

in **Environmental**

Studies

Harold Ward, volume editor

Edward Zlotkowski, series editor

Sty/us

STERLING, VIRGINIA
Originally published by AAHE

Acting Locally: Concepts and Models for Service-Learning in Environmental Studies
(AAHE's Series on Service-Learning in the Disciplines)
Harold Ward, *volume editor*
Edward Zlotkowski, *series editor*

Opinions expressed in this publication are the contributors' and do not necessarily represent those of the American Association for Higher Education or its members.

About This Publication

This volume is part of AAHE's Series on Service-Learning in the Disciplines. Copyright © 1999 American Association for Higher Education. Copyright 2006 © Stylus Publishing, LLC. All rights reserved. Printed in the United States of America. For information about additional copies of this publication or other AAHE or Stylus publications, contact:

Stylus Publishing, LLC.
22883 Quicksilver Drive
Sterling, VA 20166-2102
Tel.: 1-800-232-0223 / Fax: 703-661-1547
www.Styluspub.com

ISBN 1-56377-013-X
ISBN (18-vol. set) 1-56377-005-9

Memorial Note

One of the intended contributions to this volume does not appear due to the untimely death of its prospective author, on October 6, 1996, at age 39.

Julie Roque received her undergraduate degree in chemistry at the University of California, San Diego. She completed a master's in chemistry (with an environmental specialty) and a special doctorate in environmental risk policy, both from Brown University. She was a postdoctoral fellow at the University of North Carolina, and then joined the faculty of the School of Public Policy and Social Research at the University of California, Los Angeles as an assistant professor of urban planning. At UCLA she was a cofounder of the UCLA Pollution Prevention Education and Research Center, and served as associate director for research for the Lewis Center for Regional Policy Studies.

Julie took a leave of absence to work as a senior policy analyst in the Office of Science and Technology Policy in the White House during 1994-95. At a ceremony to plant a tree in Julie's memory in the White House garden, John Gibbons, the assistant to the president for science and technology, said:

> *Julie was an influential force in evaluating and devising policies related to regulatory reform, the impacts of toxic substances on human health and the environment, and risk assessment and management. She was an established leader in the field of environmental justice, and worked with experts in other federal departments and agencies to guide the Administration's policies in this important area of environmental policy.*

Julie Roque was a strong environmental advocate, and in her own work and in her teaching was a vigorous proponent of service-learning.

This volume is dedicated to her memory.

Contents

About This Series

by Edward Zlotkowski

The following volume, *Acting Locally: Concepts and Models for Service-Learning in Environmental Studies*, represents the ninth in a series of monographs on service-learning and academic disciplinary areas. Ever since the early 1990s, educators interested in reconnecting higher education not only with neighboring communities but also with the American tradition of education for service have recognized the critical importance of winning faculty support for this work. Faculty, however, tend to define themselves and their responsibilities largely in terms of the academic disciplines/disciplinary areas in which they have been trained. Hence, the logic of the present series.

The idea for this series first surfaced late in 1994 at a meeting convened by Campus Compact to explore the feasibility of developing a national network of service-learning educators. At that meeting, it quickly became clear that some of those assembled saw the primary value of such a network in its ability to provide concrete resources to faculty working in or wishing to explore service-learning. Out of that meeting there developed, under the auspices of Campus Compact, a new national group of educators called the Invisible College, and it was within the Invisible College that the monograph project was first conceived. Indeed, a review of both the editors and contributors responsible for many of the volumes in this series would reveal significant representation by faculty associated with the Invisible College.

If Campus Compact helped supply the initial financial backing and impulse for the Invisible College and for this series, it was the American Association for Higher Education (AAHE) that made completion of the project feasible. Thanks to its reputation for innovative work, AAHE was not only able to obtain the funding needed to support the project up through actual publication, it was also able to assist in attracting many of the teacher-scholars who participated as writers and editors.

Three individuals in particular deserve to be singled out for their contributions. Sandra Enos, former Campus Compact project director for Integrating Service With Academic Study, was shepherd to the Invisible College project. John Wallace, professor of philosophy at the University of Minnesota, was the driving force behind the creation of the Invisible College. Without his vision and faith in the possibility of such an undertaking, assembling the human resources needed for this series would have been very difficult. Third, AAHE's endorsement — and all that followed in its wake — was due largely to then AAHE vice president Lou Albert. Lou's enthusiasm for the monograph project and his determination to see it adequately supported were critical to its success. It is to Sandra, John, and Lou that the monograph series as a whole must be dedicated.

Another individual to whom the series owes a special note of thanks is Teresa E. Antonucci, who, as AAHE program manager for the Service-Learning Project, has helped facilitate much of the communication that has allowed the project to move forward.

The Rationale Behind the Series

A few words should be said at this point about the makeup of both the general series and the individual volumes. The present volume is the first not tied to a specific traditional discipline. As a field on which many disciplinary perspectives are routinely brought to bear, environmental studies may seem to provide an ideal example of the "natural fit" possible between community service and academic study. "Natural fit," however, has not been the determinant factor in deciding which disciplines/interdisciplinary areas the series should include. Far more important have been considerations related to the overall range of disciplines represented. Since experience has shown that there is probably no disciplinary area — from architecture to zoology — where service-learning cannot be fruitfully employed to strengthen students' abilities to become active learners as well as responsible citizens, a primary goal in putting the series together has been to demonstrate this fact. Thus, some rather natural choices for inclusion — disciplines such as anthropology, geography, and religious studies — have been passed over in favor of other, sometimes less obvious selections from the business disciplines and natural sciences as well as several important interdisciplinary areas. Should the present series of volumes prove useful and well received, we can then consider filling in the many gaps we have left this first time around.

If a concern for variety has helped shape the series as a whole, a concern for legitimacy has been central to the design of the individual volumes. To this end, each volume has been both written by and aimed primarily at academics working in a particular disciplinary/interdisciplinary area. Many individual volumes have, in fact, been produced with the encouragement and active support of relevant discipline-specific national societies. In the case of this Environmental Studies volume, I wish to acknowledge the encouragement lent to the undertaking by the North American Association for Environmental Education (NAAEE). Indeed, Peter Corcoran, a former NAAEE president, has generously provided a special afterword.

Furthermore, each volume has been designed to include its own appropriate theoretical, pedagogical, and bibliographical material. Especially with regard to theoretical and bibliographical material, this design has resulted in considerable variation both in quantity and in level of discourse. Thus, for example, a volume such as Accounting contains more introductory and less bibliographical material than does Composition — simply because there is less written on and less familiarity with service-learning in accounting. However, no volume is meant to provide an extended introduction to service-learning *as a generic concept*. For material of this nature, the reader is referred to such texts as Kendall's *Combining Service and Learning: A Resource Book for Community and Public Service* (NSIEE, 1990) and Jacoby's *Service-Learning in Higher Education* (Jossey-Bass, 1996).

I would like to conclude with a note of special thanks to Richard Wilke, dean of the School of Natural Resources at the University of Wisconsin-Stevens Point, for the feedback he provided on the manuscript.

March 1999

Introduction

Why Is Service-Learning So Pervasive in Environmental Studies Programs?

by Harold Ward

As the rich variety of experiences recounted in this volume demonstrates, service-learning is a common feature in a wide range of environmental studies programs. Faculty in community colleges, schools with religious affiliations, teaching colleges, and research universities include service-learning as a regular — often required — part of their environmental studies curriculum. In this chapter, I briefly categorize the types of service-learning described by the contributors to this volume and summarize the benefits these programs provide and the consequent natural fit between environmental studies (ES) and service-learning (SL). I then explore some of the challenges that ES/SL programs face, many of which arise from tensions between interdisciplinary, applied programs and traditional, more-theoretical/abstract disciplinary academic departments. Finally, I speculate on the future of ES/SL and how it might be made even brighter.

To assist the reader who has clearly defined interests — perhaps someone who is contemplating options for next semester's courses — I begin with a categorization/identification of the volume's chapters. Although all chapters are ultimately project-based, they differ considerably not only in the kinds of projects/courses on which they are based but also in the degree to which they explore broader ES/SL-related topics. Hence their titles, however thoughtful and intriguing, do not always provide a sufficient guide to their concerns.

In the table that follows, chapters are each denoted by institution and first author (the latter in italics), to allow the reader to identify relevant contexts more easily. In my subsequent discussion, I indicate pertinent institutions parenthetically, the codes consisting of the first letter(s) of the institution's name — e.g., Allegheny College (A) or Dickinson College (Di). Chapters are listed in the table in the order they appear in this volume.

In general, the arrangement of the chapters reflects a tri-partite grouping. Hornig, Firmage/Cole, and Ongley et al. not only share a common focus on the ES/SL course as "consulting company" (Hornig), they also attempt to draw from their experiences a variety of lessons and perspectives that will be of interest to anyone considering work in the ES/SL area. Fitch et al. and I also identify a variety of broad lessons, but our chapters revolve less around internal academic considerations and more around issues related to successful academy-community partnerships. Korfmacher's chapter is unique in its emphasis on junior faculty risks and rewards as they pertain to

Institution		Intro Course	Upper-Level Course	Internship	Consulting Model	Noncredit Experience	K-12 Partners	Thesis
					Relevant Context			
Dartmouth College (Da)	Hornig		X		X			
Colby College (C)	Firmage		X		X			
Bates College (Ba)	Ongley		X	X	X			
Loyola University of Chicago (L)	Fitch		X					
Brown University (Br)	Ward	X	X				X	X
Denison University (De)	Korfmacher	X	X					
Allegheny College (A)	Pallant		X		X			
Flathead Valley CC (FV)	Alexander	X		X			X	
Middlebury College (M)	Elder		X		X		X	
Univ of Pennsylvania (P)	Giegengack		X				X	
Univ of Redlands (R)	Jenks-Jay	X	X	X	X			X
St. Lawrence University (StL)	Exoo			X			X	
Univ of Vermont (V)	Hudspeth		X		X			
Univ of Michigan, Dearborn (UM)	Gelderloos			X		X	X	
Dickinson College (Di)	Wilderman					X		
John Carroll University (JC)	Diffenderfer					X	X	

ES/SL involvement.

The next seven chapters, while clearly sharing many interests with the first six, tend to focus more exclusively on the particulars of the projects/programs/courses being discussed. Here the reader will find not only a range of course and program types but also a range of institutional settings — from the community college and the liberal arts college, to research and comprehensive universities. The last chapter in this grouping is again unique. Instead of a course description/analysis, Hudspeth provides — with introduction and commentary — the actual syllabus his students receive.

The final three chapters offer still more program variety, moving to models in which internship and cocurricular experiences play an especially important role. Gelderloos's chapter is not the only one to explore the ES/SL internship experience, but it is the only one to focus on this experience. In the cases of Wilderman and Diffenderfer, much of the work described actually takes place outside of the credit-bearing curriculum altogether.

Clearly, the dominant model described by contributors is an upper-level course, usually entirely devoted to a single environmental problem of concern to a local constituency. Students in these courses are often environmental studies majors who have taken prerequisite courses. This allows the choice of more-challenging service opportunities and increases the probability of a productive outcome. Sometimes the course is required for an environmental studies major (Br, De, M, V), but in other cases the course is elective and may include upper-level students from other majors (Da, P). Such courses seem to undergo a fairly rapid evolution as on-the-job training introduces the faculty to some of the special characteristics of ES/SL (L, C, Br, P, V).

Several of these upper-level courses explicitly follow a consulting-company model (Da), even to the point of including job descriptions for different tasks in the consulting "team" (C), or time lines, contracts, and budgets (R). The degree of active direction the faculty member gives varies widely, from a relatively laissez faire (Da) to "lead consultant" (A) or "project manager (Ba), with detailed preplanning of the path the course will take (C). While a model with such a preprofessional connotation might have been expected to attract criticism from traditionalists at liberal arts institutions, only one concern is reported (Ba). Perhaps careful attention to reflection and context has provided a protective shield from critics.

The next most frequently described type of course links college and university students with elementary, middle, and high school students in cooperative environmental education programs. Some of these take the elementary-secondary students out of their schools to a special environmental education site (UM), but most send college students into elementary-secondary classrooms to work with the teachers there (Br, FV, M). These experiences appear to be particularly popular with the college students, and seem to present lower risks than partnerships with community groups. Perhaps for these reasons, the schools' programs continue in similar patterns from year to year.

The aspect of this table most likely to surprise the reader familiar with general experiential education is that the internship, traditionally the mainstay of off-campus experiential learning, is not the most frequently mentioned category. Some programs require internships for the environmental studies degree (Ba, R, UM). At least in some cases, environmental internships are available, and some programs even have internship offices (A). Perhaps contributors chose to describe other models in part because internships are so familiar; but I suspect that it is also because linking learning to service is facilitated by keeping the students more closely connected to the faculty than is usual for internships.

Why Do We Do It? Who Benefits?

While the mission of higher education is traditionally considered to include research, teaching, and service, these are usually not accorded equal status. The balance between research and teaching shifts as a function of the character of the institution, with universities giving more weight to research and colleges to teaching. Rarely if ever is service given more than token acknowledgment. At Brown, for example, in accord with its self-description as a university-college, teaching and research are given equal weight in faculty merit reviews (45 percent each), leaving only 10 percent for service. However, some schools, at times because of a religious affiliation, have an explicit service mission (FV, JC, L), and service-learning on these campuses obviously has a different standing. In one case, service-learning is required (FV).

Although contributors are concerned that the effects on the community should be positive (C, L), the benefits of ES/SL emphasized in this volume are consistent with a much higher priority for teaching than for service. Since service-learning usually (always?) places greater and less-familiar demands on the faculty, that environmental studies faculty so commonly choose to include service-learning is strong testimony to their belief that it leads to better education. This is quite unlike the situation generally, in which "few faculty actually establish community connections or work with students to tie together classroom curricula with community content" (Davidson 1997:26).

While the contributions of service-learning do not appear to have been evaluated formally by the contributors (R), there is a strong shared belief in the additional benefits available through service-learning. Reported benefits to students range from integration of disciplinary information to the satisfaction and motivation that come from helping others.

Integration and Validation

Devising appropriate responses to environmental problems is generally acknowledged to require skills, knowledge, and modes of analysis drawn from disciplines ranging across the academic spectrum (Kormondy and Corcoran 1997: 11). Most environmental studies programs lack the resources to teach all of the necessary information in an integrated fashion, and instead must rely on courses taught by disciplinary faculty from other departments — courses usually designed to serve those disciplines' own majors, for whom interdisciplinary understanding is not a priority and may even be seen as a distraction.[1] An ES/SL experience can bring this segregated material together (C, Da). At the same time, it can help students identify gaps in their background, and thus assist them in course selection. Often after an ES/SL experience students are more willing to undertake the challenge of courses they avoided before because of intimidating reputations (e.g., chemistry, economics) (Di). In many programs, the ES/SL experience, usually in a senior seminar or a thesis, is a device to integrate the entire major as a "capstone" experience (C, Da, De, M, R, V).

Cooperation

Most classroom higher education is a solitary experience for students, with the emphasis on individual performance in response to exams and assignments. It provides no experience in group problem solving, and instead often leads to competition. In contrast, ES/SL commonly relies, like most professional environmental work, on the shared expertise of groups to provide a broader range of skills and knowledge. The team spirit resulting from these efforts is thought to build a sense of unity in the majors. Some programs work explicitly with students on group-process skills (Da).

Some of the ES/SL examples in this volume involve partnerships between students and community groups or government agencies (Br, R). When these are successful (by no means every case), they can lead to an even broader sense of cooperation. The sensitivity necessary to work with individuals and groups with different goals, skills, priorities, and resources can greatly ease a graduate's entry into the environmental workplace. External contacts are also a source of education in their own right (C), giving a perspective that the supervising faculty might not have. Indeed, ES/SL projects are thought by some to work better when the topics are suggested by community groups or agencies (C, Da), although generally faculty control the choice of topics. Sometimes the cooperating "agency" is another part of the college or university. Four schools have created very successful recycling programs in this way, based on planning work done by students (Br, Da, FV, M).

Confidence, Satisfaction, Motivation

To students, a challenging ES/SL problem may at the beginning appear out of their reach. After all, if environmental specialists have not yet attended to the problem, how can less-experienced students be expected to make any headway on it? When an ES/SL problem yields to the efforts of a class, students' sense that their efforts can make a real difference gets a boost (C, Da, Di, FV, M, R). That their work does more than provide a means of evaluation, and can be of real assistance to others, can be a significant motivator and can provide an incentive to continue with environmental work after graduation. Although the contributors to this volume do not mention it specifically, I suspect that this gratification of beneficial service might also motivate them, in addition to the satisfaction that their teaching has been more successful because of service-learning. Thus, while the primary goal of ES/SL may be an enriched learning experience, the satisfaction of having helped others is not an incidental component of that experience.

Sense of Place

Most of the schools represented in the volume draw the majority of their students from some distance, so these students typically have a very limited sense of the community in which they are spending four years. Unfortunately, many of these students see no reason to become acquainted with their host communities. Service-learning can take such students out of their academic shelter and help them begin to develop a sense of place — something that is particularly important for developing the stewardship needed to protect environmental quality (JC).

Communication

Naturally enough, when a class have done something relevant that they are proud of, they want to talk about it. A shared feature of many of the ES/SL experiences is some kind of public forum in which the students present their work to an interested community (C, Da, R). This practice in presentation has an obvious value, and is all too rare in standard classroom education.

An Effective Combination

When environmental studies graduates can demonstrate the ability to work in groups and to integrate material across disciplines, are confident of their ability to solve environmental problems and are motivated to do so, and can clearly explain the work they have done, they have clear advantages in competition for entry-level positions with otherwise comparable students who lack service-learning experience (L). Some students find employment with the organization or agency with which they have worked on a service-learning project, or follow leads provided by contacts in the group (Di, R, Br).

Faculty Benefits

Some of these same types of benefits are mentioned by contributors or can be discerned as accruing to faculty. The excitement of motivated students leads to more-engaged teachers. Connections made outside the campus during a service-learning experience lead to a broadened sense of possibility (A) and also open access to information otherwise not available (C). These positive experiences have led some faculty to recruit other faculty on their campus (FV) or at other schools (Da).

College Benefits

Town-gown tensions (off-campus students drive up rents, have noisy parties, don't follow local conventions; colleges don't pay property taxes, but benefit from local services) provide an incentive to administrations to demonstrate some direct paybacks to the host community. Obviously, a college or university has a very direct self-interest in improving the quality of its local environment (Harkavy and Puckett 1995). Some contributors are quite explicit about these motives (Ba); others recognize them in passing (L).

Community Benefits

Virtually all contributors report that community partners perceived benefits from the service-learning experience. This is most clearly evidenced by continued requests for assistance over the years (C, Da). The benefits are various — some programs provide higher-quality science than is usually available to citizen groups (C, Di, L, P); others serve as facilitators to bring groups and agencies together (R). Where the service-learning experience provides training to the community, the community may be empowered as a result (Di). When technical data are produced, faculty seem to accept the responsibility for quality control before data are released (Da, L, C). One contributor in particular is concerned with ethical issues that are raised by providing technical data to nontechnical community groups (L).

Challenges and Barriers to ES/SL

In their enthusiasm for the benefits of ES/SL work, only a few contributors to this volume discuss institutional barriers they encountered or additional costs they incurred (L, De). Although these deterrents vary among schools (some schools have an explicit public service priority — JC, L) and individuals, in my experience they can be significant and probably are a source of apprehension for those who contemplate adopting ES/SL strategies.

The Two-Master Conflict

The majority of environmental studies faculty hold a joint appointment in a traditional academic department. Often, tenure exclusively in the environmental studies program either is not possible or is available only if a relevant department is supportive. Annual reviews for merit salary increases generally involve evaluations by both academic units. Thus, in situations where the ES program and a cooperating department apply different criteria of excellence, the jointly appointed faculty member will at least feel the tension of this conflict, and may suffer from failure to satisfy both masters.

Excellence in interdisciplinary work may come from the skill of integration across fields — of selecting just the right tools from a number of disciplines to create a toolbox appropriate for the problem at hand. High achievement in a traditional academic field is more likely to result (to continue the analogy) from the development of very specialized tools specific to that discipline, and the use of these tools in a tightly focused manner that can be appreciated only by others trained in that discipline or, more usually, that subdiscipline. While ES/SL may reveal interesting insights into the nature of environmental problems, it is unlikely to advance the understanding of an individual discipline as effectively as would be the case if all the faculty member's energies had been devoted to work on problems or techniques relevant to that discipline alone.

An ES/SL project report typically (and appropriately) will be crafted to present information in a manner most likely to enable action on the environmental problem at hand. This is seldom in the same style that a traditional discipline uses. Such a report may, for example, be written as testimony for an administrative hearing or be a report written in a language appropriate for a community group. Both style and content will be unfamiliar to most academic disciplines, and may not be valued by them. At the end of an ES/SL course, a faculty member often must invest additional individual effort to bring the product of the course into a truly useful form. Calculations must be checked and consistency between group reports achieved. Since the result is unlikely to appear in a refereed journal that is respected by a discipline, the work may not be valued by a cooperating department, or worse may be seen as a waste of time (Di). This concern is particularly vivid for junior faculty (De).

These challenges apply generally to interdisciplinary work in an academic world where the power still largely resides with traditional departments, as well as to ES/SL activities. One obvious approach, to create an independent department, center, or institute with tenure capability, can be effective;

but the option is not available to many, and may not be a full solution, since a college-wide tenure committee might still apply traditional criteria. Such an approach may also reduce any influence a more interdepartmental effort might have to encourage cooperation from traditional departments. The key to any enduring resolution of these tensions is *respect* — which must flow in both directions, but particularly must be shown by the usually more powerful departments for the interdisciplinary activity. I know of no universal formula for gaining respect, but have noticed that the process can be aided by tactful support from the college or university administration.

Uneasy Partnerships

Most ES/SL programs focus on issues of relevance to the local community, although one international service project is discussed (Ba). Some assist local schools in environmental education programs (JC, M, FV, Br); others work with government agencies (R, FV); and still others with community groups (L, C, Br). The schedules and priorities of these partners are rarely exactly congruent with those of the college or university, and adjustments must be made. For a challenging SL project to be completed in one semester, it must accelerate quickly and maintain a fast pace to the end (A). Some programs achieve this by careful advance planning (C); others by keeping in-house control of the pacing of the enterprise (A, L, P).

Projects in which a grass-roots group is a necessary partner can be particularly problematic (Br) because the partner may not be able to deliver according to a negotiated schedule or may shift its priorities midstream. Furthermore, successful partnerships that prove the value of the service that students can provide (usually at no cost to the partner) naturally will lead to requests for further service. These may be difficult to accommodate, since service-learning courses often change topics each year. Continuity in an environmental education program is somewhat easier, because of the congruence of school schedules, and some programs (JC, UM, Br) have continued similar education partnerships for a number of years. Making the limitations of continuity clear to prospective partners at the outset is prudent.

More Work for the Weary

For reasons already noted, ES/SL generally asks more of a faculty member than does a traditional class (De, R). Some schools have provided assistance through creation of service-learning centers (Ba, Br, De, JC, P, R, StL). Service-learning courses also can require more time from students (C, R, StL), perhaps to the detriment of other courses (L). Some administrations have indicated a willingness to take this extra effort into account in assigning teaching loads (A).

Reflection

The service-learning literature is replete with references to reflection. Indeed, "the most commonly accepted and used approach to facilitate the conceptual connections of service-learning is reflection" (Williams and Driscoll 1997:33). I found it striking that only one contributor made reflection a significant element in the service-learning course, and he is a director of a service-learning center, not an environmental studies faculty member (StL). This may in part be merely a matter of vocabulary — environmental studies faculty, having come to service-learning by natural evolution, are generally not well acquainted with the service-learning literature and have not adopted its vocabulary. However, I suspect that reflection might be more necessary when service-learning is added into a traditional course and making the connection between traditional education and service-learning is a greater challenge.

Student Evaluation

Since work is often done in groups, it may be difficult to evaluate the contribution of each student (V). Students who have worked hard resent receiving the same project grade as a classmate who has been less engaged and has made only minor contributions. Faculty have devised creative approaches to this problem (C, Da, M), usually involving both self- and peer evaluation.

The Future of ES/SL

The enthusiasm of the contributors to this volume makes clear the strong base of service-learning in a wide range of environmental studies programs. Most new environmental studies programs create some kind of "senior experience" — a seminar or a thesis — as soon as their resources allow, and often these experiences begin as or evolve to a service-learning focus. Programs that initially offered minors or certificates (C, Di, Da) have moved to majors, with expanded curricula that have more room for service-learning. As both the number of environmental studies programs and the number of students in these programs increase (Kormondy and Corcoran 1997; Martin 1997), service-learning opportunities seem likely also to grow.

There appears to be plenty of work for all these programs. While a growing majority of U.S. citizens profess to be environmentalists, their actions demonstrate a naïve understanding of the term. All too frequently these environmentalists are driving their bottles and newspapers to recycling centers in low-efficiency sports utility vehicles. As J. Robert Hunter's (1997) book title argues, "simple things won't save the Earth." Profound changes in values will be necessary if we are to avoid overtaxing the Earth's abilities to absorb our waste products — changes that are opposed by all sectors of the U.S. economy. Virtually all industrial and commercial sectors joined together to oppose U.S. subscription to a meaningful treaty to reduce carbon emissions as proposed in Kyoto in December 1997[2]; and while 65 percent of the public say they believe that greenhouse gas emissions should be reduced now, only 2 percent favor the gasoline taxes that will surely be required to achieve these reductions.[3]

Herman Daly (1996) has argued for a decade that this country needs to replace its definition of "progress" and "the good life" as the consumption of ever more material goods with more environmentally benign goals. Bowers warns that universities must abandon "classes [that] are based on cultural assumptions that have contributed to ecologically and culturally destructive practices in the past" (1997: 225). Similarly, Orr cautions that "education can equip people merely to be more effective vandals of the Earth" (1994: 5).

Those who would attempt this change face the extraordinarily challenging and perhaps dangerous task of turning a roaring economic engine in a radically new direction. Those who remember President Carter's attempts to raise energy conservation to the moral equivalent of war will also remember the political hazards of interfering with the apparently insatiable appetite of Americans to consume. Clearly, education with a firm sense of purpose will be required to assist in such a dramatic change. The message for ES/SL may be to favor programs that assist K-12 education, and to move away from nature education and recycling programs and toward more-basic issues of defining "the good life" in terms of a simpler life. As Brian Trelstad has said in explaining why the environment needs national service: "The process of building a constituency of young people who understand environmental problems at the community level may turn out to be more important than the scientific advancements that we also need to reverse our present and unsustainable course" (1997:220).

Notes

1. A fine example of a faculty member who takes a much broader view is given in the Loyola chapter, where a section on ethics was incorporated into an analytical chemistry course to help students engage more productively with issues raised by concerns that data they had produced would be used inappropriately by their citizen-group "client."

2. Advertisement, New York Times, September 28, 1997, p. 30, and www.climatefacts.org.

3. New York Times survey, conducted November 24-25, 1997, reported in New York Times, November 28, 1997, p. A36.

References

Bowers, C.A. (1997). *The Culture of Denial: Why the Environmental Movement Needs a Strategy for Reforming Universities and Public Schools.* Albany, NY: SUNY Press.

Daly, Herman. (1996). *Beyond Growth.* Boston, MA: Beacon Press.

Davidson, Sherwin L. (Spring 1997). "Divide and Flourish: Nurturing the Nucleus of Faculty Change." *Journal of Public Service and Outreach* 2: 26-32.

Harkavy, Ira, and John Puckett. (Summer 1995). "Lessons From Hull-House for the Contemporary Urban University." *Service* 1: 9-20.

Hunter, J. Robert. (1997). *Simple Things Won't Save the Earth.* Austin, TX: University of Texas.

Kormondy, Edward J., and Peter Blaze Corcoran. (1997). *Environmental Education: Academia's Response.* Troy, OH: North American Association for Environmental Education.

Martin, Paula J.S. (1997). "Report of a Survey of 17 Environmental Studies Programs." Unpublished report.

Orr, David. (1994). *Earth in Mind: On Education, Environment, and the Human Prospect.* Washington, DC: Island Press.

Trelstad, Brian R. (1997). "Why the Environment Needs National Service." *National Civic Review* 86: 219-225.

Williams, Dilafruz, and Amy Driscoll. (Spring 1997). "Connecting Curriculum Content With Community Service: Guidelines for Facilitating Student Reflection." *Journal of Public Service and Outreach* 2: 33-42.

An Undergraduate Course as a Consulting Company

by James F. Hornig

In the late 1960s, before invention of the environmental impact assessment mechanism, a faculty member at Dartmouth's Thayer School of Engineering was contacted by a lawyer employed by the State of Vermont to help evaluate the likely impact of a proposed nuclear power plant in Vermont. The lawyer and engineer found their collaboration as a small but very interdisciplinary team so productive and exciting that they conceived the idea of transferring the experience to the classroom. Using a convenient mechanism for introducing experimental courses, they offered a project-oriented seminar course that explored the environmental impact of and the public policy issues raised by the proposal for Vermont's first nuclear power plant.

As it happened, other faculty and students were at the same time discussing the need for an environmental curriculum at Dartmouth College. Quickly they recognized in this seminar a model of what the environmental curriculum needed if it were to include a course in which the class as a whole could be given the responsibility to (1) analyze some community environmental problem, (2) identify policy options, and (3) make specific recommendations. When the Environmental Studies program was officially launched at Dartmouth a year later, in 1970, that course emerged as the program's capstone experience. It has maintained that role for nearly 30 years.

Over these three decades, the course has been taught by a variety of instructors, with many variations in technique and format. In this chapter, I reconstruct the experiences of that history and identify some of the teaching and learning principles — good as well as bad — as reported by the six instructors who have been responsible for most of those 30-odd course offerings.

Course Design

Students know the course as ES 50, and in the college course catalog it is listed as follows:

Environmental Studies 50:
Environmental Problem Analysis And Policy Formulation
Students working together in groups will formulate and justify policy measures that they think would be appropriate to deal with a local environmental problem. The purposes of this coordinating course are to (1)

give students an opportunity to see how the disciplinary knowledge acquired in their various courses and departmental major programs can be integrated in a synthetic manner; (2) provide a forum for an in-depth evaluation of a significant environmental policy problem; and (3) give students the experience of working as a project team toward the solution of a real-world problem. Considerable fieldwork may be involved, and the final examination will consist of a public presentation and defense of student-generated policy recommendations.

Although it has never been explicitly described in such terms, the course could quite accurately be characterized as a community-oriented consulting service. Students take on a local environmental issue, analyze it, identify options for action, and make recommendations to the public and the client. The balance between analysis and policy recommendations depends on the nature of the project. Over the years, there have obviously been many, many variations in each of those steps. As I interviewed the instructors I found that some "innovations" had been tried more than once, and that no one had a sense that the course had always improved over this period — or, indeed, that it had improved at all. However, common themes did emerge as to what worked well and what worked less well.

We believe that students are uniquely motivated to learn by involvement in a real problem, and we also believe that by working together as teams they learn the importance of depending on the diverse skills of their colleagues. Most of the college experience is focused on the solitary pursuit of personal achievement, individual testing, and primary identification with a particular field of concentration. A culminating college experience such as the one described here, by contrast, emphasizes teamwork and group responsibility by working on a real problem of community interest whose analysis depends on skills from many disciplines.

Selecting a Course Topic

There is unanimous agreement among instructors that the best topics emerge when a community group solicits our help in a problem it has identified. This establishes a clear client-consultant relationship, and an unrivaled sense of reality, even urgency, for the students as they go about their analysis. At the first class meeting, the instructor might typically introduce the client, describe the problem, and tell the class that they are scheduled to give a public presentation of their results in the town hall at 8:00 pm in exactly nine weeks. A quick description of what must be accomplished before that deadline usually gets the students off to a fast start. The Dartmouth term is only 10-weeks long, so there is a sense of rushed compression, but students are responsible for only three courses at a time, so that 33 percent (and frequently much more) of the time of a group of perhaps two dozen talented and motivated college seniors for 10 weeks is a substantial resource.

A list of the topics selected over the more than two dozen offerings of the course is included at the end of this chapter. Several cases illustrate particularly effective student-client relationships. Norwich, Vermont, is a town even smaller than Hanover, New Hampshire, located immediately across the Connecticut River from Hanover, and home to many Dartmouth employees and some students. In the mid 1980s, Norwich decided to replace the town water supply, until then a surface reservoir, with a deep well. This decision was driven by problems related to the quality and quantity of the water supply. The problem the Norwich selectmen brought to the Environmental Studies faculty was what to do with the old reservoir. The fact that the dam holding the reservoir was showing structural problems requiring relatively prompt attention precluded the easy solution of doing nothing.

At the opening class session, students were told that they would be presenting their analysis and recommendations at a public meeting of the town and the selectmen in exactly nine weeks. The community need, the clearly defined focus of the problem, and the responsibilities attendant upon a scheduled presentation of results before an intensely interested and perhaps critical audience were immediately clear to the students and provided powerful motivation.

The Norwich dam case had another virtue in that it called on a variety of skills to reach a solution. The nature of the dam's structural problems was not really clear, nor were the costs of various repair options — obviously a problem for engineers and scientists to analyze. At the same time the selectmen had only anecdotal information about what kind of solution the townspeople would prefer. Options ranged from complete repair of the dam and creation of a lakeside park, to drainage of the reservoir and construction of a shopping mall. Identifying the town's preference was obviously a problem for students with social science skills.

A frequent client for ES 50 has been Dartmouth College itself. Perhaps the most successful experience with that client occurred in 1988. Actually the case began without a client, when the instructor decided independently to examine the management of solid waste at the college. The project was approached with some trepidation, because recycling was not yet a common or very popular idea and it is well known that facilities management offices generally do not (or, I should say, did not) welcome advice from students and faculty about how they should run their operations. However, serendipity intervened, because Dartmouth's facilities office had just hired a new employee, who was told that a major part of his responsibility was to look into the possibilities for more environmentally progressive operational policies at the college. He was not clear about where to begin, and he was equally apprehensive about the pitfalls of trying to tell faculty and students how to change their behavior. Some tentative inquiries by the instructor to the facilities office quickly identified the mutual interest, and the rest is history — one of the best long-term records in all of academia of effective cooperation between an academic department and an office responsible for managing physical facilities. As the students conducted their early-morning inventories of waste bins around the campus and began to develop a flow inventory of the campus, the "client" employee from Buildings & Grounds was on the telephone almost daily for the latest results. That particular offering of ES 50 led to establishment of Dartmouth's solid waste recycling program. Two of the students in the course were hired by the college for the summer after graduation to design and implement the program, and one was later hired by the Town of Hanover to begin design of a municipal recycling program.

Students themselves can become clients. Interested students used the ES 50 format to demonstrate the feasibility of starting an organic farm at the college, and then used the study to harangue and persuade all of the various administrative offices necessary for gaining support for the project.

Not all problems and not all clients have worked as well as these examples. Problems were judged less successful when they did not provide the multidisciplinary challenge of engaging the variety of student backgrounds in the class. For example, a survey of radon gas in area homes was designed to identify the scope of a possible problem. Due to its technical nature, the project did not engage the interests and skills of the more policy oriented students, who are, in fact, usually the majority in the class. The difficulty was probably exacerbated by the fact that there was not a well-defined client in this case — just the recognition that recent publicity had generated a concerned community "out there." We have also learned to avoid projects that are too bland, because data collection appears likely to be the primary task. The 1989 examination of energy use at Dartmouth, for example, revisited old territory and did not elicit student enthusiasm.

Fortunately, the absence of a client is not fatal. Indeed, it is far less crucial than the choice of topic. One of the all-time most successful offerings of the course did not have an obvious client. In the mid 1970s, an out-of-state company announced that it was interested in building a paper pulp mill somewhere along the upper Connecticut River Valley. Towns with high unemployment were soon offering incentives for the right to host the project, while other towns were devising strategies for keeping the mill out of their community. Many questions about likely impact were directed to various members of the Dartmouth faculty, who soon recognized that no one had a real idea of what the overall impact might be on a typical medium-sized New Hampshire or Vermont community. Developing such an impact analysis was selected as the class project. As it happened, the subject elicited great interest — and assistance — from a variety of faculty around the campus. One faculty member from the Tuck School of Business Administration accompanied several of the students to New York to analyze the nature of the company proposing the project. An engineer accompanied students to Canada to view the most modern pulp mill constructed by the company. The final oral presentation was recorded and was featured on public television. It gave a comprehensive picture of the likely impact on schools, roads, employment, and the environment, besides identifying the fact that the sponsoring company would relinquish all responsibility for operation once the project was built.

As the existence of the course has become known in the community, more and more potential clients have approached us with suggestions for projects. Not all proposals are acceptable. Generally, we have tried to steer away from projects in which conflict resolution, rather than analysis and the development of options, appeared likely to become the main theme. There have, for example, been community problems of expanding the local airport or of approving construction of a Wal-Mart store, which we elected not to take on. In both cases, analysis of options had already been extensive and had been publicly debated such that individual positions had solidified to the point where little could be added. The potential contribution of students (with marginal credentials as community residents) seemed minimal.[1]

Conduct of the Course

Although the faculty have always agreed that ES 50 should be a student-run course with the goal of teaching teamwork, self-organization, and cooperation, the level of faculty involvement has varied enormously over the years. At the hands-off extreme, the instructor might appear at the first class session, describe the problem and its background, make a few suggestions about organization, announce the schedule for the final report, then tell the students that they were on their own, with the instructor readily available, but only if help was requested. That approach takes courage on the part of the instructor, and a great deal of subtle observation and involvement. At the other extreme, some instructors have been present at all class meetings, offering suggestions and advice while attempting to give the students a free hand.

Within this range of teaching styles, several distinct instructional approaches have emerged. Outside experts are always needed to introduce the case, and frequently to provide advice during the analysis. The first outside briefing is usually by the client, if there is one, but often additional briefings follow by representatives of the concerned community, and frequently it becomes desirable to consult technical experts. It saves time if most of these briefings are arranged ahead of time by the instructor, so that they can be scheduled for one of the first class periods. On the other hand, having the class decide what advice is needed and to select and invite the experts has obvious pedagogical advantages, and it also frequently leads to the most productive longer-term relationship between the students and the consultants. Most instructors end up using some combination of these two approaches.

Faced with the prospect of a more or less student-directed course, students have an even more than usual concern about how grades will be assigned. To deal with this concern, Environmental Studies has adopted a fairly consistent procedure, which is presented at the first class meeting. The class is told that part of their lives after graduation will quite certainly involve the ability to assess and make judgments about the performance of their coworkers and to assess honestly their own performance. Therefore, they will be asked at the end of the course to submit both a self-evaluation and a detailed assessment of people with whom they have worked closely. Usually they are given a copy of the evaluation forms that will be used. Although not standardized in the department, these forms generally require students to submit judgments on all the students in their own subcommittee, as well as on others whose work has been visible to them. They are asked to make both qualitative and quantitative judgments in a number of categories, and to recommend a course grade for themselves and for the students they evaluate. It is made clear to them that the instructor will weigh these evaluations very heavily in determining a final grade, but that the ultimate responsibility for grade assignment still lies with the instructor. Should there be glaring differences between a consensus of the student recommendations and the faculty evaluation, the instructor will arrange additional individual interviews.

Generally, this grading system works fairly well, though both students and faculty find it a trying experience. Experienced faculty report that the most common problem is that student judgments of peers tend to extremes, leading to a bimodal distribution of A's and C's or even D's. Generally the rank order emerging from the student evaluations coincides quite well with the instructor's impressions, so that the instructor's main task becomes converting the rank-ordered list to an acceptable distribution emphasizing B's. As might be suspected, self-assessments are less useful than peer evaluations, since the former tend to cluster in the middle rather than at the extremes. It is probably modesty that leads some of the best students to understate their contribution, but it is interesting to speculate whether the overly optimistic self-assessment of the poorest students results from a calculated self-serving strategy or from a genuine deficiency in assessing their performance relative to their peers. To the extent that it is the latter, this may be a particularly useful part of the learning experience. Interestingly, some of the best performances each year are turned in by students whose overall academic performance has been undistinguished. Apparently the participation in the real-world problem-solving process of the course both motivates these students and draws on talents not so highly valued in conventional courses.

Perhaps the most important and most difficult organizational problem is helping the students organize themselves into appropriate teams and helping them to understand the nature of a cooperative team effort. In the early offerings of the course, this process was sometimes approached very explicitly. For several years, part of the first class period was used to play "the Tinker Toy game," in which small teams were each given a Tinker Toy set and told to compete in building the tallest tower possible. They were given only a very short time to organize themselves, plan strategies, and execute the plan. We have also experimented with inviting the assistance of professional consultants purportedly skilled in the dynamics of team behavior. One year a sociologist conducted an exercise in which half of the class analyzed the social dynamics of the other half, which was involved in a role-playing discussion of a difficult personnel problem within an organization. The observers noted how gender, position at the table, and other variables influenced the consensus-building process. Recent publications have described various team-building games and exercises.[2]

None of these devices has shown enough success to become institutionalized in the course, but all instructors do spend some time alerting students to the importance and difficulty of building an effective committee structure. Designing committee structure usually goes along with preliminary attempts to analyze the problem. In cases where the policy options seem fairly clear from the beginning, or emerge quickly, the teams may be constituted as individual special-interest teams. More commonly, however, policy options are not clear at the outset, and the teams are developed on the basis of natural needs of data gathering and analysis. Groups are warned that it will quite likely be appropriate to redefine the committee structure after the first week or so, as the problem analysis becomes clearer.

Most instructors agree with the importance of having an executive committee, whose function is to maintain an overall monitoring perspective on progress along the extremely tight time line. Depending on the closeness of the instructor's day-to-day participation in the course, the executive committee can also serve a liaison function of keeping the instructor informed about progress and potential problems, as well as serving as a conduit for transmitting the instructor's advice back to the group. An important role for the instructor, either directly or through the executive committee, is to identify and encourage natural leaders in the group, and sometimes to deal with the self-appointed leaders whose contribution is more disruptive than productive.

A very useful device has been midterm use of an abbreviated version of the final peer evaluation form. This is particularly useful in serving a warning, with documentation, to the small number of students who by design or accident imagine that their lack of contribution is going unnoticed. The peer evaluation system serves to deliver a very specific, high-impact message.

Perhaps the most consistent challenge for the instructor is to find ways of keeping the project on schedule. Compounding the all-too-common human failing of procrastination is the fact that in prior courses students have generally been able to bail themselves out with all-nighters before final exams or paper deadlines. In the group project, only a small part of the progress is under the students' own direct control. This proves as frustrating for the compulsive planners as for the procrastinators, and has threatened the productivity of otherwise cordial working groups. The answer, more easily prescribed than executed, is to persuade the group to set up a realistic time line early in the course when objective evaluation is still possible. Unfortunately, in our situation this problem is greatly exacerbated by the fact that this "capstone" course is most commonly taken during the spring term of the senior year. As can be imagined, this challenges the quality standards of the project not only by virtue of the distractions of spring and impending graduation but also by an occasional sharp deterioration of personal standards in even the most conscientious students. Almost invariably, the subgroups of students charged with writing the final report and those preparing the final public presentation do end up with a series of all-night sessions.

Some specific warnings about pitfalls related to the final synthesis are in order. In the worst case, the writing team receiving reports from the contributing committees past the due dates finds itself trying to assemble policy recommendations that are incomplete or even inconsistent. By default, the synthesis team becomes the policy team, often with very unfortunate consequences.

For better or worse, and somewhat contrary to the advertised theme of student responsibility for the conduct of the course, all faculty have assumed responsibility for ensuring the quality of the final product, and this presents difficult questions of when and how to monitor and to intervene. We have found no simple and satisfactory answer to this dilemma. One experienced instructor insists that the individual subgroups give detailed progress reports to the entire group on a prearranged schedule, and that the overall schedule include a specific time at which recommendations of the subgroups will be presented and voted upon by the entire class. This not only provides a focus for the synthesis process but also establishes a pre-deadline such that a little slippage can be tolerated without disastrous consequences. Despite such measures — and others — all-night sessions do seem to happen routinely as copy is prepared for the printer and the public presentation. All too often the instructor ends up in the office well after midnight reading, rejecting, and approving final copy.

Overall, instructors report that even though the course involves few lectures, it requires at least as much time as a lecture course, and also demands a completely different teaching technique. It takes a delicate touch to honor the philosophy of class independence and yet to intervene, as gently as possible, when it is necessary to avoid irrevocable blunders of organization or strategy. Because the course is such a central part of the curriculum, we try to rotate it as widely as possible among the department's faculty. Not surprisingly, there is wide variation in the comfort level faculty report in teaching the course.

The Faculty Perspective

It is clear from the nearly-30-year history of the course that it has established a valuable place in the curriculum. What is it about the course that is so consistently valued by the faculty? There are certainly many answers, but fundamentally they resemble faculty motivation for that very first offering focused on the proposed nuclear plant. The Environmental Studies curriculum exists because of an interest in the complex, applied problems of the environment and society that are seldom addressed directly in the traditional academic disciplines. This course uniquely addresses the processes that groups must use to solve such problems. Past instructors of the course identify various aspects of the process that they think important and relatively unique to this teaching format. They report that students:

• Learn to analyze a problem, and to ask the right questions. There is an incredible focus on the need to know, the need to get at the relevant facts by all means possible.

• Learn to work in teams, and to utilize strengths and skills of other people and at the same time learn to appreciate the complex social dynamics associated with group projects.

• Learn that defining goals and tasks and meeting deadlines in a team project are very different from their usual experience as independent students.

• Develop skills and learn to appreciate the importance of oral and written expression in persuading both teammates and the target audience.

• Learn to appreciate the importance of personal appearance and style, as they gather information by interviewing public and college officials and members of the business community.

• Return as alumni and report that this course has been of outstanding value as a transition to their professional activities after graduation.

Thus, although the course has taken on various forms over its 30-year history, it remains uncontested as a unifying experience that epitomizes, for both faculty and students, the core values of environmental studies in a liberal arts context. It is interesting that the Dartmouth faculty recently voted a change in the graduation requirements to stipulate that each major field of concentration must provide a senior-level "culminating experience." Been there, done that!

Notes

1. At one time we did offer an experimental course, following somewhat the same methodology as ES 50 though with substantial lecture component, in which conflict resolution *was* the advertised focus of the course. The topic selected was the large, proposed James Bay hydroelectric development plan in northern Quebec, which caused intense conflict among environmentalists, native peoples, and the provincial government. Despite the success of that special offering, competing priorities have so far precluded additional offerings of the course.

2. See, for example: Harrison Snow, (1992), *The Power of Team Building Using Ropes Techniques* (San Francisco, CA: Pfeiffer & Co); Steven L. Phillips and Robin L. Elledge, (1989), *The Team-Building Source Book* (San Francisco, CA: Pfeiffer & Co.); Dennis Meadows and Amy Seif, eds., (1996), *Creating High Performance Teams for Sustainable Development: 58 Initiatives* (Durham, NH: University of New Hampshire).

ES 50 Projects

A Nuclear Power Plant in the Connecticut River Valley

A Zoning Plan for the Town of Plainfield

Energy Management and Production at Dartmouth College

The Impact of a Pulp Mill on the Upper Valley Region

Farming, Forestry and the Future: A Study of the Connecticut River Valley in New Hampshire and Vermont

Stewardship of Dartmouth-Owned Lands

Growth in the Upper Valley: Dartmouth College and the Hitchcock Medical Center

Energy From Refuse: A Proposal for the Upper Valley

Salt as a Deicer: A Study of Costs and Benefits to the Upper Valley

The Hart Island Dam Project: Assessment and Recommendations

Toxic and Hazardous Substances in the Upper Valley

Charles Brown Brook Dam and Watershed Lands

Assessing Indoor Radon: A Case Study of the Hanover-Lebanon Area

Reduce, Recycle, and Educate: A Solid Waste Management Program for Dartmouth

Electricity Use at Dartmouth: Small-Scale Changes, Large-Scale Payoffs

Household and Small Quantity Generator Hazardous Waste in Vermont and New Hampshire: A Study of Integrated Waste Management

Household and Small Quantity Generator Hazardous Waste in Landfills: A Contamination Threat to Water Supplies in New Hampshire and Vermont?

Dartmouth Organics: A Proposal for the Dartmouth Organic Farm

Land Use Recommendations for Coos County, New Hampshire

Management of the Northern Forests: A State-Oriented Approach to Conservation

The Electric Vehicle in New Hampshire: Technology & Feasibility

Alternate Fuels: Analysis and Recommendations for Dartmouth College: The Upper Connecticut River Valley, and the State of New Hampshire

The Connecticut River Watershed: An Environmental Assessment

Sustainability at Dartmouth: Analysis of and Recommendations for Change on Campus

Toward Sustainability: Recommendations for Reducing Energy Use in Dartmouth Buildings

Saving Energy: An Analysis of Window and Lighting Efficiency at Dartmouth College

"I'd Like My Order To Go ... And Easy on the Packaging": Analysis and Recommendations for the Reduction of Food-Related Waste at Dartmouth College

Evaluating, Maximizing, and Maintaining the "Green Stream": Implementing the Hanover/Dartmouth Composting Facility

Planning for New Hampshire's Future: Recommendations for Sustaining the State's Forests

It's Not Easy Being Green: An Environmental Audit of Five New England Schools

Farming in the Upper Valley: Is It Sustainable?

The Challenges of Integrating Service-Learning in the Biology:Environmental Science Curriculum at Colby College

by David H. Firmage and F. Russell Cole

Over a number of years, we have developed a course that provides a capstone research experience for senior majors in our Biology:Environmental Science program and does so through the mechanism of service-learning. A service-learning course should both meet community needs and give the student an understanding of course content, a broader appreciation of the discipline, and an enhanced sense of civic responsibility (Bringle and Hatcher 1996). We believe our course fits this description very nicely.

The purpose of this chapter is to describe the nature of our Problems in Environmental Science course, to discuss the problems and pitfalls we faced in its evolution as a service-learning experience, and to present some of the solutions we have found to those problems and pitfalls. Additionally, we will describe ways in which service-learning concepts have helped us to accomplish our course goals.

Biology:Environmental Science is an interdisciplinary program that helps students acquire a strong background in biology with an emphasis on ecology and environmental science. The capstone course in this curriculum is the practicum Problems in Environmental Science. This required course was created when we initiated our biology/environmental science major in the fall of 1979. Our experience with service-learning has been gained through the evolution of this course rather than through the development of a new course specifically designed to provide a service-learning opportunity for our majors. We incorporated service-learning into the course as a technique to help us accomplish our goals and to add for our students relevancy to the research experience. Initially, the practicum consisted simply of a collection of independent research projects with no common theme other than being environmentally related. As the number of majors grew and our ability to supervise myriad and varied projects was taxed, we changed from that approach to one utilizing a group project with a common theme.

In 1980, the Problems in Environmental Science class investigated causes for the eutrophication of a nearby lake. The student report that resulted from this study stirred the interest of lakeshore owners and provided impetus among landowners to organize a lake association. Several years after our first lake project, one of us (Firmage) worked with an environmental consulting firm as part of a sabbatical leave. This experience and the background this provided led us to the idea that we could treat the Problems class as if it were itself a consulting firm. We believed that this approach would enable us to provide the course with more structure and better organization, but still encourage students to serve as the driving force behind project design, implementation, and write-up. We also sought to simulate a real-world context by "contracting" with the consulting firm to study the environmental problem we identified.

The studies conducted by students in this class quickly caught the attention of local community groups. Because the professional-quality reports the students generated included considerable useful data, we soon began to receive requests for our class to work on specific environmental projects. It was at this point that our Problems class really entered the realm of service-learning. As we learned more about the benefits and techniques of service-learning through discussions with colleagues at other institutions and through literature reviews, we discovered that our course met many of the criteria that others have set for service-learning programs. We believe that this outcome is testimony to the success of the service-learning process, and it demonstrates that the academic goals of a course can blend very effectively with those of service-learning.

Course Goals

The goals for Problems in Environmental Science evolved along with the course as we gained a better understanding of what could be accomplished by the students within the framework of a semester, as we developed more efficient and accurate methodologies, and as we discovered new possibilities in interacting with state and local agencies and offices. The current goals for this course include these:

- *To provide a research experience for students.* We wanted students to be very involved in the planning process and to work independently on some component of the project.

- *To apply knowledge learned in other courses to the study of a local environmental issue.* We expect students to apply their general background in ecology, experimental design, and data analysis to investigate the environmental issue assigned as the class project.

- *To become acquainted with a specific methodology related to the assigned project and typically used in the field of environmental science.* This course provides a means of expanding student exposure to field and laboratory techniques, as well as encouraging them to draw on knowledge gained in previous courses.

- *To enhance oral presentation skills.* We wanted to provide communication opportunities that stretch students beyond their typical coursework.

- *To become better acquainted with literature-searching strategies and typical sources of environmental data.* Beyond the standard bibliographic sources, students should be able to locate relevant technical reports and government documents published by federal, state, and local agencies/offices.

• *To enhance writing skills.* Students prepare and edit text, tables, and figures for the class report.

• *To understand some of the state and local regulations related to specific environmental issues and how these regulations are applied.* Students have little exposure to specific regulations and their implementation prior to this class.

• *To learn about the role and capabilities of state and local agencies and offices.* Students consult and work with people in offices and agencies such as the Planning Board, Code Enforcement Office, the Council of Governments, and the Department of Environmental Protection.

• *To gain perspectives on how consulting firms and government agencies function.* Students are provided with at least a glimpse of what such work is like, as they consider career opportunities. Students also learn the advantages and disadvantages of team research and the importance of group dynamics to the success or failure of a project.

• *To understand better the interactions of public and private landowners with groups attempting to address environmental issues.* This course is designed to enable students to interact with the public and observe interactions in public and private meetings to help them gain a broader understanding of the diversity of opinions on a particular issue.

Choice of Projects and Community Involvement

Several years ago, community leaders and local residents began to make requests of us to undertake projects of local interest. In addition to identifying possible projects for the class, the requests provided several pedagogical advantages. First, they heightened student interest in the projects by creating the realization that student work could have real application and effect in the local community. Many student learning experiences prior to this class taught concepts and methodologies without involving original work. By tackling a project requested by citizens in the local area, students know there will be people outside the college who will be eager to hear and read their report.

Over time, the Department of Environmental Protection (DEP) has developed confidence in our data-collection and data-analysis procedures, and it adds data our students obtain to the DEP databases. The acceptance by DEP has developed through our strict adherence to methodologies delineated by the state and the U.S. Environmental Protection Agency and by duplicate testing of our water quality samples in DEP laboratories. The DEP has suggested some projects for the class and works with us to provide background data. DEP personnel serve as resource consultants for the students. Responding to local requests has also meant that the students receive greater cooperation from local officials (e.g., town managers and selectmen, town office personnel, code enforcement officers, and plumbing inspectors). This good working relationship has developed because of a shared interest in projects and the pattern we have established of providing objective assessments based on empirical evidence. Such individuals have become tremendous resources for our students, because they can often explain procedures and regulations as well as specific implementation methods beyond an instructor's personal knowledge.

Our students also have won increased cooperation from interested residents, who have allowed them access to study sites and boat launches. The support of local lake associations and their leaders has been invaluable in developing this relationship.

Finally, student work on local environmental projects has generated greater interest in the final product on the part of both the college administration and the local press. Reporters frequently write articles describing class projects near the beginning of a semester and then go on to cover final presentations. This press coverage has enhanced student appreciation of the importance and relevance of their work; it has also motivated them to increase the quantity and quality of their work.

Our class has conducted a variety of research projects over the last 15 years. Projects have included a natural resource inventory of a National Natural Landmark, a site evaluation of a potential wildlife preserve, the design of a greenway trail for the town, evaluation of potential environmental impacts of a proposed gravel mining operation, several wasteload analyses of a local stream used for the outfall of a town sewage treatment plant, and numerous lake watershed studies. The last includes several investigations of the lake that provides drinking water for most of the local towns.

The service-learning component of the course appears in several forms. Because the chosen project has been requested locally, the entire focus of the students' work is on providing a service to others. Students work with groups such as town councils, clubs, private associations, town office personnel, regional and state agencies, and private landowners. The students provide a service to these groups and individuals, as well as learn from them. Almost every year, some students who complete our Problems in Environmental Science course continue specific or related aspects of their study by working directly with state or local agencies during the January miniterm or spring semester.

Course Components

As the last observation implies, Problems in Environmental Science is offered in the fall semester (but not in the spring, due to weather constraints). There are a four-hour laboratory session and two 75-minute or three 50-minute lecture/discussion periods per week.

We have developed a number of course components to accomplish our pedagogical goals, all of which we believe are important in order to make a course of this nature successful. Over the years, we have increased the effectiveness of these components by responding to problems we recognized and to suggestions made by students on course evaluations. The actual environmental problem investigated is different from year to year. In recent years, the course has investigated the impact of land-use patterns on lake water quality for several local watersheds, so in this chapter we will illustrate the importance of selected course components using a local watershed study.

Organization

Many of the necessary materials (e.g., various maps, overlays, aerial photographs, specific types of equipment) are gathered during the summer so that these critical resources will be available during the initial planning stage of the project at the start of the semester. Contact with resource people outside the college who are willing to work with the students is also typically made during the summer. Summer preparation is critically important and may be the single most important factor in determining the success of that year's project.

Study Area Orientation

Although the project and its location are chosen by the instructors, the students are asked to develop the project's specific work plan, so we have found it necessary to provide them with an initial overview of the study area and the issues to be investigated. During the first laboratory period, we take the class to the study area for a "reconnaissance." We provide U.S. Geological Survey topographic maps of the area, local road maps, and any vehicle or boat transportation needed. We begin with a brief orientation at sites that provide broad views of the lake and watershed areas, which we follow by a statement of the environmental problem and a description of possible contributing factors. After the orientation, the class is divided into small groups for an examination of the lake and watershed. Student groups travel over assigned portions of the watershed identifying and describing conditions to be explored in more depth (e.g., problems in erosion control, areas with a high density of development, industrial operations). They also label all fire roads to summer cottages and lakefront homes on maps provided and examine the lake shoreline from boats to identify potential problem areas, as well as locate significant tributaries for future sampling. These experiences help to make the project "real" rather than an abstract concept. Our next class period is devoted to discussing what they found and teaching them how to develop a work plan.

Writing the Work Plan

Students are asked to prepare a work plan (including a time schedule), detailing what they will do during the semester and how each component of the project is to be accomplished. The components of the work plan include the study objective, summary of relevant background data obtained, results of the reconnaissance, proposed study sites, and proposed field tests and measurements. The work plan document, once accepted, becomes their "contract" with us, as their clients. To save time, the work plan is written in outline form only. It is also orally presented to us during one of the lecture/discussion periods.

Visiting Lecturers

Early in the semester, we invite outside experts (e.g., from DEP, the Fish & Wildlife Service, the regional planning commission, local conservation groups, private companies) to speak to the class. These lectures provide relevant information and introduce students to people willing to serve as informational resources. The information and advice the students receive help them avoid pitfalls that others without prior experience would typically encounter. Students also learn that projects are often complex and involve multiple branches and levels of government. Some lecturers visit our class almost every year. The contacts made during these visits to our classroom and in our subsequent visits to agency offices can also be helpful to the students when they begin their job searches.

Techniques

This course is designed to incorporate a number of advanced techniques students may not have encountered in previous classes. Although these vary somewhat from year to year, they typically include the following:

• GIS (Geographic Information Systems) — mapping soil types, elevation, land use, slope, and drainage and using these to create other maps (e.g., septic suitability).

• Land-use mapping — designating areas by use type (e.g., agricultural, industrial, urban, grassland, forest type, roadway).

• Aerial photography — using photographs from state agencies, survey firms, and sometimes our own flyovers in constructing land-use maps and trends.

- Computer modeling — using models appropriate to the specific project. Our watershed studies utilize a phosphorus-loading model to obtain future loading projections based on specific growth assumptions.
- Water (including storm event) sampling.
- Water chemistry analysis using EPA standard methods.
- Map reading — interpreting and utilizing topographic, tax, road, soils, and wildlife maps.
- Road surveys — helping to refine a survey method developed for the state to determine the quality of dirt camp roads leading to shoreline areas and their potential for phosphorus loading into the lake.
- Searching local records for information on things such as buildings, septic systems, and lot sizes.
- Computer graphics — using figure production, drawing, and photo scanning and manipulation in producing the class report.

Job Assignments

Division of work responsibilities using job assignments is important and beneficial in three ways. First, job assignments help to identify and divide the work equitably among class members so that a sizable project can be completed. Second, they give the students defined responsibilities that are theirs alone and provide them with ownership of a portion of the project. Third, job assignments help the faculty to define the scope and evaluate the quality of each student's work with regard to a grade.

Assignments are made in the following way: Job descriptions are posted for assignments in two major areas: field/laboratory work (e.g., GIS supervisor, land-use analysis supervisor, chemical analysis supervisor) and report construction (e.g., table and graphics editor, science editor, preliminary and final draft editors). Students must apply for these, stating their reasons and qualifications. In fact, students list four choices in each area and rank them by interest. We then review these applications and "hire" each student for a job in each area. Most students receive their first choice, and only rarely does one not get his or her second choice. This procedure allows us not only to divide the workload but to do so based on each student's preferences, talents, and experiences. At times, we may initially not place students in jobs for which they are most experienced in order to encourage them to expand their horizons. A full listing of the jobs assigned for the past year with their duties and qualifications can be found on the course webpages (http://www.colby.edu/biology/BI493/BI493.html).

Report Process

The report is based on an outline established by the class and submitted in stages. Students choose or are assigned to write certain sections of the report. We review and edit early drafts of that material when requested by individual students. Each student submits his or her text to the student editors for consistency, accurate science, format, and prose editing. The report sections are then put together based on the report outline and the first draft is submitted to us for detailed editing. Typically, there are a few areas of analysis that are not complete at this point and are not included in the first draft. After we make extensive comments on the first draft, the process begins again. At least one full and several partial reviews of selected sections occur before the final report is produced at the end of the semester. During our January mini-term, we employ one or two students to complete the final corrections and necessary formatting before the report is published and distributed. The faculty are actively involved in this process as well. Approximately 50-60 copies of the report are distributed, including copies for the laboratory and library.

Oral Presentations

Students are asked to make several oral presentations during the course. Near the beginning of the semester, we provide a list of background topics for the study and allow each student to choose an area of interest to him or her to report on to the class (10 minutes). If the class is large, we create teams for this effort, but everybody eventually presents a report. Near midsemester we have the students present progress reports on their work. These progress reports not only provide more opportunities to present material before a group but also help to keep the class informed about all aspects of the project. Additionally, the presentations and resulting class discussions encourage students to evaluate critically the information they have gathered and to identify areas for further work.

At the end of the course, students are asked to make a formal oral presentation describing their findings and recommendations. This presentation is open to the public, and special invitations are extended to people who have served as resources for the project, members of local groups that are associated with the project area (e.g., lake associations), interested landowners, college officials, and the local press. In recent years, students have used computer-enhanced presentation methods and have achieved very professional results. The presentation typically lasts two hours with a refreshment break in the middle. Depending on class size, students may be divided into topic groups, each of which works on one aspect of the presentation, though only one student in each group actually presents the material. The class is made aware of the final presentation on the first day of the course so that students know their work will have an impact and they will need to be accurate in conducting their study and reporting their findings.

Problems Encountered and Suggested Solutions

The Problems in Environmental Science course is different from the traditional science course in its service-learning design, providing numerous advantages but also several challenges. During the years since the inception of the course, we have found a number of ways to help overcome many of the problems presented. Six problems are identified below, with the solutions that have worked for us.

Grading

One challenge we have faced is evaluating student work fairly when assigning grades. This problem is exacerbated by the fact that many assignments are completed by small or large groups, not individual students. We have had to identify ways to evaluate the work of each student. The job assignments discussed above include individual responsibilities that can be evaluated. We also evaluate the oral presentations given by each student during the semester; informal progress reports given periodically as updates to the class are not graded. The project report is submitted first as a draft and then as a final report, and each of these is graded. Individual students write assigned segments of the report and their names are kept with their sections until the final report is produced for distribution, allowing us to assign individual grades. Finally, there is a grade for participation. Students complete written self- and peer evaluations of their performance in each of their respective field- and report-related assignments. We assign a participation grade to each student based on this information and our own observations of his or her performance. These four project categories, providing seven grades during the semester, give us adequate information to assign a course grade to each student.

Overseeing Multiple Independent Projects

It is difficult to monitor the progress of each subgroup of students effectively and to correct problems successfully before they consume too much time. One way we address this problem is through in-class progress reports. Another way is by dividing oversight responsibility for different aspects of the class project. This approach requires coordination between teaching faculty, as well as the ability to orchestrate multiple student groups. We hold frequent faculty discussions so that we can point students in the right direction regardless of their assigned group. We also schedule frequent meetings with each group to discuss its progress in addition to the time we spend with students in the field and laboratory on regular meeting days. Finally, we provide the class with email addresses of all students at the beginning of the semester and require them to use email. As groups send messages about organizational matters, we receive copies. In this way, we can follow group activities effectively and correct inaccurate information quickly.

Landowner Concerns

As students gather information throughout the watershed, landowners sometimes become concerned about the activity, particularly since the timing of this activity coincides with the closing of summer cottages and the movement of seasonal residents south for the winter. Landowner concerns may be expressed through conversations with student field teams and telephone calls to the college, or by reports to local police and county sheriff departments. Some residents are uncomfortable just having an "environmental group" working in their area.

We attempt to address potential landowner concerns in several ways. Publicity prior to beginning our study can help. In the case of watershed projects, we attend summer lake association meetings to explain the components of our project and outline the potential benefits to the community. In addition, we alert the press to our proposed project, often resulting in the publication of a newspaper article near the start of the project. The Department of Environmental Protection also informs interested groups of the class project and possible benefits. We ask lake association officials to inform the county sheriff's office of our planned activities; just before the watershed surveys begin, we re-contact local and county officials to remind them of our project. Outreach programs to local school and community groups have enhanced community awareness, as well as educated some youth regarding lake eutrophication issues. Finally, we instruct students to be very respectful of private property and courteous to people they meet during their work. All students wear blaze orange vests to appear as obvious as possible.

Work Load Levels

To design and complete a research project, produce a professional-quality report (often approximately 200 pages), and organize a public presentation requires a heavy work load for one semester. In the early years, we probably tried to accomplish too much, especially in years with a small class size. To reduce the student work load, we send labor-intensive water quality tests (e.g., BOD) to a local laboratory for analysis. We collect the maps and existing data from the appropriate agencies so that the students will have access to them at the start of the class rather than having to seek out this information.

The class report includes a background section that provides general information for readers lacking experience with the project issues. Originally, this section was newly written each fall, but now we treat this section as property of "the consulting firm." Students are allowed to use this background material from prior reports, modifying it as needed for their own report. This procedure allows students to concentrate on the project design, data collection and analysis, data interpretation, and formulation of recommendations.

Team Research

The class project is tackled by a team of students with different abilities and interest levels. This is an advantage in that diverse views may generate more ideas for possibly broader coverage of the topic. On the other hand, there can be problems if the group members do not get along. We stress the importance of good group dynamics throughout the course. Nevertheless, occasionally interpersonal disagreements arise. Typically, these issues are resolved quickly by the class members, but there have been times when the faculty needed to counsel individual students. Constant faculty vigilance is necessary to help identify potential problems and work with students to resolve them.

Space

Over the years, we have found a need for dedicated space for the varied types of laboratory work conducted (e.g., water quality, reading of aerial photos, and mapping) and the computer work (e.g., report writing, graphics, GIS, and database management). We have also needed a staging area for organizing equipment to be used by student teams in the field. Thanks to the construction of a new science center, we now have dedicated space providing a large laboratory with substantial bench space and computer stations, a chemical analysis room, and a data analysis center designed specifically with this course in mind. This space has made an enormous difference in student morale and productivity The new spaces also serve as gathering and studying locations, helping our majors build group solidarity.

Benefits of the Course

- Students have an intense research experience.
- Students become familiar with team approaches to research problems.
- Student participation in a research project may encourage interest in graduate school.
- The team approach helps to build solidarity within the major.
- The course experience provides a good topic for job interviews.
- The service-learning component strengthens student interest in local affairs and attracts campus-wide attention to the course.

The Fit With Service-Learning Goals

The Alliance for Service-Learning in Education Reform (1993) has produced a list of "standards of quality" in service-learning. We believe these standards state nicely what service-learning should accomplish. We regularly review the 10 pertinent standards below and evaluate our course in their light:

1. *Effective service-learning efforts strengthen service and academic learning.* We believe our course has accomplished both of these objectives.

2. *Model service-learning provides concrete opportunities to learn new skills, think critically, and test new roles in an environment that encourages risk-taking and rewards competence.* Service-learning is not an end in itself but an effective means to learn new skills. Our students learn new skills and gain experience through their contacts with community leaders and professionals besides providing real service to the community. They "take risks" not found in the traditional classroom by having their work scrutinized by members of the local community. Additionally, the rewards that come through recognition and gratitude from the community outweigh those provided in the usual pedagogical structure.

3. *Preparation and reflection are essential elements in service-learning.* The early part of the course uses lectures, discussions, and readings as well as visits by outside experts to provide students with the background they need. Students are forced to reflect on what they have found and describe in a logical manner their findings and conclusions in both the oral presentation and the final report.

4. *Students' efforts will be recognized by their peers and the community they serve.* The publicity generated by the press and the public final presentation help to bring recognition to the students and the course. The course's reputation also means that peers, college administrators, and people in the community give the students positive feedback.

5. *Students are involved in the planning.* While they do not choose the project itself, students develop the work plan and are encouraged to take the initiative in all phases of the study. The faculty provide guidance when needed, but the project is student-driven.

6. *The service students perform will make a meaningful contribution to the community.* The information and recommendations students make are important both to the local community and to state agencies that receive the report. Many of the recommendations from past studies have been implemented by local or state organizations.

7. *Effective service-learning integrates systematic formative and summative evaluation.* Our own assessment of the course during the semester and at its conclusion along with student feedback through interviews and course evaluations have brought about many changes.

8. *Service-learning connects the school and its community in new and positive ways.* There has been a very positive benefit in terms of town/gown relations, with a greater respect for what the college is accomplishing and a better feeling about the college's concern for the local area. Local agencies have hired students to gather the summer data to be used in the next fall's course and to implement some of the recommendations made in the previous year's report.

9. *Service-learning is understood and supported as an integral element in the life of a school and its community.* The college has recognized the value of the course both to the students and to college/community relations and has funded it adequately. The dean of the college typically attends the final presentation and sends a letter of commendation to the students. Articles describing the course and students' efforts have appeared in college publications.

10. *Skilled adult guidance and supervision are essential to the success of service-learning.* Over the years, we have been able to develop a pool of experts on environmental issues as well as administrators who are willing to help us work with the students during the semester.

In short, our experience with this course has proved to us that service-learning is an extremely effective tool for teaching environmental science and developing skills in students that will aid them greatly in postgraduate pursuits. Students have enthusiastically endorsed the service-learning component of the course and consequently have been eager participants in our environmental investigations.

References

Alliance for Service Learning in Education Reform. (1993). "Standards of Quality for School-Based Service-Learning." *Equity and Excellence in Education* 26(2): 71-73.

Bringle, R.G., and J.A. Hatcher. (1996). "Implementing Service Learning in Higher Education." *Journal of Higher Education* 67(2): 221-239.

Evolution of the Consultant Model of Service-Learning, Bates College, Lewiston, Maine

by Lois K. Ongley, Curtis Bohlen, and Alison S. Lathrop

The tradition of hands-on course activities in geology and environmental studies at Bates College began more than 60 years ago. Beginning from a simple desire to get students out into the real world to "pound on rocks" as an innovative learning technique, experiential learning activities have evolved to include community collaboration with project design and implementation. A number of geology and environmental studies courses at Bates are now explicitly designed around service-learning projects.

Proto-service-learning has always been pervasive in the geosciences and environmental sciences at Bates, often in contexts where faculty were not consciously incorporating "something new" into the curriculum. Good faculty have long recognized that placing learning in a larger context enhances student appreciation of the complexity of knowledge. The success of this pedagogical approach has led to its widespread, informal use in laboratory-type exercises, thesis research, and courses. These projects could be considered service-learning — but for the lack of one key component: community involvement.

A "consultant model" of service-learning has been increasingly used by faculty in the Department of Geology and the Environmental Studies program over the last five years. In this approach, students develop a relationship with a client and apply the specialized knowledge and skills they acquire through their class work to address community needs. Learning and

The international work described here was supported by NSF grants EAR 94-24249 and EAR 96-19810 "REU in Hydrology: Maine and Mexico." Ongley and Lathrop would like to acknowledge their debt to Dr. Aurora Armienta for inviting us to participate in this worthwhile and exciting project. We are also grateful for the collaboration of Dr. Ramiro Rodriguez, Ms. Guadalupe Villaseñor, and Dr. Helen Mango, the other faculty involved in the REU project.

Offices at Bates College that foster service-learning include the Center for Service Learning (Dr. James Carignan and Ms. Margaret Rotundo, director and associate director, respectively, have been particularly helpful), the Office of the Dean of the Faculty, and the Office of Career Services. None of our service-learning projects could take place without the willing and active collaboration of local government officials and employees. Just goes to show: Everyone is a teacher.

application are closely coupled through the production of "deliverables" that meet the needs of a specific client. This model of service-learning contrasts with other approaches, to the extent that the students are explicitly being asked to apply specialized knowledge to the solution of societal problems. Learning happens not solely or even primarily by participating in service activities but by placing the specialized knowledge acquired in the classroom into a context where its significance to the students and the community becomes clear.

One of the benefits of this consultant model is that technical understanding is linked to practical application. In addition, by performing these projects, students learn skills they otherwise might not gain from their college experience. These include project- and time-management skills, learning to cope with immutable deadlines (the same sort of time crunch that many environmental consultants experience in their professional life), and understanding and analyzing the needs of a specific group (other than their professor for a particular course). The consultant model also requires that students communicate their work to an audience beyond the classroom. This wider communication strengthens the connection between Bates College and its surrounding communities. Such a model is especially appropriate for geology and environmental studies courses because substantial professional communities of consulting scientists now exist in these disciplinary areas. Thus, consultant-model projects provide an opportunity for students to get a taste of what life as a professional geologist or environmental consultant might be like, and in this way offer them a chance to develop not only as scientists but also as professionals.

About Lewiston and Bates College

The Lewiston area is located in central Maine and is characterized by aquifers in fluvio-glacial deposits and fractured bedrock. Interbedded clays, silts, and sands give rise to many wetlands. The Androscoggin River's history of and continued industrial use makes it an ideal site for the study of geological, environmental, and land-use issues.

Lewiston is a former mill town across the Androscoggin River from its sister city, Auburn. The combined population of the two cities is about 60,000. Although many administrative functions are separate, Lewiston and Auburn share a drinking water source (Lake Auburn) and wastewater treatment facilities.

Bates College is a coeducational private liberal arts and sciences undergraduate institution with a student population of about 1,600. The campus consists of 109 acres in a residential neighborhood of Lewiston. Bates College uses a 4-4-1 academic calendar in which students take only one class during the Short Term (five weeks in April and May).

Service-learning is strongly encouraged at Bates. The Center for Service Learning (CSL), housed in the Office of the Dean of the College, actively supports efforts to develop service-learning projects both within and outside the context of courses (Carignan 1998). CSL produces a newsletter that highlights recent service-learning efforts across the curriculum. Students are encouraged to apply for one of several internships and service grants each year and to relate their experiences to the rest of the Bates community by participating in an annual poster fair. Faculty are supported with brown bag luncheon seminars to discuss service-learning efforts, with assistance in locating potential collaborating organizations and individuals outside of the college, and with financial support for developing service-learning projects. Interest among faculty in exploring new pedagogical approaches is also strong. The sense that creative teaching methods and service-learning are valued has helped establish an atmosphere in which experimentation with various types of projects has been possible.

The Geology Department

The first reference to a department of geology is to be found in the President's Report for 1931-32 (communication with Mary Riley, special collections librarian, 1997). Prior to that time, geology was half of the Department of Astronomy and Geology. Majors are now required to take two chemistry or two physics courses, eight geology courses, and one geology Short Term unit and to undertake a two-semester senior thesis project in order to earn a B.A. The B.S. degree requires both chemistry and physics, as well as two semesters of mathematics. There are currently four faculty members, who advise 12 to 20 graduating majors each year.

Bates professors have always tried to get geology students into the field to observe and describe natural phenomena during weekly lab sessions, even in the introductory courses. This experiential focus maintains its significance throughout a student's academic career. Traditionally, the Geology Department's Short Term units are field-intensive and provide an ideal opportunity in which to implement a service-learning project.

Senior theses have always been a part of the Bates geology degree. Geology's oldest theses date back to 1933. Even then some students chose what could now be construed as service-learning projects. Early examples of proto-service-learning projects would include "The Geology of Thorncrag" (a bird sanctuary) (1935) by Dorothy Randolph and John Albertini; "Survey of Opportunities for Women in the Field of Geology" (1950) by Dorothy Cotton; and "Water Problems in the Poland Quadrangle" (1965) by Curtis Talbot. In 1996, 10 of 13 senior theses included some component of service-learning.

The current geology thesis experience includes a public defense and optional presentations at the Geological Society of America Northeast Region annual meeting and/or the spring meeting of the Geological Society of Maine. Bates geology majors now consider such presentations of their thesis research an "ordinary" but vital part of their research activity.

Geology students traditionally enjoy the outdoors. Few student lab activities, projects, and other learning exercises ever were exclusively do-it-in-the-lab-or-library activities. Long before "service-learning" became a popular concept, Bates College geology students were doing it, though perhaps with a slightly different focus than is understood today.

The Geology Department at Bates has a extensive history of activity in the Lake Auburn watershed, which is an ideal and convenient locale for class laboratory exercises at all levels of teaching. Many students at Bates have conducted independent class projects and senior thesis research in the area. We began working in the watershed as a natural consequence of service by professor emeritus of geology Roy Farnsworth on various local governmental boards, commissions, and task forces (see Kiley 1986, for example). Initially, undergraduate students performed much of the watershed work as research for required senior theses. It was, however, a small step from laboratory exercises and thesis research to collaborating with members of the Lewiston and Auburn water departments and the Lake Auburn Watershed Commission (LAWC) to address issues of direct interest to the community.

The Environmental Studies Program

The Environmental Studies program was officially established in 1996. Numerous faculty from diverse departments worked for more than eight years to get the program going. Currently, there are four tracks through the major: Culture, Society, and the Environment; Earth and Ecosystems; Environmental and Natural Resource Policy; and Geochemistry. Students are required to take a set of core courses that include ES 202-Introduction to Environmental Studies, ES 181-Working With Environmental Data, two science courses, one social science course, and a humanities course from prescribed selections. Each track requires six to eight additional courses. A two-semester thesis is required, as is an internship.

Students entering the environmental studies major at Bates often bring to their education a contagious enthusiasm for working for practical changes that address environmental concerns. These students are motivated as much by environmental concern as by curiosity. Traditional teaching methods provide students with information and theory that can help them understand environmental problems, but sometimes fail to connect with students' eagerness to address real problems. Service-learning in environmental studies provides a powerful approach to motivate students to learn.

From the inception of the Environmental Studies program, faculty intended to create a close link between theory and practice. Service-learning is one way to emphasize such a connection. As a result, service-learning has been extensively incorporated into the program. Environmental studies majors have several opportunities to take part in service-learning projects during their time at the college.

The Context of Service-Learning

At Bates, we have developed a framework that allows us to think broadly about different aspects of service-learning. We classify service-learning projects by locating them on a ternary diagram (*on the next page*) that emphasizes how they embody in different proportions three key "end members": life experience, research, and coursework.

Each end member represents an archetypal context for service-learning, and within each context there exists a continuum of opportunities: a life experience–based opportunity, such as an internship, not tied to any one course; a research project; and an exclusively curricular project done as part of a course. Thus, a 100 percent research-based service-learning activity might be undertaken in the lab or field with no associated class work or non-research component. One example of this might be working to determine the phosphate loading in a watershed without going to public meetings (life experience) or attending lectures on eutrophication (coursework). In reality, few service-learning projects occur in only one context. Most involve components of each end member, such as a class project that involves significant research or an internship that relates directly to coursework. Examples of projects that tend toward the apexes of this ternary diagram are discussed below.

Life Experience–Independent Internships

The environmental studies major at Bates has been structured to convey more than fact and theory. The major also develops analytic and practical skills of effective environmental citizenship in students. As one component of building those skills, the Environmental Studies program has established a requirement that all majors undertake an internship related to the environment. The internship experience, which must be approved in advance, may take many forms, from work on environmental education in local schools to a legal internship working on environmental law. In such cases, the central purpose of the internship remains the same: to provide students with practical experience applying to practical problems the

A paradigm for the contextual basis in which service-learning occurs at Bates College. Life experience, research, and coursework can each form an archetypal context of a service-learning project. Most service-learning projects include some aspects of each end member. The closer an activity plots to an apex, the greater the relative proportion of that end member in the activity.

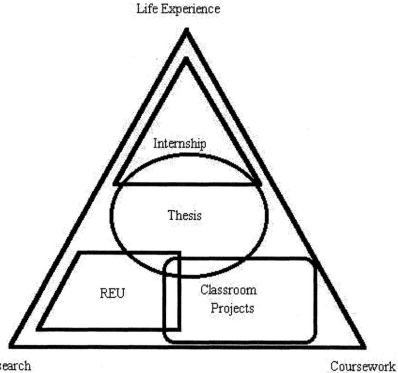

knowledge, theory, and tools learned in classes. The Environmental Studies program is currently developing a database of environment-related internship opportunities with businesses, government agencies, interest groups, and schools. The database of internship opportunities will help students recognize the full range of options they have in developing an internship experience and help with the logistical process of bringing students together with potential sponsoring organizations.

Examples of internships undertaken through the Geology Department include a land-use study and Geographic Information Systems (GIS) technical assistance. In 1997, a student assisted the cities of Lewiston and Auburn in the development of a consistent, comprehensive GIS that met both cities' needs. In 1996, a student undertook to determine the land-use distribution in 1992 of the Townsend Brook sub-basin of the Lake Auburn watershed as an independent study/internship project. His academic goal was to learn to use a GIS system and to construct a model of phosphate input into the lake from that sub-basin. During the course of his study, he and Lois Ongley noticed a discrepancy between the apparent surface water divide and the divide mapped by the Lake Auburn Watershed Commission. After his report to the commission, they were asked to check into the surface water divide discrepancy. This independent work segued into a class project and ultimately into a senior thesis.

Research – With International Flair

A fortuitous circumstance led to an international service-learning project in Mexico. Ongley met Aurora Armienta, research investigator and head of the Analytical Chemistry Laboratory at the Geophysics Institute of the National Autonomous University of Mexico, at an Association for Women Geoscientists board of directors meeting. Armienta described a service-learning project that she was just beginning in Zimapán, Mexico. Her involvement came at the request of residents and local authorities. In April 1993, she and other researchers found that 22 of 50 groundwater samples were contaminated with arsenic (concentrations greater than 0.028 mg/L), 19 with concentrations greater than 0.050 mg/L, the U.S. Environmental Protection Agency's drinking water limit.

The Zimapán Mining District in Hidalgo, Mexico (about 250 miles northeast of Mexico City), has been the site of active mining and smelting activity since the late 1500s. Arsenic is a contaminant in the ores mined in the area. Zimapán is located in a semiarid region, with annual rainfall of about 20 inches, and its residents get their drinking water from privately dug wells and from the municipal potable water system. The municipal system relies on four deep wells (more than 300 feet deep) and one shallow well (less than 100 feet).

This project had three goals: first, to locate and evaluate a reliable and safe drinking water aquifer for the town of Zimapán; second, to identify the arsenic source; and finally, to involve undergraduate students in a service-learning research project of genuine scientific interest with the possibility of an immediate beneficial impact on the local community.

Armienta and others proposed that the arsenic contamination was derived primarily from a natural source and that less significant problems (in terms of public health issues) were associated with two anthropogenic sources. The natural source was dissolution of arsenic-bearing minerals associated with economically important deposits of lead, silver, and zinc and/or disseminated throughout limestones, and the highest groundwater arsenic concentrations appeared to be related to this source. Arsenic might also have leached from arsenic-rich solid wastes from mineral processing plants and/or from smelter fume particulates that settled on the ground. Ongley, Armienta, Alison Lathrop, and Helen Mango (of Castleton State College, Vermont) proposed a collaborative group service-learning project to the National Science Foundation to evaluate the relative contributions of these three sources and assist in understanding the hydrogeologic flow regime. This Research Experience for Undergraduates (REU) program ultimately brought faculty and undergraduate students from the United States to Zimapán to work with Mexican faculty and students. In a project such as this, it becomes difficult if not impossible to separate student work from that of the faculty. All work was done collaboratively; no one worked in splendid isolation.

In the end, REU participants were thrilled to learn that they had had an immediate and significant impact on the municipal water quality in Zimapán. Shortly after the 1995 summer field season, one of the five wells (El Muhi, more than 1 mg As/L) was retired and a new well (San Pedro) was put on line as a direct consequence of the group's work. The San Pedro well had been drilled but had not been completed for lack of a pump and distribution system. REU participants insisted on testing the San Pedro well for arsenic contamination and found no detectable arsenic in the well water. This new information encouraged municipal officials to complete the San Pedro well.

REU participants also assisted Enrique Ortiz, the director of public works, with various water quality tests he needed. The team demonstrated that microfiltration (0.1 micron) would not remove the arsenic from untreated well water and that arsenic was desorbing from the distribution pipes that had been removed from the El Muhi well and used in the San Pedro system.

Lathrop, Mango, Ongley, and other Mexican colleagues have discussed the possibility of collaborating on an extended service-learning project in Mexico that would bring U.S. and Mexican students together for about six months. Normally Mexican undergraduate students are required to perform six months of social service, and most assist in adult literacy programs. However, science and engineering students might be able to provide additional technical help to the rural communities of Mexico.

Coursework

During Short Term 1996, students in Geo s32 — Hydrogeologic and Environmental Problems in Maine's Watersheds — students returned to the Townsend Brook sub-basin, walked the surface water divide (with a relief of less than 1 foot), and verified the Lake Auburn Watershed Commission's map. The class determined that Townsend Brook's course no longer matched the course on the topographic map. The class also determined, through water budget analysis, that there might be a sand aquifer that transports water into the Lake Auburn watershed from the Nezinscot River watershed. The class report was presented to the LAWC, with copies produced for each resident who interacted with the students. In the event that further work verifies the existence of an aquifer system importing water to the Lake Auburn system, the LAWC might wish to hire a consultant to evaluate the evidence and consider extending the water quality protection regulations that have protected that pristine water source.

In 1997, students in ES 202 — Introduction to Environmental Studies — completed a report for the Maine Land Trust Network on land trust organizations in Maine. The compilation of information on the size and location of land owned, managed, or otherwise protected by land trusts had not previously been attempted. Students planned the data-collection strategy and wrote the survey instrument. Students contacted nonrespondent land trusts, compiled the data, developed state-wide and regional maps of land trust holdings, reported case studies, and designed, wrote, and produced the final report. Students were so engaged with the project that their efforts continued (voluntarily) past the end of the semester. Several students attended a regional land trust meeting to present the study's results.

During Fall 1997, Curtis Bohlen and Lois Ongley coordinated two courses, one on groundwater hydrology and one on wetland science and policy (Burns and Watkins 1998; Ongley and Bohlen 1997). The focus of the interdisciplinary collaboration was the examination of Garcelon Bog, a wetland complex located within the city of Lewiston. The courses both used laboratory exercises and projects that focused on the bog. Students gathered data on the structure, function, and values associated with the wetland area.

The Garcelon Bog wetland area contains a wide range of wetland types, from riparian swamp forest to an actual bog. These diverse wetland habitats reflect the complex hydrology of the wetland and the surrounding, largely urban environment. The area is of interest to the city of Lewiston because a road has been proposed that would cross the wetland, and thus would require environmental reviews under federal and state law. We approached James Lysen, Lewiston's director of planning, with a general concept of the laboratory and field projects we would carry out in our classes, and he actively helped us select our work site. The proposed projects included field examination of groundwater flow patterns, correlation of water chemistry with surrounding development and surface vegetation features, delineation of wetlands, application of wetland assessment methods, and so on.

Students in Wetland Science and Policy delineated the wetland area and performed wetland functional assessments using standard assessment protocols. They examined relationships within the wetland complex between surface vegetation and water chemistry, and nutrient dynamics within the wetland system. Students in Hydrology looked at surface and groundwater hydrology both within the wetland complex and in the largely urbanized watershed. They identified effects of nearby urbanization on water flow and chemistry, and examined the effects on surface and groundwater of alteration of the wetland. Students from both courses examined the relative environmental impacts of alternative road alignments across the wetland, and worked together to develop options for compensatory mitigation of the environmental impacts of any development activity in the bog. Joint presentation of the results to community residents and city officials (including the city manager, city planning director, and director of public works) was the culminating activity for both courses.

Cooperative geology and environmental studies courses, coordinated with discussions with the city's planning office, offered a richness and depth of understanding about Garcelon Bog and its physical and social context that would be difficult to achieve in traditional courses. Focusing on this site ensured that students would understand that hydrological, ecological, and policy questions can all relate to a single area.

The Consultant Model

Consultant-model projects can sometimes be difficult to place on the ternary diagram, as consultancy requires work that occurs in all three contexts. Indeed, it is the very practice of tying coursework to research and life experience that makes these projects so effective. Most of the consultant-model projects with which we have been involved over the last several years have tended to emphasize either coursework or independent research. Our students often note, however, that it is the life experience context of these projects that affects them most strongly.

Implementing the Consultant Model

The specific organization of a consultant project will differ depending on whether the project in question emphasizes coursework, research, or life experiences. It will also differ depending on the academic preparation of the students involved. In lower-level classes, the instructor acts as project manager, responsible for project planning and budget. The students are responsible for the bulk of the work, while the instructor ensures that a timely and appropriate product is delivered to the client. The consultant model requires that the instructor select clients and projects of a complexity and scope to fit class needs and student capabilities; allocate enough classroom time on a regular basis for project coordination; and plan carefully. Critical planning issues include identification of key tasks, ensuring these tasks are completed on time, management of the project budget, and monitoring the level and quality of effort contributed to the project by each student. The same model implemented with a single student as an upper-level research project or senior thesis could be managed by the student in consultation with appropriate faculty.

We have been careful in exploring potential projects to make clear to potential collaborators (the "clients") that we are looking for a mutually beneficial partnership, but that our bottom line must be achieving pedagogical or scholarly objectives. The collaboration process requires a frank discussion leading to a mutual understanding of the distinct interests of the faculty and the outside collaborator, including specification of all deliverables. Although we often provide analysis that because of lack of funds would otherwise be unavailable to our clients, we do not promise up-to-date literature reviews or comprehensive implementations of cutting-edge theory. The client commitment often includes a substantial investment of time meeting and working with students. The final project may represent a compromise, one that provides some benefits to the outside collaborator and also achieves reasonable academic goals.

The best project is one that can readily be broken into parts that can stand alone. This ensures that each student has a sense of individual responsibility for the project. In addition, if one student is unable to complete an assigned task (or does so poorly), the remaining components will still be of value to the community. Where a project cannot be readily subdivided, clear assignments and unambiguous information on the criteria by which students will be evaluated are essential to keep the project on track.

Evaluation of the Consultant Model

We believe that the consultant model works well for our students, faculty, and community. However, there are many significant challenges to using it.

Miller (1994) has reported that psychology students involved in service-learning projects reported an enhanced ability to apply concepts learned in the classroom to the real world. While we have not carried out a similar controlled experiment, we have seen this happen. Based on our conversations with service-learning participants, their advisers, and written evaluations, students clearly have gained inspiration and a sense of dedication to earth science and related disciplines. Clearly, service-learning projects impact the lives and careers of student participants. Student evaluative comments of the Research Experience for Undergraduates have been especially clear:

> Now I understand why you told me that it all fits together.

> I left the program with a love for geology, which I had never experienced before.

> I am inspired about chemistry for the first time in my life.

> After this project I can say that I want to become a geologist.

> [This REU] has made me more aware of things I need to do . . . like getting published, going to [Geological Society of America meetings], doing independent research. . . .

> Doing research for the sake of doing research is one thing; however, doing research and knowing it will improve people's quality of life is much more motivating.

> I felt I was living an experience that will stay with me forever . . . one of the most positive and rewarding experiences I could ever have.

In the consultant model, students are producing a product for the community based on specialized knowledge that may affect the community's life. As noted earlier, such an application of specialized knowledge to community needs helps differentiate the consultant model from some other approaches to service-learning. Preparing a report on pollutants in the Androscoggin River is qualitatively different from serving food in a soup kitchen. A student providing social services gains new insight into the community without necessarily changing community policies or practices. A student consultant, on the other hand, provides services that may do so. As a consequence, the consultant model risks placing students in an apparently privileged position vis-à-vis the community — a position to which they may not be entitled. Students may lack the expertise to do work of the caliber that clients had hoped for and are used to seeing from professional consultants. Students often lack the sophistication necessary to recognize the limited role their contribution may play in an overall search for solutions. Issues beyond their control may arise because of political, engineering, financial, and social constraints faced by the community.

In the consultant model, students are placed in situations in which they are also asked to learn professional skills. Successful project completion requires a variety of such skills: placing cold calls to collect information, developing professional presentations, working in a group, managing time, and reflecting on project progress and making decisions on task sequencing. Students must integrate skills and knowledge from many different sources. Students must learn to appreciate skills brought to the project by others.

Furthermore, faculty may find it challenging to evaluate student work in consultant-model projects. Even when projects are going well, it can be difficult to allocate fairly credit for work done. Students will each have different strengths and be assigned very different tasks. For instance, it may be hard to compare the contributions of a student who puts in long hours preparing a final report with those of one who develops a detailed Geographic Information Systems application or one who struggles to learn and apply a sophisticated analytic technique.

In spite of these challenges, students, faculty, and community members who participate in consultant-model projects emerge with a better understanding of how earth and environmental scientists think, study, and work. Students gain an infectious enthusiasm not only for the consulting project but also for learning in general. Projects contextualize scientific thinking, thereby reducing the sense of irrelevance felt by some students, especially women and minority students, in traditional science classrooms (Rosser and Kelly 1994). Student participants may discover new or renewed interests not only in geology and environmental studies but also in other disciplines relevant to solving environmental problems. In particular, students (and often faculty) acquire an appreciation for how information from many disciplines can contribute to wise decisions in the face of limited or incomplete information.

Summary

An excellent liberal arts undergraduate education is one that transforms students' lives and that connects classroom learning to community and global issues. This education must also help students to find their place in the world and must include activities and habits of mind that lead to better and/or more-active citizenship. Fulfillment of these goals requires that students venture off campus, intellectually if not physically, so that they come to grips with issues that affect their lives and the lives of those around them. Service-learning is appropriate, even critical, in a liberal arts setting.

Consultant-model service-learning projects involve student participants in activities that can have an immediate impact on the communities around them. Students can connect with individuals in the community and build a grass-roots basis of working together. Students can acquire understanding of the working world and get an idea of the life they would like to live after they emerge from their own school's version of the "Bates Bubble."

References

Burns, H. Jay, and Alana Watkins. (Winter 1998). "Boggling the Mind." *Bates Magazine* 96(2): 18-21.

Carignan, James. (1998). "Curriculum and Community Connection: The Center for Service Learning at Bates College." In *Successful Service-Learning Programs, New Models of Excellence in Higher Education,* edited by Edward Zlotkowski, pp. 40-57. Bolton, MA: Anker Publishing

Miller, Jerry. (1994). "Linking Traditional and Service-Learning Courses: Outcome Evaluations Utilizing Two Pedagogically Distinct Models." *Michigan Journal of Service Learning* 1(1): 29-36.

Ongley, Lois K., and Curtis C. Bohlen. (1998). "The Road in Garcelon Bog — A Collaborative Service Learning Project." *GSA Abstracts With Programs* 31(1): 64.

Rosser, Sue V., and Bonnie Kelly. (1994). *Educating Women for Success in Science and Mathematics.* Columbia, SC: Division of Women's Studies, University of South Carolina.

The Ethics of Community/Undergraduate Collaborative Research in Chemistry

by Alanah Fitch, Aron Reppmann, and John Schmidt

This article describes ethical issues related to service-learning in Instrumental Methods of Analysis, a course for junior and senior chemistry majors. In this course, we have chosen a community service-learning context for the unknown analysis in response to our school's mission statement:

> Loyola University of Chicago is a Jesuit Catholic university dedicated to knowledge in the service of humanity. . . . The university strives to develop in its community a capacity for critical and ethical judgment and a commitment to action in the service of faith and justice. . . . An urban institution, Loyola benefits from Chicago's exceptional cultural, economic, and human resources. In turn, the university affirms its longstanding commitment to urban life — and works to solve its problems. . . .

The project's "variable community" of student-mediated interaction with urban community activist groups (themselves fluid in membership) has created a unique set of both *planned* and *unplanned* ethical issues. The planned ethical issues are relatively simple ones and are easily dealt with. They consist of discipline-centered or *constitutive* values (deciding between competing theories or experimental methodologies) (Longino 1983) — values that have been defended in various formulations of the philosophy of science as *value-neutral* (Procter 1991).

This class grew with the interest of several "generations" of Loyola undergraduates. Funding comes from an Anheuser Busch award in environmental education to the Fall 1995 class and from the Policy Research Action Group's MacArthur Foundation award. The inductively coupled plasma-mass spectrometer was a gift of Chemical Waste Management Corporation, and Loyola University has supported bringing this instrument on line. Postdoctoral associate Dr. Yunlong Wang and Alanah Fitch's graduate students Susan Macha, Simona Dragan, Scott Baker, and Sean Mellican helped in developing the lab sequence. Drs. Jameson and Crumrine assisted in the NMR lab. The 300-MHZ NMR was supported by a National Science Foundation ILI grant to Dr. Jameson. Undergraduate Peggy Kalkounos validated the wet-wipe digestion procedure. Loyola's Center for Urban Research and Learning has provided an umbrella organization for institutionalizing community/university relationships. John Knox at the Lead Elimination Action Drive was very helpful. Karen Croteau worked on developing a children-based lead curriculum. Alanah Fitch is grateful to the university for a semester fellowship with the Center for Ethics.

More crucially, this collaboration between fluid participating groups (student/urban) yields other issues linked primarily to the class's community *context*. As Hollander (1991) writes: "'Good' science is not enough for professionals to fulfill the requirements of moral responsibility." Here we encounter those ethical, ideological, and cultural values that Longino (1983) has defined as *contextual values:* the social context in which science and technology are practiced.

For example, the Incinerator II study, carried out in Fall 1995, raised issues of *ownership* of data and of *scare science*. In this study, students sampled soils near the City of Chicago's municipal solid waste incinerator, which was located in a predominantly minority community. Despite finding some "elevated" soil lead values, we were unable to answer the simple question does the incinerator deposit lead, for we had not adequately sampled in appropriate places. Furthermore, the background levels of soil lead in urban Chicago are sufficiently high that lead from an incinerator would be difficult to identify, unless deposits were quite large, as might occur only within a tight radius of the incinerator.

More troubling, and linked to a key ethical issue, was the fact that the significance of our findings could easily be massaged by manipulating the data after the fact. If we drew the "close" population of soils in tightly enough, there was a statistical correlation of high soil lead with the incinerator. If we drew the "close" population farther out, as we had originally intended, then there was no correlation. Students had a difficult time wrestling with this dilemma. Scientifically, the answer was clear: We needed to re-sample on a smaller gridline with a tighter control over our question: What is the contribution of the incinerator to total lead in soil samples? Ethically, the answer was not so clear. The semester ended, and the data were ready to be compiled and returned to the community group. The students had had no direct contact with the community group: for them, the group existed only as an abstraction with the stated political agenda of shutting down the incinerator. Many of the students felt that the data should not be turned over to representatives of the community group, because, if one were fuzzy with the map lines, it would be quite easy to interpret the data to mean that lead had been deposited. Some students felt a sense of ownership of the data, ownership that presupposed their technical superiority in interpreting it, and assumed a propensity to use "scare" science on the part of the community group. Other students felt that it was up to the community members to do their own data interpretation, and that it was paternalistic to assume that the community would make inappropriate choices.

These student debates highlighted the fact that student/community collaboration requires manipulation of the course content to allow specifically for ethical exercises that provide a framework for decision making, thus expanding the scope of course management required by the faculty member.

Other *contextual* ethical issues have arisen with other classes and their projects. To what extent are we required to study them? Should projects be completed to the standard of a peer-reviewed article? Do we include community participants as members of that "peer" group? Are we obligated to confront the image of *public* science; i.e., the rapid, rational test of a hypothesis? Such science has been called "normal" science by Kuhn (1962) and differs from "private" science, which imagines or constructs reality (Popper 1975). On still another front, does working with the community in order to motivate our undergraduates mean that we are treating the "community" as means to an end (better education for undergraduates)? And is there not also some as yet undefined responsibility on the part of the community to make an effort to participate fully in the project? Where does this responsibility reside: in the hands of so-called community activists? or in the hands of the individual members of a community association? The remainder of this paper will focus on these contextual ethical problems.

Professional Guidelines for Contextual Values

We can begin to address contextual ethical problems by turning to the *Chemists' Code of Conduct* and *Academic Professional Guidelines of the American Chemical Society*. Professional codes are set up precisely for the purpose of helping members of the profession to resolve dilemmas: "The *Chemists' Code of Conduct* is for the guidance of society members in various professional dealings, especially those involving conflicts of interest." A similar statement is made in the *Academic Professional Guidelines of the American Chemical Society*. These guidelines articulate reciprocal responsibilities of professors, undergraduate and graduate students, postdoctoral associates, and administrators, but they are silent on the issue of public- or community-based research.

The *Chemists' Code of Conduct* outlines various responsibilities of the chemist to the public, the science of chemistry, the chemical profession, employers, employees, students, associates, clients, and the environment. Several of these interactions could encompass community-based research. One could conceive of the community as an "employer" or as a "client," which would imply a fiduciary relationship with the community, one that does not exist given the voluntary nature of the association. One could consider the community a "student," although this seems tenuous, since the "community" has not explicitly agreed to assume a "student" role vis-á-vis a professor. The final category that might be relevant would be to classify community collaborators as "the public." The *Chemists' Code of Conduct* states that

> [C]hemists have a professional responsibility to serve the public interest and welfare and to further knowledge of science. Chemists should actively be concerned with the health and welfare of coworkers, consumers, and the community. Public comments on scientific matters should be made with care and precision, without unsubstantiated, exaggerated, or premature statements.

The earlier part of this statement suggests that community collaborations should be actively encouraged. The latter implies that, given the tentative or incomplete nature of the data that we supplied to the community in the case of our incinerator study, no type of community collaboration could be envisioned within the space of a single semester of a single class.

Thus, we conclude that the code and the guidelines are too vague to be of help in resolving the *contextual ethical issues* involved in chemical community/collaborative research. We must use some other source of ethical reasoning to resolve some of the issues raised by such research.

Ethical Reflections: A Consequentialist Perspective

In this section, we proceed by adopting a cost/benefit (consequentialist) perspective, beginning globally and working back to particular affected parties.

As a discipline, chemistry can be seen as advancing through its being actively introduced to a new generation of developing scientists (growing scientists?) and through communication with the public that may result in increased funding for science. The assumption underlying this position, that the promotion of education for public understanding of science is something good, suggests the (mis)leading "premise that if we all understand science, we would all make the same decisions" (Harrison 1986). Furthermore, though in the case of the incinerator study, real, defensible data were obtained, the data were not obtained as *efficiently* as in a normal research arena. Lead was mapped near an incinerator, and a leaded house dust map with isotope ratios was initiated. Eventually these results might be publishable. However, one could also argue that much more efficient science could be achieved through a normal grant-supported research effort (although funding for such research may be problematic). The cause of science would also be adversely affected if incomplete data were used for political ends.

Clearly, such a class is more costly and labor-intensive than a traditional course. It requires additional resources such as money, supplies, teaching assistantships, and services/time/teaching that the faculty member could otherwise have devoted to other purposes. Economically, the department would be better served by placing a full-time professor in a lecture section of 100 tuition-paying students than in a project-based course with only 10-15 students. Furthermore, the department potentially loses national recognition as a research institution within the discipline due to less publishable data. A significant redirection of instructor energies could occur, which, in turn, could entail less individual research productivity and grant funding. It is also possible that the university would become legally liable if false negatives and positives are reported.

On the other hand, the department has already benefitted by being able to justify the cost of maintaining the inductively coupled plasma-mass spectrometer used in chemical analysis (approximately $10,000/year). It has further benefitted from external publicity (the class was featured on national prime time television). The university as a whole gains through services provided to its Center for Urban Research and Learning and by a tangible contribution to the university mission.

More particularly affected parties are the undergraduate students, the "community," and participating faculty. With regard to the students, they can be said to enjoy a significantly enriched curriculum: They learn problem solving better; they better appreciate analytical skills; they have a framework in which to learn. They also learn, some for the first time, the difference between public (that which is reported) and private (that which is carried out in laboratories and recorded in personal notebooks) scientific activity (Aikenhead 1985; Benson 1989; Hodson 1986). This helps avoid the narrowness of teaching solely "public" science, which can propagate myths about the scientific enterprise (Gauld 1982). In addition, the caliber of the written material presented by the students shows significant improvement. There is a testable increase in understanding of the principles of instrumentation and mastery of the current literature. All classes participating in the project have had a rate of 15 to 30 percent voluntarism (work outside of class or after the semester ends) associated with the project. Two years after completion of the first lab, students began to return with comments that indicate this project was the most important factor in their obtaining a job. (One student currently works on a United Nations–sponsored project for monitoring lead pollution in Croatia, a job obtained because of his lab experience here.) One class submitted its results for a national environmental award and won third place. This, in turn, has facilitated support within the university for the program. Still, it is interesting that these positive indicators have not directly translated into superior course evaluations: Values on teacher course evaluations have remained relatively unchanged.

Negative consequences to the students include less time available for traditional subject matter. As one participant remarked, "If students sign up for science courses, they have a right not to have their science time used for ethics" (Mahowald and Mahowald 1982; Walters and Zoeller 1991). Time must be allotted for reflection. This could be as minimal as a lab on quality control or could include some planned segment on ethics, as described above. One challenge in encouraging reflection is the fact that each "community" experience is quite different, on account of both the technical question answered and the type of collaborative interaction experienced. Consequently, the nature of ethical reflection also varies.

Outcomes for the community group include increased access to some level of scientific expertise. Given appropriate safeguards, the community would appear to be enriched by the process. Our collaboration with After School Action Programs (ASAP), a network of 30 Chicago community organizations — churches, HUD buildings, and ethnic associations — seeking to strengthen the capacity of smaller, community organizations to work effectively with youth and children, illustrates this point.

One of ASAP's most successful projects is Science Seekers, a community-based, hands-on science initiative. It is a 12- to 15-week science program that takes place each academic semester at as many as 10 sites throughout our urban community. ASAP coordinates curriculum development, recruits and places student interns from local universities, and manages regular field trips and semiannual Family Science Day celebrations. ASAP member organizations recruit 10-15 fifth and sixth graders, provide space, and identify a parent, youth-worker, or other adult to team teach science curriculum with a university student.

In Fall 1996, the first two weeks of the project were spent on lead testing. During this time, the children learned about the presence and dangers of lead in homes, schools, and other structures. They also learned how to take samples from their own homes, gathering a control sample, a sample of an untreated surface, and a sample of a washed surface. Through this process, they learned not only that lead may be present and that tests can be conducted to test for its presence but also how samples need to be gathered scientifically and how to present findings to a broader audience. After the samples were gathered at each site, all 70 children participated in a field trip to Loyola to learn about the chemistry of lead and the kinds of machines that analyze the content of the samples.

Even without the assistance of the university and its professors, students, and laboratory equipment, the lead-testing portion of the curriculum might still have been a learning experience. However, what made the experiment provocative was the hard science used to back it up and to turn it into an experience with broad sociopolitical consequences. Part of the attraction of this project was that it helped children to determine the safety of their own homes with respect to the presence of lead. ASAP saw this as a wonderful opportunity to address programmatically an important environmental issue that has important public health implications. Children engaged in a process of discovery, especially valuable since "science learning is of lasting values when the student is motivated by [his or her] own curiosity" (Silverman 1989: 44).

There are, however, situations in which the community may not benefit. These may occur when there is a mismatch between community expectations of "public" science and the ability of an undergraduate class to meet those expectations. The community may have expectations based on a popular view of science that data should be instantaneous, limitless, definitive, and risk-free (Covello, Sandman, and Slovic 1991; Mingle 1989). Students themselves may harbor such a misconception, but it is perhaps a more serious problem with community collaborators.

There are also costs associated with these community and undergraduate benefits that the faculty member must bear. In order to provide valid data to the community group, the instructor must personally check all of the student lab books and calculations, as well as provide a running analysis of the statistical boundaries of the data. He or she must either train in ethics or receive the assistance of ethicists in order to develop the planned ethical reflection portion of the coursework.

The faculty member must also take on a new educational "role" with regard to the community. His or her interaction with it cannot simply be viewed as providing a learning experience to the college students, for then the community becomes merely a "means." Education in conjunction with the community includes education about the public and private nature of science. At the initiation of the collaboration, the instructor should attempt to clarify the "learning" aspect of the collaboration. Data returned to the community must be accompanied by some assistance in interpreting it. In the case of the dust-sampling done at homes, the participating children's parents may, depending upon local law, have legal and financial responsibility (estimated cost of lead remediation is $15,000/housing unit) thrust upon them as a result of the findings. Some interpretations of local law would require that awareness of the lead found in this study be reported in all subsequent real estate transactions. In view of these considerations, we deliberately designed the dust sampling to illustrate the differences in the content of the dust after the surface had been cleaned by wet-mopping methods. In this way, we were able to show that cleaning diminished the lead content in the dust in each individual home from 70 to 100 percent. This helped the instructor to fulfill the obligation to the community in a nonthreatening way.

The task of community education is made more demanding by the fact that the situation varies from collaboration to collaboration. To whom are the materials delivered and how do they get to the larger "community"? This educational component may be the most problematic in widespread adoption of our model. It implies a wide expansion of the responsibility of the instructor to become a community educator, not typically part of the job description of a professor of chemistry. Some of these problems could be solved by establishing a long-term relationship with a local school teacher. We have yet, however, to find a local school teacher to take this project on as part of his or her *own* curriculum. Positive outcomes for the university instructor include a chance to exercise creativity, to learn in a new environment, and to have extended relationships with undergraduates that break the normal classroom boundaries.

In summary, there are clear benefits to the undergraduate students and the university at large. There may be benefits to the community. There are corresponding debits on the part of the individual faculty member, the department, and the efficient functioning of science. On the surface, it appears that a simple valuation of costs and benefits would preclude a chemistry professor from organizing this type of "teaching/research" for a class. The fact that there is little community-based research at Ph.D.-granting chemistry departments points to the "cost" of this program. Does this consequentialist argument then doom community-based research in the physical sciences?

Critique of the Consequentalist Argument

The problem may be not with the task of community-based research itself but rather with the cost/benefit approach to ethical reasoning. A cost/benefit analysis assumes a single scale on which all values can be ranked, and that all affected parties create identical lists of consequences. It further assumes that all moral considerations can be reduced to a cost/benefit analysis, and that the "value" attributed to each consequence will be equivalent even when this is done by different individuals or groups. This is clearly the case only when those generating the lists have similar backgrounds and commitments. These assumptions have been broadly criticized. A full ethical analysis of community-based research needs to consider the possibility of more than one scale of values (Taylor 1982); other moral attitudes (commitment to community or to personal integrity) that did not appear above (Williams 1973); and the responsibilities imposed on a person or group in encounters with a person or group *different* in fundamental ways (academic research science versus church group community) (Peperzak 1997). A full reconsideration of community-based research from such a perspective is too large a task for this article. We do, however, take a first step by reexamining the *relationship* between the community and the professor.

A Different Approach

Weighing the competing interests of "community" versus professor requires that the relationship between the community/layperson and the expert needs to be better defined. Hardwig (1994) pinpoints the role that "trust" or "faith" plays in the ethics of expertise by describing the steps involved in appealing to authority:

1. Layperson knows that Expert says [proposition].

2. Layperson has good reason to believe that Expert (unlike Layperson) is in a position to know what would be good reasons to believe [proposition] and to have the needed reasons.

3. Layperson *believes* that Expert is speaking truthfully.

Belief is an important component in community/expert relations. Even experts are involved in trust within their own field, believing in the integrity of a previous body of knowledge. Because of this element of trust, the ethics of expertise cannot rest on a voluntary relationship among equals as embodied in contract theory. Contract theory assumes each party will look after its own interests equally. In a nonequal relationship — e.g., expert and layperson; budding expert (student) and urban group — the needs of the party surrendering autonomy are given greater weight. This does not imply that the instructor is morally required to embark upon a sacrificial relationship. While May (1996) says that social responsibility is not governed by "cost/benefit" systems and the vulnerability of the dependent person should be given greater weight, he also writes that "self-sacrifice is not required to be an integrated professional" (203).

How lopsided is the relationship between "community" and "expert"? How much can the community ask from the expert? If it had become necessary, how could the university have helped the After School Action Program? While ASAP has important experience in bringing diverse constituencies together to work with youth, ASAP doesn't have the ability to analyze complicated scientific data. Should it have become necessary, the political clout and the scientific expertise of the university would have helped in seeking relief from lead poisoning. ASAP acknowledges that the university is asked to step outside of its normal role of research, but suggests that such collaboration is critical when the well-being of the community is at stake.

This perspective contains two important points. The After School Action Program has *important experience* to bring to the table, and *collaboration is critical when the well-being of our community is at stake*. This suggests that the expert/layperson relationship, while not among "equals," is not entirely one-sided either. It may be helpful to view this relationship as similar to the mentoring that goes on between a graduate student and a faculty member. The faculty member brings ideas, money, and support to the project. The graduate student, initially, brings labor, but during the *development* of the relationship moves to become a contributing member of the team who eventually assumes ownership of the research plan. The community brings an expertise in "living with lead" and in "forming community alliances." It is not solely a recipient of expertise. The two-way nature of this relationship is valuable. May (1996) writes that "mutual (rather than unilateral) vulnerability and dependence is the hallmark of social relationships like citizenship" (110). Such a mutual dependence or commitment to the common good is linked to community involvement and *identification*.

This brings us to one final point. Professionals normally participate in a reward structure (prestige, grant support, honors) set up by the professional community with which they identify. Such expanded responsibility to community education can only be sustained when the academic chemical community supports these efforts. A change in the professional code should include some definition of community relationships. Baum (1994) has argued forcefully for changes in the engineering code of conduct to begin the process of "public" decision making:

> *The strongest argument that engineers and other professionals should play a major and perhaps leading role in making changes to their codes is self-interest. The code imposes an impossible burden of responsibility on individual engineers (while at the same time usurping the rights of all other affected parties). . . . The only morally justifiable procedure for making decisions in complex cases is for all affected parties or delegated representatives to be provided with all of the available information relevant to the decision and for them to have an equitable say in the final decision.*

We end with a similar plea for a reexamination of the *Chemists' Code of Conduct* to explore issues of pro bono and/or community-based research.

References

Aikenhead, G.S. (1985). "Collective Social Decision-Making: Implications for Teaching Science." In *Science Education and Ethical Values,* edited by David Gosling and Bert Musschenga, pp. 57-63. Washington, DC: Georgetown University Press.

Baum, R.J. (1994). "Engineers and the Public: Sharing the Responsibility." In *Professional Ethics and Social Responsibility,* edited by D.E. Wueste, pp. 121-137. Lantham, MA: Rowman and Littlefield.

Benson, G.D. (1989). "The Misrepresentation of Science by Philosophers and Teachers of Science." *Synthese* 80: 107-119.

Covello, V.T., P.M. Sandman, and P. Slovic. (1991). "Guidelines for Communicating About Chemical Risk Effectively and Responsibly." In *Acceptable Evidence: Science and Value in Risk Management,* edited by D.G. Mayo and R.D. Hollander. New York, NY: Oxford University Press.

Gauld, C. (1982). "The Scientific Attitude and Science Education: A Critical Reappraisal." *Science Education* 66(1): 109- 121.

Hardwig, J. (1994). "Toward an Ethics of Expertise." In *Professional Ethics and Social Responsibility,* edited by D.E. Wueste, pp. 82-101. Lantham, MA: Rowman and Littlefield.

Harrison, A. J. (1986). "Roles of Scientists, Engineers, and the Public in the Resolution of Societal Issues." In *Ethics and Social Responsibility in Science Education,* edited by M.J. Frazer and A. Kornhauser. Oxford: Pergamon Press.

Hodson, D. (1986). "Philosophy of Science and Science Education." *Journal of Philosophy of Education* 20(2): 215-225.

Hollander, R.D. (1991). "Expert Claims and Social Decisions: Science, Politics, and Responsibility." In *Acceptable Evidence: Science and Value in Risk Management,* edited by D.G. Mayo and R.D. Hollander. New York, NY: Oxford University Press.

Kuhn, Thomas. (1962). *Structure of Scientific Revolutions.* Chicago, IL: University of Chicago Press.

Longino, H. (1983). "Beyond Bad Science: Skeptical Reflections on the Value-Freedom of Scientific Inquiry." *Science, Technology and Human Values* 8(1): 7-17.

Mahowald, M.B., and A.P. Mahowald. (1982). "Should Ethics Be Taught in a Science Course?" In *The Hasting Center Report,* p. 18. Briarcliff Manor, NY: The Hastings Center.

May, L. (1996). *The Socially Responsive Self: Social Theory and Professional Ethics.* Chicago, IL: University of Chicago Press.

Mingle, J.O. (August 1989). "Inchemacy: An Ethical Challenge for Chemical Engineers." *Chemical Engineering Progress:* 19-25.

Peperzak, Adriaan. (1997). "Before Ethics." Atlantic Highlands, NJ: Humanities Press.

Popper, Karl. (1934). *The Logic of Scientific Discovery.* London: Hutchison.

Proctor, Robert N. (1991). *Value-Free Science? Purity and Power in Modern Knowledge.* Cambridge, MA: Harvard University Press.

Silverman, M.P. (1989). "Two Sides of Wonder: Philosophical Keys to the Motivation of Science Learning." *Synthese* 80: 43-61.

Taylor, Charles. (1982). "The Diversity of Goods." In *Utilitarianism and Beyond,* edited by A. Sen and B. Williams, pp. 129-144. Cambridge: Cambridge University Press and Editions de la Maison des Sciences de l'homme.

Walters, J.C., and D.A. Zoeller. (Spring 1991). "Developing a Course in Chemical Engineering Ethics, One Class' Experiences." *Chemical Engineering Education:* 68-73.

Williams, Bernard. (1973). "A Critique of Utilitarianism." In *Utilitarianism: For and Against,* edited by J.J.C. Smart and B. Williams, pp. 82-88, 116-17. Cambridge: Cambridge University Press.

Evolving a Service-Learning Curriculum at Brown University, Or What We Learned From Our Community Partners

by Harold Ward

I wish I could say that our Center for Environmental Studies carefully planned and methodically developed an integrated environmental service-learning curriculum for Brown students, but it wouldn't be true. We do have such a curriculum now — with service-learning opportunities in our introductory class, a practicum seminar, and for many students a year-long senior thesis on a service theme, but these had unrelated origins and evolved over time to reach their current level of integration. The purpose of this chapter is to explore this evolutionary process, with the idea that service-learning programs starting now might reach their goal more directly by reflecting on our experiences. In the course of this evolution, our successes and our failures in working with community partners taught us some valuable and sometimes painful lessons. I hope that a recounting of these experiences may ease the learning process for programs newer to service-learning.

Origins of the Program

Brown's Center for Environmental Studies was created in 1978 in response to requests from undergraduates, many of whom had self-designed environmental majors. The bachelor of arts degree in environmental studies (ES) retained several of the features of an independent major — requiring a thoughtful proposal and an integrating final project. Of the 15 courses

Funding for the work described here was provided by an endowment grant from the Ittleson Foundation; a grant to support CEServe from the Surdna Foundation; and five Eisenhower Professional Development Grants from the Rhode Island Office of Higher Education, to support our work with the Providence Public Schools. CEServe coordinators were Nicole Rolbin and Arthur Handy. Faculty colleagues involved in the integration efforts are Caroline Karp (senior lecturer), Christina Zarcadoolas (adjunct assistant professor), and Steven Hamburg (Ittleson associate professor). Rachel Ede and Luke Driver from the Mayor's Office in Providence provided essential assistance in our work for the past two years. Our work on urban environmental indicators has been supported by an Urban Environmental Initiative grant from the U.S. Environmental Protection Agency, Region I.

required for the major, roughly half were defined as a core, and the remainder were chosen to support the senior thesis — viewed as the keystone of the major. There is a strong preference for thesis topics allowing primary research, and thus for practical reasons a bias toward investigation of local issues. Subsequently, a bachelor of science degree in environmental science (ESci) and a master of arts degree in environmental studies were added. Both also require a year-long thesis, and retain the preference for primary (and thus often local) research.

The Introductory Course

The gateway course to environmental studies is the Environmental Issues course, ES11 (one of Brown's idiosyncrasies is to refer to courses only by numbers). Typically, this course is taken in a student's first or second year, and has an enrollment of 80-130. To provide more direct instructional contact than the lecture/discussion portion of the course allows, sections of 16 students each are formed, coordinated by a senior undergraduate or graduate teaching assistant. These sections meet each week for 90 minutes, with roughly half of the sessions devoted to a section project. The other sessions engage students in activities that relate to and extend the lecture portion of the course. In the 1980s, section projects were primarily focused on improving Brown's own environmental performance. We reasoned that before we presumed to advise others on environmental issues, our own house should be in order.

In 1990, a representative of Rhode Island's Office of Higher Education (RIOHE) met with Brown faculty to ask our help in improving the quality of local K-12 education. The rapid growth in demands on faculty time from the Environmental Studies program left little space for ES faculty involvement in this initiative, but bearing in mind a peer-assistance project that Brown had developed to improve undergraduate writing, I wondered whether Brown students might be of assistance to local schools. Writing fellows take a course on how to offer constructive criticism on writing and, as part of that course, review and comment on papers written by students in other courses — including ES11. I thought that ES11 students could work with teachers in the Providence Public Schools to present a unit on an environmental issue, and in that way learn the material they would teach at a deeper level. The RIOHE gave us a small grant to hire a student coordinator and a consultant teacher to identify cooperating teachers, and to pay students to assist in developing an appropriate unit.

We selected the prevention of childhood lead poisoning as the focal issue, since at that time more than half of the children under six years of age tested in low-income Providence neighborhoods were classified, according to the Centers for Disease Control standards, as lead-poisoned. Because significant public education had been conducted in these neighborhoods, we thought this issue would resonate with the public school students, and since these students are often in charge of younger siblings their better understanding of protective strategies could reduce poisoning rates. Pairs of Brown undergraduates visited public school classes for five or six sessions — they gave basic instruction on lead poisoning, asked students (with their caregivers' permission) to collect samples of the soil and dust their siblings might contact, prepared these samples for X ray fluorescence analysis, and tabulated the results. Data for all classes were combined for the purposes of class discussion. Caregivers were mailed the results in envelopes they provided, along with Department of Health literature with cleanup recommendations. We offered to speak with caregivers in whose homes high lead levels were found, made clear that these results were preliminary, and explained how further testing could be obtained.

We had not anticipated the variety of responses Brown students and the public school teachers would have to the detection of high lead levels in soil/dust samples. Some teachers were vigilant in their follow-up to the mailed results, to be certain that remedial action was taken. Others were apprehensive about discussing even the aggregated results in their classes. Some Brown students shared this apprehension, concerned that the younger students would conclude they themselves had likely been exposed to high lead levels and that the realization of the possibility of a developmental handicap would be harmful, perhaps reducing the children's academic efforts. Such different opinions led to heated classroom discussions on these very real and immediate ethical issues.

Pre- and posttests suggested that the schoolchildren had increased their understanding of the lead poisoning issue substantially. Evaluations by their teachers were positive, and Brown students were so enthusiastic that several of them continued to work in the schools as volunteers during the following semester. In subsequent years, topics have been expanded to include the health of the urban forest, urban open space, and indoor air quality. The ES11 sections focused on public education projects are always the most popular, and suggestions of reducing the numbers of these sections have been resisted vigorously by Brown students and teaching assistants and the public school teachers.

I caution that these projects do require additional effort — to prepare the units, coordinate with the teachers, and schedule the visits. We have been fortunate to obtain continued funding from the RIOHE, which allows us to pay the schoolteachers for workshops and to hire teacher-consultants. Teacher training clearly enhances the quality of the project but is not essential, so long as teachers are willing to devote time to coordination.

The Practicum Course

All environmental studies majors and all master's candidates without field experience are required to take a practicum course (ES192); this course is an option for environmental science majors. Undergraduates usually take the course in their sixth semester, in preparation for thesis research. The course always is focused on a single local environmental issue, and the class — usually between 15 and 25 students in size — is divided into teams to address critical components of the issue. During the 1980s, I selected topics that had a strong regulatory or agency flavor — e.g., a feasibility study of a comprehensive permitting process for Rhode Island, a comparative study of the licensing process for several proposed coastal developments, and a proposed reorganization of the Department of Environmental Management. In the early 1990s, partly in response to a growing interest among our majors in environmental justice issues, and partly to see whether a focus on these issues would make the major more attractive to minority students, I began to choose topics that had a more urban character. One year, we did the baseline study for a greenway proposed along the first industrial river in Rhode Island, now running through one of Providence's most distressed neighborhoods. Another year we studied a community development corporation's plans for low-income housing in an area that had been devastated during racial unrest in the 1960s.

In each of our urban practicum projects, we identify a community partner well in advance of the time the class begins, and work with that partner to structure the questions the class will address so that the results will be of use to the partner. What the class has to offer is hard work from a significant number of bright, energetic, but not yet expert researchers and the technical resources of the university, including information sources and computing and mapping capabilities. The community partners offer local information, access to members of the community, reduced cultural and language barriers, and, most important, the "clients" for the project — the folks who will use the information the class produces and give that information meaning.

I have chosen for discussion here a project that in some aspects was one of the least successful among our urban issues — because it nicely illustrates some of the important considerations that often seem to arise in working with community groups. Our partners for this class were a neighborhood housing group located in a neighborhood with very high childhood lead poisoning levels and the Rhode Island Department of Health (RIDOH). RIDOH had obtained a sizable federal grant to fund the group to carry out a systematic program to reduce lead exposures in an eight-block section of the group's neighborhood. In order to conserve as much of the funding as possible for actual lead remediation, we offered to perform the initial baseline studies against which change would be measured. After numerous meetings, a written document that set out a schedule and defined responsibilities was agreed to by all parties. The schedule was not ideal from the academic perspective, because it left much of the important work to the end of the semester and allowed no margin for error, but it was the schedule the housing group wanted.

Our students prepared a protocol to guide a visual assessment of the conditions of the housing in the target area, conducted the assessment, and entered the results in a database. A Geographic Information Systems map was prepared and used, together with census data, to produce a suggested priority list for risk-reduction efforts. To calibrate the visual survey, we developed protocols for interviews with residents and an interior survey that included testing for lead concentrations. The calibration was a key step — without it there would be no assurance that the other work of the class was valid.

This particular class was large, energetic, and well-motivated, and rather quickly began to produce materials that the housing group had agreed to review. From our own grant funds, we provided support for the group's staff to carry out this function, but as the semester went by, the group's responses came back more and more slowly. As we reached the critical stage of calibration of our risk estimates, the group became unresponsive, and finally acknowledged that it had not been able to make the necessary arrangements for us to gain the access to the community that we required. Even though much of the work the class produced had value to the group, many felt that the group's failure to live up to its agreement had prevented us from reaching our goals.

What lessons can be drawn here? First, in setting the schedule for the class, in order to accommodate the housing group, we had to buy into an arrangement that we knew put at risk full completion of the project. It is our experience that working with community partners almost always requires sharing with these partners decisions that otherwise would be reserved to the faculty member alone. Second, a class is likely to be bound to a rather rigid time line. Work needs to be completed by the semester's end, and students move on to other courses and often other locations. A community group takes a much longer view, and is much less invested in any particular schedule. That means the community group may not be able or willing to make the same extraordinary effort to meet deadlines that we often expect of students, and this calls for some adjustment of student attitudes.

In the instance discussed here, a key staff member of the neighborhood housing group took an unannounced vacation at a critical time, a decision our students found hard to accept. From the group's perspective, after being exposed to the intense interest displayed by the Brown students during the semester, the students' complete withdrawal after the semester's end may seem to evidence a lack of sincerity and dedication. Even if another class continues with the same project the following year, there often is an interruption of a semester and a summer, and then there is an entire new cohort of students to meet and train. Also, during this period a faculty member may be fully occupied with other courses and cannot devote significant time to maintaining contacts. Community groups often complain about this lack of continuity. These same issues arise in cooperative projects with agencies, but because agency staff are full-time, have greater resources, and are comfortable with a faster pace, complications are less severe.

We were fortunate to obtain grant funds from a private foundation to support a coordinator for our service-learning programs — part of our Community Environmental Service (CEServe) initiative. When a coordinator is available full-time and can stay in reliable contact with community groups, the continuity difficulty can be somewhat eased. The coordinator can also spend more time than I ever was able to in defining the issues that a practicum course can address, and he or she gains a more realistic sense of what a community group can provide. We have had two people with different backgrounds in our coordinator's position — a recent graduate with a degree from the program has the advantage of knowing what students in the program are able to do but must learn a great deal about the community; someone familiar with the community needs to learn quickly about the academic program. Our experience is that both approaches can be effective, but the former is preferable.

Another lesson from experience is that, whenever possible, one should avoid working with a single community group. Then, if one group falters, at least some chance exists that another partner group can pick up the slack. I caution that this may require some tactful mediation, since community groups do not always have compatible goals or even much affection for one another.

An experience from another class illustrates two other lessons worth recounting. A grass-roots partner group had identified the creation of a park on a vacant lot in its neighborhood as a priority. A project group of students in the practicum researched the issue and identified an administrative process they believed would pressure the parks department to comply with the community's wishes. Another student project group prepared a proposed design for the park, including a playground using recycled materials and a community garden with permaculture features, all to be surrounded by lush greenery.

The grass-roots group rejected both ideas quite firmly, explaining that its primary interest in creating a park was to demonstrate community power, which was better effected by occupying the office of the parks director than by an administrative process, no matter how effective. Indeed, it mentioned that a demonstration of community power was even more important than getting the park. Further, the grass-roots group's preference for a park design was, to our students' horror, an enclosure with a chain-link fence on three sides and a lockable gate, its key to be held by a neighbor. There would be a heavy brick wall between the back of the park and the alley, to prevent drug dealers from cutting through the fence; the ground would be entirely covered with asphalt, to make broken glass removal easier; and the entire park would be brilliantly lighted. So the park would be fully visible, there would be no trees. The group's highest value was safety of its children — park aesthetics were secondary. This humbling experience made us much more careful to discern the subtext of stated community desires and chary of assuming that we shared tastes or values.

Because the entire practicum class is devoted to a single project, we have the luxury of being able to dedicate several class periods early in the semester to discussions of how to approach the community (always with humility, and with at least as much expectation of learning as of teaching). We bring in a staff member of Brown's Swearer Center for Public Service to lead a discussion of service-learning issues, and at several points in the semester hold small-group discussions of issues that arise at the university-community interface. These sessions provide opportunities for sharing the experiences we have gained (sometimes painfully) from earlier classes.

The Thesis

Quite often, students who have taken the practicum class elect in their thesis research to continue and extend a project that the class could not complete. This happens somewhat more frequently when the class views their service project as a success, but even in the case of the "failure" described above three students continued to work on aspects of the project for their theses. This extension can go a long way toward reassuring the community of the sincerity of student interest. It also often provides a much more useful product, because these students build on experience and community contacts and have an additional year (and sometimes a summer) to complete their work. On occasion, we have been able to arrange internships or work-study positions (funded by Brown) with community groups, which allow students on financial aid to follow this path.

The practicum course is only one way in which students identify service-related thesis topics. For reasons completely analogous to the benefits of working with a community partner in our practicum course, we have for years suggested potential thesis topics that are of interest to someone outside of Brown, usually someone in an agency or a nonprofit organization. These connections provide easier access to information and people, offer the incentive of potential utility for the work, and not infrequently lead to job offers after graduation. Frequently, the outside contact is asked to be an additional reader for a standard thesis or one of the three readers required for an honors thesis. This ensures that the thesis is read by someone who can use it, and it gives the outside contact a stronger stake in the thesis process.

A thesis several years ago examined the thermal efficiency of low-income housing being built for a local housing authority. The thesis writer persuaded the director of the housing agency to be a reader, with the result that the next generation of housing was built to a significantly higher energy standard. In the second chapter of this story, another student four years later surveyed these more-efficient houses to see whether the predicted energy savings had occurred. She discovered that inadequate ventilation had been provided, so that moisture buildup was a problem, and that some tenants had an energy subsidy that encouraged excess energy consumption. Once again, the director of the housing agency was a reader of the honors thesis, and again was persuaded to correct the problems.

The thesis process begins for our undergraduate majors in their fifth semester, shortly after they have declared their major. First-semester juniors are matched with a senior (a thesis buddy) who usually is just beginning thesis research and they accompany the senior to meetings with her or his faculty thesis sponsor, typically half-hour meetings each week. Not all juniors take advantage of this opportunity, but those who do find that it demystifies the process and makes their own search for a thesis topic easier.

One technique for identifying service opportunities is to organize a thesis fair at the beginning of the spring semester. Representatives of all agencies and groups with which we have worked (successfully) in the past are invited, as are all juniors and beginning master's students. Our guests each make a short presentation on work they would like to have done, and then the formal session is ended and interested students discuss the ideas in small groups. We caution that suggested projects should be of interest to an organization but not part of the organization's essential functions, because student efforts can never be guaranteed to be successful. Once a match is made, the organization representative usually agrees to be a thesis reader.

Early in his or her sixth semester, each student submits one or more thesis topic proposals. These are reviewed and commented on by the faculty, and faculty sponsors are assigned, based on commonality of interests, the student's preference, and the need to balance faculty workloads. Sometimes we are able to arrange a summer experience that is relevant to the thesis, but most thesis work begins in the student's seventh semester. A significant piece of written work is due at the end of this seventh semester and goes to all readers for comment.

All students present their work in a seminar given to the entire Center for Environmental Studies sometime during their final semester of thesis work. Dates are assigned by lottery, and if the date a student draws is at the beginning of the semester, the presentation necessarily is of a work-in-progress. Community organization and agency representatives who might have an interest in the topic are invited to attend. Seminars are held at noon, and if the student draws a Thursday, the presentation is part of our Soup Seminar series — soup (prepared by student staff), bread, and juice are available at modest cost. We find that providing food significantly enhances attendance. All majors are "expected" to attend at least half of the thesis seminars, and most attend more regularly. Some examples of service-related theses done by the graduating classes of '95-'97 are provided *on the next page.*

Although students are encouraged (indeed, required) to identify their own thesis "central question," they quite naturally build on past experience, and often look to earlier service-learning courses. The influence of the service-learning seminars on the Woonasquatucket River Greenway and on housing issues in South Providence is clearly visible in the thesis titles. The environmental education initiative and the lead poisoning prevention projects in ES11 also have been influential.

Integration

Although there have been some substantive themes shared among our service-learning efforts (e.g., our schools project and our practicum course have both dealt at various points in time with childhood lead poisoning prevention), there has until recently been no Center-wide attempt to integrate these efforts across classes. As the next step in our evolution, we have begun to work simultaneously on the development of indicators of urban environmental policy in several of our courses, and we believe this has the potential to harmonize our service-learning efforts.

In Fall 1996, the Environmental Perception course explored the attitudes and values of Providence residents toward environmental amenities and risks. Three senior theses looked at various aspects of urban environmental indicators — at the potential for socially derived indicators to be adopted by environmental agencies, at the use of indicators by an industry-sponsored good-government group, and at the attitudes and values of the Southeast Asian community (titles are included in the list above). In Spring 1997, students in the practicum course, working with community partners and the Providence Mayor's Office, developed a suite of indicators and began to map

Some Service-Related Theses

- Environmental Education in the Urban Setting: An Investigation in a Providence Classroom
- Rebuilding a Neighborhood Movement: Low-Income Housing in South Providence
- A Sense of Place: Cooperative Housing in Providence, RI
- Prospects for the Surveillance of Occupational Illness in RI
- Re-Creating Providence: Preventing Childhood Lead Poisoning in Low-Income Rental Properties
- Fruit of the Woon: A Look at the Urban Planting Component of the Woonasquatucket River Project
- The Health Effect of Radon and Policy Implications for Rhode Island
- Entrepreneurial Inner-City Gardening Programs and Adolescents
- Limbo, Liens, and Litter: Policy Solutions to South Providence's Abandoned and Vacant Land Problem
- Lead Poisoning Prevention in Rhode Island: Achieving Better Compliance
- The Prospects for Active Community Support for the Woonasquatucket River Greenway
- Re-Creating Riverside Mills: A Chance for Alignment of the Ecological and Social Improvements on the Woonasquatucket River Greenway?
- Mujeres en Accion (Women in Action): Strategies for Lead Poisoning Prevention and Health Promotion in Rhode Island's Latino Populations
- Are Turner Reservoir Fish Safe to Eat? A Risk Assessment of Rhode Island Southeast Asian American Fishers
- Looking for Lead in All the Wrong Places? An Examination of the Environmental Protection Agency's Integrated Exposure Uptake Biokinetic Model Using Rhode Island Case Data
- Zoning the Woonasquatucket: Using Zoning for Long-Term Land Protection Around Greenways
- Urban and Community Forestry in Rhode Island: Incorporating Trees Into the Plan
- Designing Effective Strategies for Environmental Education: An Evaluation of the Center for Environmental Studies' Partnership With Providence Public Schools
- Southeast Asians in Providence and Their Urban Environment: Establishing Connections, Assessing Perceptions, Influencing Policy
- Urban Environmental Indicators: A Framework and Application, Providence, RI
- Juggling Priorities: Philosophies on Urban Water Quality Indicators for Providence
- Analysis of Ecosystem Restoration Potential: An Impounded Salt Marsh in Barrington, RI

the city to allow neighborhood comparisons. In the summer of 1997, four students were awarded university research assistantships to extend this work, and several of these students focused on related topics in their theses. The schools project worked with the Providence schoolteachers to develop units on indicators for use by ES11 sections in Fall 1997. This concentrated activity has required closer coordination between faculty than had occurred in the past, and from this new ideas have emerged, including proposals for funding.

The power of such a focused approach is already evident. In May 1997, the Mayor's Office hired consultants to evaluate risks presented by vacant lots (from illegal dumping, and as rat habitats), using an evaluation protocol developed in the practicum course. In June, relying on analyses of these data by the research assistants, the Mayor's Office announced an immediate enforcement action against owners of more than 400 vacant lots and abandoned properties identified as presenting particularly high risks. The success of this partnership encouraged the city in 1998 to request assistance in setting priorities for allocating housing funds to reduce the risk of childhood lead poisoning. The practicum course identified housing characteristics that correlated strongly with lead poisoning, and the students' course report provided base information to support a successful $4-million proposal to the U.S. Department of Housing and Urban Development. Three students from the practicum class have chosen thesis topics on that "Healthy Homes" theme.

The Future?

I believe that we will continue our explorations of partnerships with urban communities, with the hope of improving both the quality of learning for our students and the service to these communities. Whether the service will be direct — in partnership with neighborhood groups — or indirect — in partnership with agencies serving these groups — is less clear. Direct service to low-income communities offers students and faculty a sense of accomplishment and understanding that indirect service cannot match. And yet, even though a partnership with an agency (such as the Mayor's Office) may provide less direct service than does work with a community group, I am coming to believe that the quality of learning for our students is sufficiently higher in the former to encourage us to continue in that direction. For an ES program just beginning service-learning, I strongly advise starting with agency partners and/or with elementary and secondary schools. Authors of other chapters in this volume appear to agree, since agency partners are mentioned far more often than are grass-roots groups.

Finally, it is important to point out that many of the program specifics presented in this chapter will be obsolete by the time they reach print. For the most current version of Brown University's Environmental Studies program, see *http://www.brown.edu/Departments/Environmental_Studies/*.

A View From the Bottom of the Heap:
A Junior Faculty Member Confronts the Risks of Service-Learning

by Katrina Smith Korfmacher

Scenario #1: As a project in Introduction to Environmental Studies, three undergraduates elect to teach environmental education. They have trouble reaching the host schoolteacher, have several miscommunications about scheduling, and finally arrange a field trip that is snowed out. It's the end of the semester and they need to write something up for their environmental studies class, so they take their lesson plan inside. They are taken aback by the activity level of the kids, who run around and won't listen to their lesson. Frustrated, the undergraduates give their environmental studies class and instructor low marks on end-of-the-semester evaluations.

Scenario #2: An upper-level environmental studies class does a small telephone survey to investigate the level of public participation in a town planning decision. The local newspaper picks up the story in its town-and-gown section. The article includes a quotation from one of the college students ridiculing the town council's handling of the matter. The university president receives a call from the councilperson.

Scenario #3: In a capstone seminar on farmland preservation, the participating seniors interview numerous agency personnel, farmers, and developers. Based on that research, the seniors write a report recommending major changes in the existing farmland protection policies of the state. As a courtesy, they send a final copy of their report to the people they interviewed. The next month, an agency staff member phones the seminar instructor expressing her "alarm" that the report misrepresented the information she had provided the students. When the instructor contacts the staffer later for some related research, she is aloof and unhelpful.

None of these scenarios happened to me. But in my first year of teaching service-learning classes at a small liberal arts college, they appeared regularly in nightmares I had about my new job. I have believed in the principle of service-learning since I experienced it as an undergraduate in environmental studies at Brown University. When I landed my first teaching job at Denison University, I remained committed to the idea that community-based learning is crucial to an education in environmental studies. All the same, in my first months as an assistant professor, I began to have qualms about being on the instructor's end of service-learning classes. The more I tried to think through assignments and projects, the more ways I imagined they might go horribly wrong.

Despite its many rewards, embarking on service-learning as an instructor introduces new kinds of uncertainties into an academic career. This chapter talks about some of the risks of service-learning as perceived by a junior faculty member. It discusses a series of questions I have often been asked by new service-learning instructors — and have asked myself. Based on my own experiences and conversations with other instructors, I offer suggestions on how universities can support new faculty in their efforts to incorporate service-learning into their teaching. My purpose is not to argue whether or not the challenges of service-learning outweigh its benefits. What interests me is how these risks are *perceived* by junior faculty, because these perceptions may determine whether, when, and how we choose to engage in service-learning.

Risks of Service-Learning

For reasons discussed throughout this volume, real-world problem solving has vast potential for teaching the skills essential to environmental careers. At the same time, service-learning is inherently riskier than traditional teaching methods. Some environmental studies instructors believe that the more realistic — and hence riskier — the project, the greater the learning. That is, as students assume more responsibility, confront more complexities, and share their findings more directly with stakeholders, the possibilities for real mistakes also multiply. This implies that we should carefully examine the uncertainties involved in service-learning and how they can be confined within acceptable bounds.

What do I mean by the "risks" of service-learning? As the scenarios above demonstrate, there are potential risks to all parties involved. The students face uncertainties in how they will be graded for this new kind of experience, how to work in unfamiliar environments, and how to deal with potential physical risks as they travel off campus. The community participants or clients may find it uncomfortable to relate to, never mind depend on, undergraduates from their neighboring "ivory tower." These student and community perspectives translate into risks for the instructor responsible for bringing them together. The tasks of teaching service-learning classes may add to the burdens junior faculty members already face of developing classes, learning about our new students, contemplating (never mind doing) new research, and adapting to new academic environments. I focus here on the challenges service-learning poses to a junior faculty member.

As I start my academic career, I find there are more complexities to integrating service-learning into my classes than I had anticipated. Establishing community contacts strong enough to bear the burdens of student projects seems to take an overwhelming amount of time. Figuring out how to play the role of facilitator for applied projects takes more mental and emotional energy than designing lectures and in-class group activities. Supporting community-based projects means diving into the intricacies of institutional issues.

Behind these concerns is tenure — the bogeyman that is the undercurrent in so many conversations of junior faculty. The time of judgment six years down the road is certainly not the only thing that matters to idealistic young faculty. However, one cannot deny that many of a junior faculty member's choices are made in light of how they will affect his or her tenure decision. Simply put, my personal goal is to help educate the students at my institution to address the Earth's environmental problems. If I don't get tenure, I can't do this for long. Therefore, although I currently find service-learning a satisfying way to teach environmental studies, I do consider the long-term impacts of my pedagogical choices.

Although the calculus of tenure decisions varies enormously from place to place according to the weight given to teaching, research, and community service, certain concerns about how service-learning affects a candidate's viability are probably common. My experience at a small liberal arts college is my primary basis for reflecting on these concerns, but conversations with faculty at other kinds of institutions have generally confirmed these ideas.

The concerns that weigh on my mind and frequently surface in conversations among other junior faculty members can be summed up in five questions:

• Will teaching service-learning classes take too much of my limited time and energy?

• Will incorporating service-learning in my classes hurt or help my course evaluations?

• What effect will service-learning projects have on the university-community relationship?

• Will being responsible for students in service-learning projects compromise or enhance my professional and personal relationship with the community?

• Will being involved with service-learning work for or against me in the tenure process?

There are certainly many other factors that determine whether and to what extent a new faculty member incorporates service-learning into his or her classes. However, I need to consider at least these questions carefully before I rely significantly on service-learning as a pedagogical mode. I reflect on each question below, including some ideas for minimizing faculty concerns.

Will Teaching Service-Learning Classes Take Too Much of My Limited Time and Energy?

Time is the unit in which the equation of a new faculty member's life is measured: time for teaching, time for research, time for advising, time for meetings, perhaps even time for oneself. This is a zero-sum game — if I spend more time on teaching, there is less time for research, writing, and going to conferences. Since starting up new courses is incredibly time-consuming in any case, it is daunting to think that incorporating service-learning might take even more time.

Service-learning instructors are in consensus that service-learning takes more time than do standard class formats. However, certain approaches to service-learning may be more improvisational than in-class lectures and so be perceived as less demanding of daily preparation. Thus, I wonder whether review committees will acknowledge the time demands of service-learning. As a junior faculty member, I must balance my ideals with how much more time I project service-learning classes will take, and with the concern that this allocation of time may not be taken into account in the tenure decision.

One of the important assumptions behind the faculty time equation is that classes take less time as they are taught over successive years, allowing more time for research. While some logistical elements and standard assignments may be reused from year to year, many service-learning projects must be determined anew by what is happening currently in the community. Not only does this require constant contact with community members or organizations, but also it means that instructors must educate themselves about new issues each year. If service-learning takes more time than in-class learning on an ongoing basis, where will the time be found for research?

On the other hand, there may be some ways to offset these time demands. First, assuming that the faculty member is interested in doing locally applied research and is in a discipline where it is possible to publish based on problem solving, service-learning class activities can lead to research projects. Second, projects can be planned to build on each other from one semester to the next. This may reduce logistical demands. Third, wise use of administrative staff and teaching assistants can also reduce the instructor's tasks.

Will Incorporating Service-Learning in My Classes Hurt or Help My Course Evaluations?

The consensus among Denison University service-learning faculty is that community experiences do not have a negative impact on course evaluations. In fact, many faculty report that they have had positive reactions. However, from time to time there are smashing failures in projects or placements that are reflected in evaluations, even if the instructor does a good job of framing and interpreting the "failure." More often, a project does not quite live up to students' expectations and goals. As an instructor, I realize that as much or more can be learned from a project that goes awry as from one that goes off without a hitch. The students do not have the same perspective, however, and I am very much aware that their short-term reactions on course evaluations will affect my tenure decision.

Knowing this, I have carefully planned group projects in Introduction to Environmental Studies intending to maximize the students' satisfaction with their experiences without compromising what they learned from a real-world experience. In the process, I have discovered that I have a lot more to learn about guiding rewarding community-based projects. In order to avoid placing students in a situation they do not want to be in, I give them a choice of an on-campus project or an off-campus environmental education experience. To give them a chance to design their own projects and set up logistics, I make group projects a semester-long experience. I assign a teaching assistant to each group to provide adequate support and set intermediate deadlines to help the groups keep on schedule.

By and large, the students have completed successful projects and enjoyed the experience. However, there have also been some significant dissatisfactions. Some students seemed to be overwhelmed by a long-term group project in addition to the week-to-week activities of an introductory course. Several of their evaluations have indicated that the students were not sure what they were learning from these experiences. Time devoted to applied projects did not seem intellectually challenging and rewarding to them. I myself have struggled with how to evaluate diverse community-based projects equitably.

Experienced service-learning faculty have made suggestions to me about how to minimize these concerns. One idea is to be extremely clear about the purpose of service-learning and one's criteria for evaluation. Another piece of advice is to spend more of the class relating concepts of environmental studies to the ongoing project work and integrating the student projects into class discussions. This seems to conflict with yet another suggestion I have received: to structure the projects to be narrower both in scope and in duration. I also wonder whether it is worth providing students with a chance to struggle with real-world issues if they might end up frustrated at evaluation time. Will new faculty leap wholeheartedly into service-learning when they are concerned about the stochastic element such projects introduce into the student evaluations? It seems safer to limit service-learning to labs or parts of a course in order to isolate the risks it poses to the students' overall experience of the course.

What Effect Will Service-Learning Projects Have on the University-Community Relationship?

Most dialogues about service-learning focus on how such interaction can improve the community-university relationship. Service-learning may help counter stereotypes on each side, improve the public image of the university, and increase understanding among the academic and local communities. Contemplating the possible outcomes of a variety of service-learning projects, however, I can imagine outcomes that might be perceived negatively by parts of the community — and by the college's administration.

The worst-case scenario for the university-community relationship is physical harm to the students. Other kinds of impacts on the people involved in service-learning are less clear-cut than the risk of physical harm. An occasional student project, interaction, or report might be perceived negatively by local groups or by the community at large. More often, the community groups involved might be disappointed that the students' product is not what the group had hoped for. Or, the community groups might become frustrated with lack of continuity when similar projects are done year after year. Occasional irresponsible behavior by students or recurrent disappointments with outcomes can contribute to the feeling that the students are getting more out of the service-learning experience than the community is, causing community groups to stop participating in such projects.

Furthermore, service-learning projects can impact local politics — especially if they are successful. Environmental problems involve value conflicts, and taking a stand for a solution is bound to be controversial. Because of this, environmental studies faculty have always had to confront the boundary between academics and activism. For most of us, being involved in addressing ongoing local environmental problems has helped motivate us to teach in this field. On the other hand, it can be difficult for a new faculty member to negotiate an acceptable and appropriate political role for representatives of the university in the community.

I have heard of few cases in which the activities of environmental studies classes have resulted in animosity with the community. Maybe this is because we tend to advertise our successes more than our failures. Maybe students' products simply are not that controversial. Or maybe faculty have figured out how to teach service-learning classes in a way that minimizes negative interactions with the community. When I was preparing a capstone seminar on farmland preservation, I thought about training students to do interviews with farmers, discussing how to talk to the press, analyzing the difference between studying an issue and taking a stand, distinguishing emotionally based activism from well-argued policy analysis. I soon realized that I could spend the entire course preparing students to do community-based work, leaving no time to actually do it.

As the examples in this volume show, the potential benefits of service-learning to the university-community relationship are enormous. However, the risks to all parties of such interactions cannot be ignored. Judging from the interest in the questions raised here among environmental studies faculty, the balance between relevance and responsibility must be seen as a recurrent issue for many of us. It is particularly important for new faculty for several reasons. First, new faculty can lack sufficient experience with undergraduates to sense how to guide their behavior without seeming patronizing. Second, new faculty may not understand the political setting of their new institution and the surrounding community well enough to filter their students' work appropriately. Third, if students' community-based work products do create an awkward situation for the university, junior faculty are in a weak position to defend their pedagogical choices. Even if an administration strongly supports service-learning, it is hard to imagine this support would include cases where projects are embarrassing to or critical of the university. Junior faculty might wonder whether they will receive credit for enhancing relations with the community through successful projects, or if negative interactions with the community will affect their standing in the university.

Will Being Responsible for Students in Service-Learning Projects Compromise or Enhance My Professional and Personal Relationship With the Community?

As mentioned above, service-learning activities can have a positive or negative impact on university-community relationships. In addition, such interactions may have direct impacts on the sponsoring faculty member. Negative interactions between students and community groups can have personal repercussions for the instructor, who is generally seen as responsible for the students' work and who remains in the community after the students have graduated. This can be a particularly daunting prospect in the small, tightly knit communities that are home to many liberal arts colleges. In addition, community members will not necessarily distinguish individual students' performance from their overall impression of their contact with the instructor and even the university as a whole. If the faculty member hopes to build on relationships with community groups for his or her research, the risk of students making a negative impression can be professionally significant, as well.

I confronted this concern in the capstone seminar mentioned above. Coming from a coastal environment, I knew little about Midwestern agricultural issues and thought leading a related seminar would be a good way to learn more. In some ways, this may have worked too well. To prepare for the course, I wrote a long-shot proposal that ended up getting funded: I was suddenly committed to doing research on farmers' perspectives on farmland preservation. As a result, my students' interactions with the local agricultural community took on a new significance. What if local farmers got tired of being interviewed? What if the community workshop the students held to propose zoning changes made residents angry at anyone connected with Denison University? On the one hand, service-learning guided me into a new research area. On the other, the continuing involvement of students in the community raised uncertainties for my planned research.

Service-learning projects may lead to positive ties with community organizations that the faculty member can build on from year to year into a major research project. However, a certain number of relationships forged in this way are bound to reach dead ends. For this reason, junior faculty might be cautious about exposing their major research projects to the uncertainties of service-learning.

Will Being Involved With Service-Learning Work For or Against Me in the Tenure Process?

This question combines the other four questions and certainly has no single answer. Because I am at the beginning of the tenure countdown, I can only report what I have experienced in relation to what I have been told. Junior faculty are immediately indoctrinated with the three criteria for tenure: teaching, research, and service. The relative importance of each varies from place to place — at Denison University, teaching is clearly the top priority.

How service-learning influences the review of my teaching is primarily a function of how service-learning affects my teaching evaluations (related to question 1), although initially I may be given credit for innovation and risk taking. Beyond teaching evaluations, I anticipate that it will be difficult for review committees to interpret service-learning. The learning part of service-learning is hard to see; that is, it is much more difficult to "sit in" on a community project than on a lecture. It is probably more complicated to assess an instructor's skill as interpreter, motivator, and facilitator than it is to evaluate his or her lecture style. Because of this, I expect it will be incumbent on me to interpret service-learning through assembling a teaching portfolio that talks about my philosophy, goals, and methods. Although it could help me to get the endorsement of community groups I work with, I will need to explore how to get such responses included in my review.

As noted above, service-learning will have its biggest influence on my scholarship if it takes too much time away from research and writing. On the other hand, service-learning could help my research, as in the farmland preservation example. I do not know at this stage whether such applied work will count as scholarship, whether I can build it into longer-term projects, and how combining research and teaching in this way will be viewed by review committees. This certainly varies by discipline. For some junior faculty, those journals that publish applied work are not respected by the departments or outside disciplinary reviewers. What journals and kinds of work will "count" could be difficult for junior faculty to decipher, especially if they consider themselves to be interdisciplinary or they hold joint appointments.

I was an embarrassingly long way through graduate school before I realized that the service aspect of the tenure criteria primarily meant serving the university community. I know that my service on various environmental groups and citizen action committees is approved of by the college, but I wonder how it will "count," since it is not direct service to the university community. I hope that colleges can expand the definition of "community service" to include such contributions to the larger community — but I'm not sanguine that this will happen before I come up for tenure.

Supporting Service-Learning by Junior Faculty

Senior faculty doing service-learning have helped me address some of the uncertainties discussed above. However, there is also a significant role for institutional support of service-learning in the form of logistical and administrative help, building networks among colleagues, and clear definition of the role of service-learning in the review process. Such support is important for the development of junior faculty who are enthusiastic about the ideas of service-learning but are skeptical about its implications for their careers. So, for any senior faculty and administrators who read this, I want to offer a few ideas about how to support junior faculty members' increased participation in service-learning.

First, mitigate the increased time demands of service-learning. Such mitigation can range from course releases to service-learning teaching assistants to administrative support of a community service coordinator, as described in the chapter from Brown University [see pp. 65ff.]. This support needs to be strong enough to provide students with the resources they need to be safe and responsible as they go out into the community. Universities should not claim credit for sponsoring service-learning without providing the logistical support needed to ensure the safety of the students and the careers of the faculty involved.

Second, support service-learning faculty networks. I have benefitted enormously from talking with service-learning faculty in other disciplines. For example, Denison University's new Center for Service-Learning recently sponsored a three-day workshop for faculty doing service-learning in all disciplines. At this workshop, we shared syllabi, evaluation methods, and placement strategies that have informed my class planning. We also discussed ways to support networks among faculty, such as sponsoring periodic workshops, faculty lunches, and faculty mentoring relationships.

Third, provide specific guidance about the role of service-learning in the institution to address some of the uncertainties discussed in this chapter. For example, guidelines on university-community interactions could help set bounds for what students can and cannot do. A clear statement of how teaching, scholarship, and service based on service-learning are treated in faculty reviews might provide reassurance. Systematic research about the effects of service-learning on faculty careers would be informative. Because service-learning is relatively new in most colleges and because many faculty do not become involved until after they have tenure, new faculty cannot simply look to their senior colleagues for precedent. Consequently, proactive statements by university administrators are especially important to encouraging service-learning.

Fourth, make service-learning count. Virtually all of the uncertainties discussed above relate in one way or another to the tenure review criteria. Service-learning does not clearly enhance a faculty member's portfolio with respect to any of the three existing criteria. That is, while service-learning can improve teaching evaluations when projects are successful, provide research opportunities in fields that accept applied research, and contribute to the service criterion at some institutions, there is also a chance that none of these will be true. Why would junior faculty embark on a major new activity that introduces more uncertainty into the morass of their tenure review process? The tensions discussed above would be significantly mitigated by making service-learning a significant criterion in and of itself in the tenure review process.

I am part of the first generation of environmental studies instructors who have experienced service-learning as undergraduates (although we did not use that phrase back then). Unlike the many environmental studies faculty who hold adjunct appointments from home disciplines or departments that do not support service-learning, my appointment is solely in the applied field of environmental studies. In fact, my colleagues in environmental studies at Denison University and elsewhere share a commitment to service-learning. As a policy scientist, my own discipline supports research on applied problem solving, which fits well with service-learning projects. I teach at a college with an administration that is very supportive of environmental studies, service-learning, and faculty who experiment to improve their teaching. Nonetheless, I still feel pressures to minimize the risks to my teaching evaluations, to getting research done, and to my standing in the community. Sharing experiences such as those discussed in this book reminds me why I am willing to confront the uncertainties of service-learning I have identified: I teach environmental studies because I want to help people learn to solve the environmental crises our society faces now and in the future. There is no doubt in my mind that actually doing so is the best way to learn.

Raising Fish and Tomatoes to Save the Rustbelt

by Eric Pallant

"Being a fishhead was a great thing."

— Becky Curtis

The Challenge

Meadville, Pennsylvania (pop. 14,900), is the home of Allegheny College and the first town in America to manufacture zippers, but it is no longer the home of Talon's zipper factory. The factory closed during the depression of the 1980s. Talon shut its doors within months of the closings at Avtex Fibers, Abex Brakeshoe, and the Conrail fix-it yard for freight trains. Avtex, a maker of rayon, left behind a Superfund dump, and only a court injunction kept Conrail from ripping up the tracks that connect Meadville to the rest of the country. With the loss of more than 3,000 jobs between 1983 and 1986, Meadville's unemployment rate shot into the teens. Stores closed. Houses were abandoned.

Steep unemployment among blue-collar workers did not breed a strong environmental ethic. On the contrary, a staunch antigovernment, anti-regulation ideology permeates local politics. Meetings to support local militias have been well attended, and northwestern Pennsylvania appears to be well prepared for any invasions directed by the United Nations. Although unemployment has dropped by two-thirds in little more than a decade, emigration has produced much of that decline. Those who could leave have left. Hard work by the regional redevelopment authorities has generated more than a thousand jobs since 1990, but many of the new jobs are low paying. Efforts to attract a major factory to revive the town have failed. Nearly one in seven residents of Crawford County still lives in poverty.

So what kind of service-learning can a 1990s department of environmental science offer to a community such as this? The service, it seemed to me, was to provide jobs: jobs that were fulfilling, and part of an ecologically restorative, sustainable economy. First, I read some big names in ecological economics: Paul Hawken, Herman Daly, Robert Costanza. I liked their theory, but struggled to try to apply it to Meadville: Could I name two businesses that would come to Meadville, create jobs, make a profit, and improve the environment all at the same time? Second, I searched the local landscape for resources that might be used both profitably and sustainably. My list included timber, water, scenery, and abandoned factory sites.

For example, more than 50 percent of Crawford County is covered with forests. Unfortunately, nearly all those forests are hacked to the ground within the hour the trees reach marketable dimensions — a practice driven by underclass landowners and unscrupulous timber haulers. So there is plenty of room for improvement in our forests. The same might be said for our weather. Meadville's nickname, "Mudville," is not just a charming local expression. It really does rain a lot here. A solar energy expert has told us that Meadville averages just 44 blue-sky days a year. However, that means streams, groundwater, and wetlands are nearly always full, and all those trees, streams, and wetlands mean our scenery is good and so is hunting, fishing, birding, canoeing, and hiking. Consequently, ecotourism has some potential. Finally, all the abandoned factory sites are perfect brownfield locations for new businesses to use without having to rip up pastures and forests.

I brought my ideas for the sustainable economic development of our resources to my departmental colleagues, and after discussion and refinement we divided them up on the basis of inclination and expertise into Junior Seminars. Junior Seminars in the environmental science department at Allegheny have long been bastions of student teamwork directed at solving real-world problems. My idea was to use our plentiful supply of water to grow fish in tanks warmed by heat wasted at a local factory. Dissolved fish excrement from the aquaculture tanks would be pumped to a greenhouse to nourish vegetables and herbs. The integrated hydroponics and aquaculture operation, sometimes called aquaponics, would create a couple of jobs and provide the rest of the town with locally produced fish, the herbs to season it, and a side of salad, all available at the BiLo supermarket. It would also serve as a model for other depressed small towns.

I employed a college junior as a research assistant the summer before my seminar to gather whatever information she could on the world of aquaponics. I even went to visit an aquaponics operation outside New York City right before classes started. The operator, Annie Farrell, of Cabbage Hills Farms, Inc., was exceptionally informative. She told me that "no aquaponics plant anywhere [including her own] is profitable. The one that is closest to being profitable has already dumped $16 million into its operation. Another has been at it for eight years without breaking even, and a third just recently lost its entire stock of fish to a staph infection." Reading between the lines, I concluded that there must be a reason why so many people were trying to get started despite the odds. Ignoring Farrell's dire predictions, I handed the charge of designing a profitable aquaponics factory to a bunch of inexperienced 20-year-olds.

The Class

I asked the 15 students enrolled in my Fall 1996 Junior Seminar, called "Sustainable Solutions," to investigate the feasibility of creating a sustainable aquaponics business in Meadville. On the first day of class, I told them (though they forgot) that they were beginning a long-term project that might take years to complete, if even then. Disappointment mounted midway through the semester when it became clear they weren't going to get to eat the fruits of their labor by finals. So I promised to continue their work (using students who would build on their successes) if they produced enough information and their feasibility study demonstrated aquaponics was worth pursuing. I urged them to infuse the project with everything they could think of that would make the factory a paradigm of sustainable development, but insisted they could not sacrifice profitability on the altar of environmental correctness, a position that grated several the wrong way for much of the semester. A student whose email to me always arrived from "SULL-DADDY" insisted in one class that "[he didn't] care whether the aquaponics plant ever makes a profit so long as it uses sustainable energy." No one refuted him, and I fell off my chair in disbelief. Though SULL-DADDY's determination to back a factory that lost money was impractical, the ensuing discussion of how far we should go to trade off sustainability for a factory in the black was excellent.

It's worth speculating, however, on what I would have done if the midsemester calculations were already showing that only a fool would bother proceeding. I'd like to believe that even a feasibility study demonstrating guaranteed financial losses year after year would have been intellectually remunerative. Students could still have proven to themselves which parts of sustainability don't cut it in the 1990s, and that would have been lesson enough. But the issue never arose, for within days of the opening bell the class confirmed my summer research. They contacted lots of people trying to assemble hydroponic and aquaculture plants, and we took that to mean that if we failed to construct a bottom line in the black our research wasn't good enough. Either that or everyone else was crazy, and the "everyone else" included the agribusiness behemoth Archer Daniels Midland. If we designed sustainability into the operation correctly, I reasoned — i.e., very efficient recycling of water, energy, and materials — it would help make our factory just a little more competitive than the others. At least that is what the theorists in ecological economics suggest, and I never let my students forget it.

We met once a week for one semester around a large table. I acted as the lead consultant in a "firm" of "consultants" and divided the students among several research teams. The groups were told to

1. Choose crops and species of fish.

2. Assess local markets for greenhouse vegetables, herbs, and *Tilapia* fish, or other fish if *Tilapia* wasn't the right choice.

3. Calculate the energy requirements to heat fish tanks, pump water to greenhouse vegetables, light and warm the greenhouse and see whether the entire operation could run off heat wasted by an existing industry.

4. Determine whether excess heat in the operation (should any exist) could be used to dry produce from the greenhouse plus fruits produced by area farmers.

5. Design the factory so the water and nutrients knew how to get from the fish to the veggies and back again, arriving with the right amounts for each station.

6. Identify several plant locations, including appropriate brownfields (abandoned factories) adjacent to surviving industries, and rank them.

7. Prepare a net present value estimate for a business under optimistic and pessimistic scenarios.

8. Write and edit a final report.

During the first class, I also made it clear that their work mattered, not just to the life of a future hothouse tomato but also as part of a larger puzzle that I and a small core of others dedicated to sustainable development were trying to assemble in northwestern Pennsylvania. To raise the stakes still further, I let them know that their research was being supported in part by the Heinz Family Endowments, that were eagerly awaiting the results before they decided whether to supply additional funding to the Department of Environmental Science at Allegheny. Raising the stakes acted as a stimulant. The students charged ahead, each working on his or her own small portion of the puzzle, tackling issues in business planning and energy efficiency for which they had no training and for which Allegheny offers little support. I relied, too, on what I had learned from earlier seminars: Students are motivated by a desire for immortality. A fish farm that consumes its own excrement would let them leave their mark on the local community, almost as if they were constructing a statue of themselves on the town square.

The integrity of the research groups lasted two weeks. By that time, students were surging into class and stopping one another in hallways and dormitories with discoveries that were more important to another group than to their own. Information poured in throughout the semester from the World Wide Web, hundreds and hundreds of telephone calls, field trips, letters, and email discussions with growers and aquaponics aficionados from Arizona to the Virgin Islands. Students invented and then perfected a method of interview that began meekly with "Hi, I'm a junior in college [giggle, giggle], and I'm doing a report about aquaculture." Five minutes into the interview, after the barricades were fully breached, students let loose with heavy artillery. "You said the coefficient of production for the low-end heat pump was 2.8, but my research shows. . . ."

About a month into the semester things really started hopping when the Small Business Administration, the Meadville Redevelopment Authority, and the Crawford County Development Corporation all responded to our requests for assistance. We were inundated with eager engineers and business analysts. I even started getting solicitations from rural electrification cooperatives trying to sell me electricity to run my factory. More than once I had to be firm: "I'm not starting a company. I'm just *studying* how to start a company."

Class meetings turned into free-for-alls. Each week as we gathered around the table, students performed concurrent brain-dumps, followed by group hand-wringing. We worried whether juniors in a college with no business school and no engineering program could really achieve anything meaningful. I concluded our weekly sessions by assigning new tasks for the upcoming week to answer questions generated during our three hours together. Still, Chrissy Scott told me:

> [She] felt a whole lot more motivation to work hard because there was a
> specific endpoint to reach and no one knew just how much work was
> required. The fact that this was a real feasibility study, and not just for
> practice or to help [students] learn, increased the determination to get the
> job done and for it to be done perfectly.

Kristen Graziano agreed: "I've never worked so hard to just go to class! Unlike any other curriculum, the material from this class will never leave me, because I have essentially taught it to myself through hands-on experiences."

Evaluation of student performance in a class where students are supposed to work in teams is normally tough for any instructor; but in this class, where the groups students were assigned to dissolved, it got tougher before it got easier. In order to complete a feasibility study in about a dozen weeks using novices, I needed to see good work and a lot of it. The good students took off like speedboats, at first pulling the slower ones behind them and then eventually forming new groups of their own. It was obvious from what each student was sending me in his or her weekly email dumps what he or she was hauling in, and even more clear during our weekly class meetings which students knew what they were doing.

What worked best of all were two narrative evaluations I had the class prepare — one at mid term and one at the end. The midterm report let participants tell me quite clearly what was going well, and what wasn't, with them, their teammates, and the class as a whole. That's when the burnout issue came up, and I took the class on a hiatus of two weeks to work on more-philosophical issues related to sustainability before pushing them to full throttle in an effort to squeeze the final bits of research out of them before finals. Their evaluations also gave me a chance to tell them what I liked about their contributions up to that point and what more I hoped they would achieve in order to improve the midterm grade each was receiving. I had to tell several students that learning is not a passive process. I told Megan Terebus, a competitive swimmer, "You will need to be just as aggressive out of the blocks in this class as you are during a meet. It won't be enough to just dive into the water. You will have to push hard with every stroke to teach yourself what you need to know for this class and in learning situations beyond this one." Then I gave Megan and several others low grades. It worked. The quality of work improved during the second half of the class, and my final grade for each student was a summation of the quantity and quality of the work presented in class, in written work, and during meetings with me and of the two self-evaluations.

The Results

By the end of the semester, my original prediction stood unamended: It would be years before my class could hold a reunion dinner of broiled *Tilapia* served on a bed of greenhouse lettuce. But the class was still a success, and for reasons I hadn't imagined.

We introduced the business community of northwestern Pennsylvania to sustainable development, and they loved it. Maryann Martin, director of grants administration for the Crawford County Development Corporation, told me:

> Allegheny College's Environmental Science students have really influenced our thinking in making the environment a priority in whatever we do. Because our offices are at a site that was a Superfund site, we want to continue to work with companies that will keep the environment clean and healthy and not deplete resources.

Martin, whose primary function for years had been to attract any old jobs, began sending me monthly progress reports on a tire recycling business she was courting. It wasn't just that tire recycling was appealing, it was that Martin knew that the process of melting the tires was going to generate enough heat and natural gas as by-products to run the aquaponics farm.

Chet Shoop, an engineering consultant from Erie, Pennsylvania, brought our way by the Small Business Administration, called our project "one of the most interesting I have ever worked on." Shoop became so excited that he brought us five more engineers with specialties in heat transfer, mechanics, and systems analysis. The engineers were fascinated by a project whose primary objective was to balance sustainability, worker satisfaction, and profit.

They had all spent careers groveling exclusively for profit. They loved tinkering with plant designs to increase energy, material, and water efficiency. Sarah Vernier, of the Small Business Administration's office in Meadville, echoed the engineers. She, too, called the creation of an aquaponics plant "a fascinating proposal," and she called me several times to be sure that I and my students had received all the support we needed. Joe Boito, the geothermal energy expert for our regional electric company, GPU, made a special trip to Allegheny to help us work through calculations and cost estimates.

The integration of aquaculture and hydroponics took on a life of its own, too. Because plants can absorb only dissolved nutrients, and much of what fish excrete is solid, the current factory design has been modified to include a mushroom room producing shiitakes and portabellas on a substrate of solid fish poops mixed with newsprint now piling up at our recycling center for lack of markets. Thus, there is a fish room, a greenhouse, a fruit drying room, and a mushroom room, with heat exchangers to take heat out of the mushroom room and put it into the food drying room.

Markets for our products are soft. Currently, *Tilapia* arrives in Meadville rarely, and only to one store. It comes from Costa Rica to Maine to Pittsburgh to our local Giant Eagle supermarket, where it sells very slowly because the name is funny. If *Tilapia* were renamed for the way it tastes, "boring-white-fish-that-Americans-would-eat," it would sell better in places such as Meadville. Lacking a local supermarket eager for our product, we called Heinz to assess its interest in buying our vegetables and fish to make soup, but got nowhere with the lead. Alas, the family endowments and the pickle people are completely divorced these days. Nevertheless, the markets we could secure were sufficient to cover production. After Roy Campbell, the business analyst for the Small Business Administration, ran our last net present value estimate on his computers, he said, "the numbers look reliable enough that I would be ready to invest in it."

There were unforeseen successes in the classroom, too. Spontaneity and chaos often overwhelmed us. Once, near the beginning, all 15 students went to the blackboard simultaneously to list their facts under 11 different categories. On another occasion near the very end of the semester, as we were trying to tie up loose ends, all the students rushed out of the room to telephones throughout the building we worked in. Few events have been as satisfying to me as a teacher as those two, when the excitement of learning overcame conventional decorum. During both events, I sat at the table alone waiting for the students' breathless return to the customary.

In addition to teaching Meadville about sustainability, the students came away with extraordinary lessons of their own. Chrissy Scott summed up the academic side of things: "Our research was fully interdisciplinary and collaborative so that we had to learn everything from the thermodynamics of heat pumps to the biogeochemical cycling of fish crap and the business of advertising." By the end of the semester Becky Curtis admitted, "I was so tired of thinking because I had never thought as much as I had in that one class. It was not just memorizing notes but actually thinking, understanding, and putting the pieces together."

Shana Stewart listed the class lessons she added to her notes. The list is interesting, because we discussed much of it but I never lectured about any of it:

> 1. *Make a good presentation of yourself — even if it means wearing dress clothes. 2. Be on time. 3. It's easier to criticize a new idea, than to run with one or come up with one. 4. Not everyone [who] looks like they know what they're doing really does. 5. Be skeptical of your sources. 6. Expect impediments, but realize that you will most likely be able to cross them if you persevere. 7. I have the ability to teach myself, and I get more out of it than when someone is feeding me information. 8. Most people are actually pretty nice and open to these sort of projects. 9. Staunch educators: You don't always have to lecture to teach or for me to learn. In fact, I probably learned and will retain more information from this class than many of my other classes, and I did not have one exam or paper on aquaponics.*

Kristen Graziano added to Stewart's list:

> *I learned a tremendous amount from failure and frustration; it's hard to believe the number of trials it took for me to get the information I wanted. I've learned to network by phone, email, and correspondence. Granted, there were days I wanted to choke someone because they criticized an idea I had spent days intensely researching. It taught me the importance of listening and presenting my information quickly, clearly, and concisely!*

The biggest successes for the students were how they, as future promoters of environmental issues, came to view their task. According to Scott Ferrenberg:

> *[There was] one unexpected occurrence in particular, which really changed the way I think about sustainable development. I altered my feelings toward business. At the onset of the class, I viewed business as an evil entity hell-bent on making money regardless of the costs to society. After our class focus began to shift from how to make a sustainable, efficient, model business toward how to make a profit, I realized that my earlier thoughts were unfounded. If a group of environmental science and studies majors could become caught up in making money and capturing a market, I could understand how people, without an environmental focus, could do so. These*

people are not inherently evil and money-minded, but rather trying to survive in a capitalist society.

Regardless of whether a *Tilapia* ever grows in Meadville, a profound change has occurred. I am now a regular collaborator with the redevelopment authorities in Crawford and Venango Counties. Together we think about redevelopment in terms of sustainable development. And in addition to whatever sustainable businesses we can bring to life in Meadville, at some other time and some other place sustainable businesses like the one my students created will grow. Becky Curtis has the skills to make her dream come true:

> *I hope to one day work with inner-city youth. I have been thinking of starting something like an aquaponics project in the city to give the youth a place to come, work a little, but especially to enjoy the beauty of wildlife right in their own backyards.*

Fulfilling and Expanding the Mission of a Community College

by Janice Alexander

Flathead Valley Community College (FVCC), located in rural northwest Montana, is surrounded by pristine areas such as Glacier National Park, Bob Marshall Wilderness, and the Jewel Basin. Our location provides many needs and opportunities for environmental service-learning. We have used our Environmental Science 101 course as the cornerstone of environmental service, and have expanded from there to tie environmental service into other courses such as General Biology, Business Communications, Micro- and Macroeconomics, Social Problems, and Introductory Sociology. However, our primary focus has been the "Waste Not" project, with expansion in 1997 to include additional environmental service areas.

The "Waste Not" service-learning project, begun in 1994-95, was designed as a collaboration between FVCC, Kalispell Junior High, Citizens for a Better Flathead (CFBF), the Retired and Senior Volunteer Program (RSVP), and the Flathead County Solid Waste Board. The "Waste Not" project is a consumer education program that seeks to heighten awareness about solid waste issues while promoting ways to reduce the volume and toxicity of Flathead County's waste stream. The Flathead County landfill board was initially quite interested in this collaborative educational project, since the Montana legislature had passed the Integrated Waste Management Act of 1991, an act that asked each county to develop strategies to achieve a waste reduction goal of 25 percent by 1996. In addition, Flathead County had no hazardous waste disposal collection facility for business or household hazardous waste. Another pollution source was Flathead County's storm-drain system, which unloads directly into lakes and streams.

At the time I was gearing up to teach the first environmental science course at FVCC. I had designed the course with service-learning as an integral part so that students would learn about and be involved in local concerns and, I hoped, not just envision the material learned in the course as relevant somewhere else. I was trying to plan a solid waste–related service project at the same time that Mayre Flowers, of CFBF, and the Flathead County Solid Waste Board were developing strategies to meet the 25 percent reduction goal. With the help of FVCC's new service-learning coordinator, we put the program together. We applied for funding for the project through an American Association of Community Colleges service-learning grant program, with matching funds coming from the Flathead County Solid Waste Board and FVCC, and we were excited to be chosen as a grant recipient.

The first year was designed to educate the public about the identification, safe use, and disposal of — as well as less-toxic alternatives to — hazardous household waste products, leading up to Household Hazardous Waste Days. These days, scheduled during the springs of 1994, 1995, and 1996, were intended to allow residents an opportunity to dispose of their household hazardous waste legally. Mayre Flowers agreed to train my service-learning students and volunteers from RSVP to give presentations on household hazardous waste in local schools and to citizen groups. Our hope was to generate some cross-generational interactions by having a college student and an RSVP member present jointly.

The First Try

The first day of class, my students were informed they would be the first official class at FVCC to have service-learning as a required part of a course. The class was split between initial excitement and fear that they would not have time to fulfill the service requirement. I explained that service-learning had been considered in the context of developing realistic class expectations, and that without service-learning a different requirement would have existed. The fact that we were to be the guinea pigs in this first effort also raised enthusiasm and lowered expectations of a perfect outcome. Since the whole class was to be involved, I arranged for Mayre Flowers to come in during class time to give a lecture on solid and hazardous waste issues in Flathead County. I also arranged the class schedule so that the students would have completed an exam on these chapters just prior to the lecture. This worked wonderfully! Students were very curious to learn how our local system worked and asked a lot of questions, since they already had some knowledge of how the system "should" work. This lecture was followed up with a three-hour training session on household hazardous waste and how to give a presentation on it. Presenters who felt the need for additional practice time met one-on-one outside of class with two trainers. Students had to be flexible with presentations, since schools were interested in 45-minute presentations but most citizen groups wanted them to last only 20 to 30 minutes. Presentations were to include basic information, a short video, a game, and a trivia quiz. Audience questions were to be addressed throughout the presentation, and listeners were encouraged to relay their personal experiences.

We found the most challenging part was scheduling the presentations. Our service-learning intern received phone calls from interested teachers and groups and tentative dates, which then had to be matched with the students' schedules. Flyers to the schools did not always get to teachers, causing more delays. In retrospect, all informational flyers should have gone directly to the teachers as well as to administrations to speed up the process. A deadline for responses from teachers and groups could then have been set to allow adequate time for scheduling, instead of the frantic last-minute scheduling that often occurred. Even so, the students loved presenting and their interactions with younger students and community groups . Often they were amazed by the level of audience interest and the number of questions asked. Those who presented with RSVP members were impressed with the wealth of knowledge these folks had acquired in their lifetimes. Feedback on presentations was received via a survey, as well as through comments by students, teachers, and citizen group members. Survey results indicated 85 percent of respondents believed the program made them more aware of how to identify and safely dispose of household hazardous waste; 88 percent indicated the presentation made them more aware of problems concerning unsafe disposal of household hazardous waste; and only 11 percent indicated awareness of Household Hazardous Waste Day prior to the presentation. Most of my students also participated in the Household Hazardous Waste Day held at the campus, by directing traffic, conducting surveys, and assisting the Flathead County Solid Waste Board. (The board had hired an external company to collect and package the waste and remove it for disposal.) Students' service grades were determined by their completion of a pre-set number of presentations and the quality of their journals.

Early Results

After talking with my students and reading their journals, I knew I definitely wanted to continue service-learning. The results were amazing. Some of their comments included these:

> My experience from doing the service project was extreme. As far as getting involved on the environmental side of the fence my views haven't changed, but they have been made more stable with education. Household hazardous waste and how to dispose of it was unknown to me prior to this experience. I poured things down the sink. . . . I have learned more in this class and enjoyed it more in this class than any I have taken prior to it. Not only to benefit myself, but also to benefit the next generation by presenting the subject.

> The "Waste Not" project's household hazardous waste collection day presentations were time-worthy projects. They allowed me to glimpse into a classroom from a different point of view, as a teacher, and taught me how I can personally contribute to an environmental project. . . . [Today] I did two presentations for seventh-graders. They were really funny. They look so small, and think themselves so big. (I remember the days!) The teacher was a nice woman. She seemed genuinely interested in the program.

Giving the presentations [was] great. I feel as though all the students got something out of it. As I gave them, I realized that some of the work we did in class applied to what I was speaking about.

Taking Next Steps

The Flathead County Solid Waste Board members were able to meet my students at Household Hazardous Waste Day, and Mayre Flowers and I presented a short summary of the semester's work to the board at its April meeting. All partners were interested in continuing the project for the following year. As part of FVCC's original grant, we had put aside some funding to entice more faculty next year into offering service-learning in their classes through the "Waste Not" project.

Faculty applied for $500 mini-grants to incorporate the "Waste Not" project into one fall and one spring semester course the following year. Grants were utilized for stipends and any course expenses. The mini-grant recipients included faculty teaching Microeconomics (fall/spring); Social Problems (fall) and Introductory Sociology (spring); and General Biology (fall/spring).

A Second Round

The second year of the "Waste Not" project involved students from the Microeconomics, General Biology, and Environmental Science courses. These students conducted a detailed waste stream analysis at FVCC and Kalispell Junior High in conjunction with the school's students and RSVP members. The waste stream analysis included solid and hazardous waste (as well as energy efficiency). The Social Problems and Introductory Sociology courses conducted a survey to assess any statistically significant differences between awareness and attitudes at FVCC and at Kalispell Junior High before and after the waste audit. These were random surveys of classes on campus, omitting the students in specific courses involved in the waste audit. Results from the FVCC survey indicated an increase in the number of students who knew what *source reduction* is, considered waste management a problem at FVCC, and said they had done something recently to reduce waste on campus. Teams of students focused on specific areas such as recycling, the use of recyclable materials, energy usage, water usage, pesticide and herbicide usage, and the use of toxic versus nontoxic supplies.

All four classes started the semester with a tour of the local landfill — an event that made quite an impression on the Flathead County Solid Waste Board's director. He and Mayre Flowers conducted the landfill tour, filling us in on its design, history, and usage. The students were quite impressed. Most had never been to a landfill before, and none had ever toured one. They were all surprised that it did not stink! Many students were also surprised to discover a separate section for composting tree branches, and a "white goods" (major appliances) area.

A second highlight of the fall semester was another trip to the landfill, this time to sort garbage. We dressed in old clothes, heavy plastic aprons, and rubber gloves, with goggles available as needed. Containers were set up to receive the different plastic and paper types, organic material, hazardous waste, different metal types, and glass. Everyone sorted bags of garbage, and when a container was filled it was weighed and emptied in the appropriate place. Students enjoyed being outdoors (even in November) and working with students from other college classes as well as with the junior high students, their teachers, and FVCC faculty. RSVP members, CFBF members, and some members of the Flathead County Solid Waste Board. The interaction between the groups was great. Everyone felt he or she was involved in an important task. One of the students, as his semester project, was assigned the task of tabulating and analyzing the data.

We ran into some unanticipated student reactions to their fall semester projects. Students prefer the hands-on, more tangible projects; but many felt that, with the exception of the landfill trips, their projects were insufficiently so. Some students were assigned to count all the light bulbs on campus and determine energy efficiency and hazardous waste disposal options. Others were required to determine energy usage on campus, or photocopy usage. These students became frustrated interviewing on-campus and off-campus information sources and researching information.

We had several classroom discussions of long-term goals for the college and the community to help increase students' understanding of why these types of projects are important even though one's individual role may seem small, boring, and insignificant. We discussed the final written report to be compiled from the student data and presented to FVCC's board of trustees. This helped the students understand the process, but they still wished they could have been involved in different types of projects. Joint update meetings with all four classes helped them feel like members of a large team but did not change their views. Students' primary concerns centered on finding the assignment sheet provided by the agency vague and unclear; believing a wider variety of choices should have been available; and preferring projects with more hand-on activities and short-term goals.

Rethinking Their Options

The students' reactions led us to rethink our spring plans. We redesigned the options to include more hands-on activities, such as a cafeteria waste audit, and offered some additional options. One option, in cooperation with Flathead County and the Citizens for a Better Flathead, involved the students in labeling storm drains and distributing literature on why it is critical not to dump most liquids down storm drains. The students, working with local high school students and the Flathead Basin Commission, were also able to collect stream water samples.

The first day of class, students were given the choice of either splitting their hours between the waste audit and one of the options or completing all their hours on one project. (Details of the service-learning requirements and options are given in the ES 101 syllabus available at http://mail.fvcc.cc.mt.us/~jalexand/syllabus/envl-101.1996.html.) This gave us more flexibility in arranging options to fit students' interests and needs. Students were excited about having a variety of options to choose from. Most split their hours between two projects, but some chose one or the other.

Once again, we started the semester with a tour of the Flathead County landfill and included a tour of the newly expanded local recycling operations in Kalispell. As before, students were very interested in and quite impressed by the tour, even though the temperature was below zero on the day of their visit. The landfill tour was actually a great "ice-breaker" to excite the students about their projects.

This semester's class ran much more smoothly, mainly due to our offering more-tangible projects. These included studying the pesticides and herbicides used on campus, tracking all use of paper in our community education department for two weeks, a one-day audit of all waste generated from food purchased in the cafeteria, other waste audit projects, and the off-campus projects mentioned earlier. The students eventually produced a summary of the year-long FVCC waste audit document and presented it to our board of trustees. The board, after reading the document, signed a resolution to adopt the recommendations of the "Waste Not" project and agreed to become a member of the Green Star program, a voluntary program that encourages businesses to incorporate techniques of waste reduction, energy conservation, and pollution prevention into their daily business activities. Exciting! The students were able to see that they actually did make a difference at FVCC and in the Flathead Valley. Some of their reactions included these:

> I talked to several people when I was leaving information at homes. They were all pleased that we were painting the drains. People stopped me to ask what I was doing and I didn't receive any negative comments from anyone. This is a neat project and I really enjoyed it.

> At the beginning of the semester I was not looking forward to this project; in fact I was feeling like it was going to be a waste of my time. . . . I do hope that the college will continue to have the inservice projects because it gives you hands-on experience that is invaluable. You have to see it to believe it

is really true in many cases. It was for me in this project. I am a recycler now, because I have found that I can make a difference.

When I was assigned to do this report, I thought I was going to find that pesticides were a good thing and that all bad things written about them were a sort of witch hunt by environmentalists. I scoured the library to find some claim to refute that pesticides had no good qualities. The only conclusion I drew from my research is that pesticides do kill and they do it . . . through the air, water, and soil. . . . Only by getting the government to acknowledge that pesticides are a real damage to our environment will there be any real hope for change. As it sits now, the college hasn't broken any laws, and it is an ethical question to use a product whose long-term effects [as a] possible cancer-causing agent have not been fully researched.

I learned from conducting this audit that numerous people seem to be very interested in sorting garbage. While we were monitoring the audit people asked questions and made comments that suggested they were very interested in this project — even on a long-term basis. Some problems we ran into . . . at one point we had to clean off tables because people purposely left their food waste rather than take a few moments to sort their own garbage.

A Third Year

Building upon this success, we made plans for the third year. The "Waste Not" project in 1996-97 focused on gathering information to estimate the waste reduction potential in the business community. A survey was designed by CFBF and reviewed by the Flathead County Solid Waste Board and area recycling businesses. The survey attempted to identify difficulties businesses face in finding and implementing waste reduction strategies. FVCC students in environmental science, economics, biology, and business communications together with RSVP members administered the survey to interested businesses and informed them of the Green Star program. Data from the completed surveys was tabulated, and the results will drive future educational programs and determine a priority of services needed.

In this year, we also expanded the program to include service projects with the Montana Department of Fish, Wildlife, and Parks; Flathead Basin Commission; and the University of Montana Flathead Lake Biological Station. Our environmental science students helped the Montana Department of Fish, Wildlife, and Parks operate the big game check stations in the Flathead Valley and tabulate the data that they collected. Economics students working with the Flathead Basin Commission are tabulating the previous year's water quality data and producing educational information. Environmental science and biology students work with the University of Montana Flathead Lake Biological Station to collect water samples for the Flathead Basin Commission. Depending on the time of year, students either cross country ski or use hip waders to collect the samples. Student reactions to the projects have included the following:

> At 2:00 pm my wife and I [both service-learning students] arrived at the hunter check station on Hwy 2 just out of town. I was not looking forward to this assignment but figured I might as well make the best of it, since I had to do it. However, I was in for a surprise. Not only did I enjoy it but I would gladly do it again. . . . After working at the check station, we got the opportunity to work on the computer system at the office. This was not near as much fun, but we learned some interesting facts. . . . I really enjoyed working with the Montana Fish, Wildlife, and Parks. . . . They have a very efficient and thorough system for gathering needed information about our wildlife.

> Throughout the service-learning project, I found many different strengths and weaknesses that I have. By contacting businesses, setting up meetings, and completing the surveys, I realized I have a hard time dealing with people face-to-face. On the other hand, I found out that I am good about getting things done on time and working by myself. This project has been a learning experience in many different ways for me. . . . Service-learning has made me think about classes that I need to take in the future to avoid the mainstream service-sector jobs such as restaurant, retail, etc. I am grateful that I learned this fact through this project before picking my major. The service-learning project has been a learning experience for me and I have enjoyed doing these surveys for a good cause.

> I learned a lot from participating in this project, including what things constitute and contribute to good and bad water quality, as well as how water testing is done. Most interesting to me, though, was the experience of being a "scientist for a day." . . . As a "creative type," science has always seemed like something I had no talent for or much interest in. But this project made me see that science is more relevant to "real life" — and to my life — than I'd imagined. . . . I know I will never again look at a creek or lake in quite the same way.

Lessons Learned

Time and practice certainly have improved the program. Indeed, each semester's project has improved on the previous one. In the future, we hope to continue to offer all of the projects described, and to expand the program to include other projects as the need arises. The "Waste Not" project ended in 1997, but we intend to continue the collaboration with the Flathead County Solid Waste Board and with Citizens for a Better Flathead, offering whatever projects best meet the current community need. I do find that for my Environmental Science course, I must know the exact nature of the service projects to be offered before I plan the semester's syllabus. Another instructor who recently taught the course also found this to be true. The projects drive the course. In the end the same topics are covered, but the order in which they are covered, the depth of coverage, and laboratory experiment choices vary depending on the semester projects.

I have been amazed by the impact of service-learning both on my students and on the collaborating agency. I now cannot imagine offering a course without a service-learning option. It has been an even greater surprise to see the impact the "Waste Not" project has had on both FVCC and the community. I had never imagined the "Waste Not" project would lead to a resolution by FVCC's board of trustees to incorporate environmentally friendly practices, nor to adopt the Green Star program with Flathead Valley. It has been exciting for the students and service-learning faculty here to see that we have made a difference in improving the environment of Flathead Valley and FVCC.

Much of our success with effective collaborations stems from our rural environment. About 70,000 people reside in Flathead County. A small community such as ours has strong connections between its college and community groups and agencies. There is a genuine desire to work together on all kinds of projects for the benefit of the community. Agencies are interested in playing a role in helping our college students expand their view of citizenship, since our students will soon become active members of the community. At the same time, our students provide needed manpower. Recently, service-learning in all areas has expanded greatly through word of mouth. More agencies have contacted us with requests for service-learning students after other agencies have told them about their positive experiences. I would guess that this kind of chain reaction is less likely to occur in a larger area.

I believe this same community spirit explains the response of our board of trustees. FVCC's president is a strong backer of the service-learning program and the "Waste Not" project. In addition, many folks on campus were interviewed during the waste audit process, giving them input into the project. The final report of the waste audit was first presented to the College

Council and the president. Upon their approval and recommendations, it was then presented to the board of trustees for adoption. As a collaborative project with government, education, and citizen-group partners, adoption of the resolution was a win-win situation for FVCC. It made us a major player in a small community, helping the county make required changes through our willingness to look first at ourselves and the changes we could make.

I believe communities and students have much to gain by incorporating environmental service-learning projects. It is very important before embarking on the service-learning journey to pay attention both to the design of the actual project and to how it will be incorporated into a given course. A wonderful project without properly worked-out details can very quickly change students' initial enthusiasm to disappointment. Student, agency, and faculty expectations can be very different. Time must be spent to make sure these differences are worked out before the project is begun. Everyone must know the expectations and responsibilities of each member.

Relatedly, during the "Waste Not" project, staff to be interviewed by students were notified ahead of time as to how many students would be contacting them and, to avoid surprises, the students' due dates. Our physical plant manager was the target of many student interviews. All of the students were impressed with how helpful he was. In appreciation, the "Waste Not" project presented him with an award — which proved to be a good method to maintain open channels on campus. Toward the beginning of the semester, we devote much time to clarifying service project expectations in class. (Short discussions over many days seem to be more effective than one long session.) Over time, the part of my course information sheet devoted to explaining service-learning has lengthened, as has the initial class time spent discussing expectations.

I now include service-learning in all of my courses and intend to continue to do so. It is required in my Environmental Science course, but is an option in my other courses. I have not found any correlation between required service and levels of student enthusiasm and commitment. I have had students in a service-required course indicate they would not have chosen service if it had been an option but ended up loving it and now strongly believe service should be continued as a requirement. Likewise, I have had students in a service-optional course who chose service believing it to be the easier choice but discovered otherwise and did not complete the option even though failure to do so affected their grade. Currently, all agencies evaluate our students with a common evaluation form. Typically, more than 95 percent of these evaluations are in the "excellent to good" range in all categories. Although students are evaluated in all service-learning courses, whether their service is required or optional, we have seen no difference in their evaluations or in service completion rates in required versus optional service courses. We do require all instructors offering a service option to assess a grade penalty for students starting but not completing that option. In service-required courses, we try to eliminate potential problems by offering a variety of choices, including on-campus or off-campus; research or hands-on; a variety of topics; time-intensive over a few days or hour-per-week over the course of the semester; and daytime or nighttime/weekend.

Service-learning will continue to be a requirement in my Environmental Science course due to the impact it has had on bringing the classroom material into the students' daily lives. That connection should not be lost. It also is important to strengthen their ties with our community, allowing them to become active members of that community through their coursework.

Connecting With Human and Natural Communities at Middlebury College

by John Elder, Christopher McGrory Klyza, Jim Northup, and Stephen Trombulak

Like the Environmental Studies program at Middlebury College in general, service-learning in environmental studies at the college is firmly grounded in the liberal arts. The chief place where such service-learning comes into play in our curriculum is in our senior seminar, Environmental Studies 401. Environmental studies majors at Middlebury take four common core courses, three cognate courses for breadth, six or seven courses in a specific area of depth (e.g., conservation biology or environmental economics), and the senior seminar. This final course is designed to bring students who have headed off in different directions back together again in an interdisciplinary and multidisciplinary culminating experience. Three sections of the course are offered each year, with the topics varying from course to course and from year to year. The only constant is that the course focuses on a local or regional environmental issue. Although ES 401 does not always revolve around service-learning, it frequently does. The decision as to what topic the course will focus on and whether or not it will be service-learning oriented is completely at the discretion of the instructor. Furthermore, the college administration has demonstrated no position in support of or in opposition to a service-learning–oriented course. Two of three cases presented in this chapter are from sections of ES 401.

In Fall 1995, Jim Northup's class worked with the community of Salisbury, Vermont, as it planned a new elementary school. Students in his class helped the community articulate what it wanted in the new school and worked in a variety of ways to incorporate the environment and a sense of place into the site, the community, and the curriculum of the new school. Steve Trombulak's section of ES 401 in 1988 analyzed the possibilities for recycling on Middlebury's campus and developed a plan that led to the birth of the college's recycling program. The final case is John Elder's class in environmental education (ES 302, Environmental Education: A Bioregional Approach). In this class, 15 to 20 Middlebury environmental studies majors are matched with teachers from grade school through junior high school throughout Addison County. The students work with the teachers and their classes to incorporate a bioregional approach to environmental education into the curriculum.

School as a Center of a Healthy Community

During the Fall 1995 semester, 18 Middlebury College students enrolled in ES 401 taught by Jim Northup took the lofty concept of community sustainability and grounded it in reality. Working as an interdisciplinary team, self-named the Sustainable Systems Group, the students collaborated with local officials and residents from the nearby town of Salisbury to develop a strategy for making a proposed new public elementary school a center of a healthy, sustainable community, as well as a place for teaching schoolchildren. From all points of view, this exercise in service-learning was an enormous success.

Early in the semester, the students met with their "clients" — Salisbury's school board, principal, teachers, staff, and pupils — to learn about Salisbury and to define a realistic scope of work and schedule. It was this early and sustained dialogue with all the significant parties (including the architect) over the course of the semester that created an atmosphere for the acceptance of the student recommendations. After several meetings and a tour of the town, the students decided they would deliver a "polished, professional report recommending ways that the new school's programs, building, and grounds could be designed to connect Salisbury residents — students and other — to their local environment and to each other."

When the Sustainable Systems Group entered the picture, Salisbury officials were working with architects on preliminary designs for the new school building. A relatively blank slate remained for the students to fill with their ideas, and that they did, to the delight of local school officials and residents.

The final report presented to the Salisbury community at a public meeting in early December 1995 described the students' vision for the public school as a center of community, and recommended innovative programs and design features for the building and grounds. Their vision began with this statement:

> A healthy community understands the relationships among its integrated components, and works to provide environmental, economic, and social security for one and all, present and future. The community school can be a place and a set of relationships that manifest a sense of dedication to the future and to the common good.

To begin work toward this vision, the Sustainable Systems Group recommended that several community-building programs be offered at the new school. They researched and described in detail programs such as annual community workshops aimed at creating a desired future; multiyear activities promoting awareness of self, environment, and community; application of Geographic Information System (GIS) technology to create awareness and understanding of place; a student-prepared annual State of the School Report for engaging residents in an informed dialogue about their school and community; and annual community celebrations of people and place. These and other program ideas were wholeheartedly embraced, and many are now being advanced by local residents.

Among the design features proposed by the Sustainable Systems Group and incorporated into the final design of the school were energy conservation via optimum use of insulation, passive solar energy, natural lighting, and smart technologies (e.g., switches and sensors to reduce unnecessary energy use); minimal use of virgin, imported, and toxic materials and maximum use of recycled, renewable, and "healthy" materials from local sources; preservation of historic stone walls and mature trees; a greenhouse to directly connect the school building to the living world; and incorporation of trails and outdoor classrooms into the landscape design. These proposals and more were accepted by local officials and incorporated into the building's design.

As a result of the research and advocacy performed by the Middlebury College students, the new Salisbury elementary school will be one of the most ecologically sound and healthiest public buildings in the country. The 10-inch walls (R-38) and ceiling (R-48) are insulated with densely packed cellulose (recycled newspaper). A superior ventilation system, abundant indoor plants, and avoidance of carpeting and volatile organic compounds in building materials will help keep indoor air quality high. Two exterior walls in every classroom bring in an abundance of natural light and fresh air through the triple-glazed windows. The list of features recommended by the students and incorporated into the school's final design goes on and on.

As of this writing, construction of the new school is still under way. However, some of the results of the students' work are already visible. For example, on a recent below-zero day and to the amazement of engineers and townspeople, the entire 25,000-square-foot building was heated to 70 degrees Fahrenheit by one energy-efficient boiler that is smaller than that most households have in their homes. During most days, adequate classroom lighting levels are achieved without using electricity.

The report prepared by the students made a meaningful, enduring contribution to Salisbury and served as a source of great joy and lasting pride for the entire student team. Their mood after the final public meeting was ecstatic. Many expressed thanks for being given the opportunity to make a substantial contribution to the town and planet, and felt confident of their ability to bring about even greater change during the rest of their lives. Most commented about how much they had learned and grown by doing the project and how different that learning was from what goes on in the typical classroom. In their view, opportunities for service-learning are valuable, if not essential, aspects of a college education.

A Recycling Plan for Middlebury College

In 1988, Middlebury's Program in Environmental Studies developed a senior capstone course for the environmental studies major designed to give our students experience in carrying out an interdisciplinary group project. One of the most successful of these projects was the very first one, in which a group of nine environmental studies majors developed a recycling plan for the college and convinced our administration to adopt it. Their plan formed the basis for the successful recycling program that we have in place today; one that this past year — combined with a composting program—diverted 64 percent of the college's waste from landfills.

The class, taught by then director of the program Steve Trombulak, was structured exclusively as a group research project, without traditional lectures, laboratory exercises, or discussion groups. At the first meeting, Trombulak gave the students their goal: to develop a recycling plan for Middlebury College, and to make an argument to the college's administration for why it should adopt the plan. Over the next few days, the class as a group developed a list of the subgoals necessary to achieve the overall goal, developed a work plan for the semester, and assigned specific tasks to each student. Trombulak acted as a facilitator, helping to keep discussions on track and answering questions when asked. He also tried to instill in the students a sense of cooperation and team spirit by emphasizing the importance of what they were doing and the "radical" nature of their goal (remember, this was 1988, before most colleges had implemented recycling programs). Other than that, Trombulak did not serve as a leader or a teacher. As work on the project progressed, the students chose their own leader, and Trombulak was viewed more as the project's primary resource person.

The students decided that to achieve their overall goal they needed to investigate the following topics:

• Previous efforts at the college for reducing the solid waste stream, and why they failed.

• What was in the college's solid waste stream, with respect to the types of waste, the volume of each type of waste, and the variation in these parameters among buildings on campus.

• Current costs to the college for solid waste disposal, and trends during the previous 10 years.

• Current procedures for handling solid waste on campus, with a special focus on how these practices could be modified to allow separation and storage of different materials.

• The current economics of solid waste disposal, and projected scenarios for how this might change over the next 10 years.

• Attitudes and knowledge among students and employees with respect to recycling, with a special focus on what kinds of educational initiatives would be necessary to make a recycling program work.

• Regional markets for recyclable materials.

Each topic was investigated by a subgroup of the students, and each student was part of at least three subgroups. Meetings of the entire group or subgroups were scheduled by the students when needed.

After several weeks of data collection, the group began to develop a proposal for a recycling program based on their results. As a group, they decided to organize their report around two topics. The first was an argument for why a recycling program was needed. After talking about the ethical justification for reducing the production of waste, they developed several scenarios for how the costs of solid waste disposal might change projected to the year 2000 in the absence of a recycling program. Variables in the scenarios were annual increases in the amount of garbage produced, tipping fees per ton in 1990, and annual increases in tipping fees.

The second topic was a detailed, six-step proposal for solid waste management. Based on the analysis of their data, the students developed plans for

1. encouraging reduction of waste at the sources of its production;
2. creating cardboard receptacles at dining facilities;
3. recycling procedures in academic buildings;
4. recycling procedures in residential buildings;
5. building a recycling center; and
6. involving the campus community, including an ongoing educational outreach program.

They calculated the cost of implementing their proposal and savings under each of the scenarios from eliminating recyclable materials from the waste stream. From these calculations, they estimated the maximum payback time for their plan to be eight years.

The subsequent report was written collaboratively, with the group creating a style sheet, individuals writing specific sections, and one person collating and editing for a common style. Then they prepared a presentation of their proposal for the college's administration. First, they developed an outline and decided who among the group would present which parts. After practicing their presentation in front of an audience of their peers, they made a formal presentation to the college's treasurer and his staff, ending with an official request that the college adopt their proposal. After a brief question-and-answer period, the treasurer granted the request and authorized the initiation of the program to begin at the end of the current academic year. (In our experience, it was the fastest decision ever rendered by a member of the administration, testimony to the strength of the students' arguments and presentation.) Additional copies of the written report were prepared for all senior administrators and the board of trustees, to accompany an announcement of the program prepared by the treasurer.

Because this project was conducted as a formal class, Trombulak needed to assign a grade to each student. He had each one write an evaluation and provide a letter grade for himself or herself and for every other person in the group. Each student's final grade was based equally on three factors: the grade the student gave himself or herself; the average grade given to the student by the other students; and a grade Trombulak gave based on his impression of the quality of that student's work. He has used this grading policy in all of his classes with a collaborative learning component, and he finds that the students take it seriously and provide responsible evaluations of themselves and one another. (The other two classes described in this chapter were not group project classes, so students were graded based on assignments that they completed individually.)

Although Middlebury College's recycling program has grown and improved based on new technologies, new markets, and expanded interest on campus, it still retains the basic form established by the students who carried out this project. None of the potential pitfalls of a project of this type developed, although problems have all occurred in other project attempts. Everybody worked well together and worked hard to achieve their goal. A natural leader emerged from the group. The size of the group was manageable. The magnitude of the project was appropriate for the time allowed. And the project related to a subject of tremendous interest to the students involved.

Experience over the years with this and other service-learning projects has taught Trombulak several rules of thumb. First, he recommends keeping the group to between eight and 12 students; fewer and it is difficult to complete a meaningful project, more and the group simply becomes too difficult to manage. Second, keep an eye open for disruptive personalities even at the earliest stage of the project's development. Telltale signs of a disrupter are constant complaints about how the project is "stupid" and about the work of others. Disrupters can usually be dealt with by calling them aside early in the process and talking with them openly about the importance of developing good collaborative skills, respect for others, and a positive attitude about the project's goal. In most cases, the disrupter is surprised to learn what he or she has been doing, and immediately shows an improved attitude. Third, let the students know that part of what they are learning is how to work cooperatively on a project that is bigger than any one of them could do alone. This makes them more responsive to input on issues such as group dynamics, deadlines, and common writing styles.

Trombulak believes that the students learned several important things during that semester, including the interdisciplinary nature of environmental problem solving, teamwork, leadership, development of work plans, and developing supported arguments both orally and in writing. But most important, he believes, they learned that if they invest the energy to do the very best job they can, they *can* make a difference.

A Bioregional Approach to Environmental Education: Connecting Middlebury Students With Local Schools

Since 1993, Middlebury College students have worked with local elementary and junior high teachers to develop and implement place-based curricula. This initiative, called the Watershed Partnerships, has had support from the Orion Society and the Geraldine R. Dodge Foundation as it integrated internships into the work of a Middlebury course called Environmental Education (ES 302) taught by John Elder. The course has followed an inductive approach. Rather than designing a curriculum at the college that would then be applied in a variety of settings, students collaborated with classroom teachers to find approaches that were distinctive and appropriate to particular communities. The result was a series of highly effective educational experiments and exciting discoveries for college students, public school teachers, and local school students alike.

The first two years of the Watershed Partnerships were focused in Bristol, Vermont, initially working with one talented third-grade teacher named Ann Straub and then extending into practically every classroom in Bristol Elementary School. Since 1995, Middlebury students have moved out into a wide range of the county's schools, including Bristol, Lincoln, Starksboro, Monkton, Salisbury, and Middlebury Junior Highs. Among the emphases of the students' collaborations have been mapping, oral histories, creation of nature trails, writing local field guides, tracking, studies of animal shelters, and agricultural history. In every case, the arts were integrated into interdisciplinary scientific research out of doors.

The success of this initiative has gone beyond its palpable educational benefits. Local children have loved exposure to college-age people, while our students have often found this their first significant glimpse into the life of the college's surrounding communities. In a number of cases, long-term connections were formed, as Middlebury students have invited their elementary-school friends up to visit the chemistry lab in the science center or have taken them to see hockey games and other events on our campus. The teachers, too, have praised the energy and insight of our student interns.

They like the connection with the college for many reasons, among them the extraordinary resources for research to which Middlebury students have access and the teachers' own pride in showing the high quality of work being accomplished in their little rural schools.

The success of our Watershed Partnerships at Middlebury has inspired a national program of the same name. Within this context, undergraduates and graduates at Oberlin College, Swarthmore College, Trenton State University [now called the College of New Jersey], the University of Vermont, Rutgers University, and the Teton Science School have all combined their formal academic work with internships in local schools. In these highly different settings, students have found the same success, and the same pleasure, as Middlebury students have in sharing their knowledge with their communities and in learning from the talented teachers of their regions.

Conclusions

These three cases are indicative of some of the service-learning that goes on in environmental studies at Middlebury College. Due to the resource limitations of our Environmental Studies program (we are currently the second-largest major on campus and are an interdisciplinary program), expansion of service-learning will be incremental at best. In addition to the service-learning that frequently occurs in the senior seminar, the greatest opportunity for such expansion will be in new courses such as John Elder's environmental education course and a new junior-level course in environmental science, taught for the first time in 1998.

The service-learning that has occurred and will continue to occur can be placed in two categories: campus-based and community-based. The recycling case illustrates the first. It seems likely that students will always have opportunities to serve the campus: it is their home for four years, and it is often students' actions that they are seeking to influence. Furthermore, the college is the largest institution and employer in the county; improving its environmental activities has significant effects in the region.

Service-learning based in the local communities surrounding the college generates two clear benefits. First, only a small percentage of the students at Middlebury are from Vermont and, similarly, only a small percentage come from rural areas. These courses help our students connect to the human communities that surround them, to the issues and concerns of communities involved in agriculture, forest products, and tourism. It helps everyone affiliated with the Environmental Studies program think more about the middle landscape often neglected by such programs. And second, service-learning connects the surrounding towns to what is often regarded as a rich and elitist institution populated by rich, elite, out-of-state students.

So, this service-learning is an important two-way path for community building both in a general sense and on environmental issues more specifically. Certainly, students going into the environmental field will be well-served by this community-building work.

Finally, these service-learning experiences — campus-based and community-based — serve our students in two fundamentally important ways. They require students often focused on abstract environmental ideas and problems to work on issues and problems in specific human and natural communities. And perhaps most important, they let students know that they can make some difference in the world, a lesson of incredible importance in the face of often seemingly incomprehensible environmental problems. Instilling a sense of accomplishment and hope in dealing with the environment is a most worthy result of any kind of learning.

An Educational Strategy to Reduce Exposure of Urban Children to Environmental Lead: ENVS 404 at the University of Pennsylvania

by Robert Giegengack, Walter Cressler, Peter Bloch, and Joanne Piesieski
and other participants in ENVS 404[1]

In January 1995, the College of Arts and Sciences of the University of Pennsylvania first offered the course Environmental Studies (ENVS) 404, The Urban Environment. The course was designed to introduce Penn undergraduates to selected aspects of urban environments and to engage them in a service-learning program that would employ children at the Anna Howard Shaw Middle School in direct assessment of some aspect of their immediate urban environment. The seminar chose to address the pervasive problem of exposure of urban children to environmental lead (Pb).

Background

The element Pb is a heavy (~207 awu), soft metal with a low melting point that is quite rare (~12 ppm) in rocks of the Earth's crust. Lead is found in eco-

ENVS 404 has received financial support from U.S. EPA Region III via EPA grants Nos. X-993351-01 and X-993351-02; from the Kellogg Foundation grant No. P0039774; and from HUD grant No. COPC-PA-96-064. Gerallyn Valls, director of the lead-abatement program in EPA Region III, and her assistants Helene Stolker, Lewis Malnak, and Enid Gerena have participated in many aspects of our program. Tom Spittler, senior research scientist with EPA Region I in Boston, has worked closely with our group, particularly in helping us acquire a field XRF instrument. Al Bichner, principal of Shaw Middle School, has welcomed our program and our students into Shaw. We have been ably assisted by 10 classroom teachers: Joyce Abbott, Dira Caplan, Maria Fitzgerald, Laurie Franklin, Clara Gay, Robert Goldstein, Sharon Harless, Mary Beth Kulp, Donna Saunders, and Patricia Whack. The staff of Penn's General Honors program, Linda Wiedmann, Cheryl Shipman, and Susan Duggan, cross-listed ENVS 404 as a General Honors course and recruited many of our student participants. Staff members of the Center for Community Partnerships assisted us in many aspects of the program: Ira Harkavy (director), Cory Bowman, Penny Gordon-Larsen, Winnie Smart-Mapp, Amy Cohen, Joann Weeks, Alicia Saslow, Karen Wheeler, Robin Hands, and Edie Page. Several members of the Penn faculty have contributed their technical expertise to the lead aspect of ENVS 404: Irving M. Shapiro, Carla Campbell, and Donald Schwartz. Richard Tobin, director of the lead-abatement program of the Department of Health of the City of Philadelphia, has freely shared with us his experiences, his data, and his enthusiasm.

nomic concentrations most often as the mineral galena (PbS), typically associated with sulfides of zinc and copper. Imperial Rome used lead in plumbing fixtures, cooking vessels, and wine goblets; as pigments; and, when it was discovered that even mediocre wines tasted better when drunk from lead containers, as a direct additive to sweeten inferior wines (see Gilfillan 1965; Eisinger 1996). The use of lead by Roman society has led at least one student of that culture to posit that the fall of Rome was a direct consequence of the exposure to the metal by Rome's ruling classes (i.e., those with the resources necessary to acquire and use it), an exposure that eventually so compromised their reproductive capacity that they were unable to keep pace with the rate of population increase among those whom they ruled (Gilfillan 1965). Studies of the inventory of lead in polar ice sheets (Moruzumi et al. 1969) have documented the long history of human use of the metal.

Ingested or inhaled, lead is distributed throughout the human body in solution in the blood stream; in many physiological processes the lead substitutes for calcium and/or iron. It has been recognized for centuries (e.g., Franklin 1786; Eisinger 1996) that occupational exposure to lead produces recognizable symptoms of lead poisoning in children and adults: abdominal pain, headaches, impairment of motor skills, impairment of cognitive skills, reduction in attention span, kidney/urinary tract dysfunction, bone damage, reproductive dysfunction, and even death.

Excess lead is excreted in the urine or stored in bone as a substitute for calcium. Thus, short-term lead exposure can be measured in a blood or urine sample; longer-term, integrated lead exposure can be determined by measuring the Pb burden in bone. The latter can be achieved noninvasively via X ray fluorescence of living bone or, far more simply, by measuring the Pb concentration in shed deciduous teeth (e.g., Shapiro et al. 1978). The stability of Pb in bone has led to numerous studies of collections of fossil bones from cemeteries and museum collections in efforts to evaluate the role of environmental Pb in historical cultures (e.g., Zonies 1997).

Clinical lead poisoning is associated with blood-Pb levels at or above 50 micrograms per deciliter (μg/dl), the level at which therapeutic action was indicated as recently as the early 1970s. With growing awareness of the fact that neurological impairment can result from far lower blood-Pb concentrations, the action level has been systematically lowered, and now stands at 10 μg/dl for the Centers for Disease Control and most other organizations that address lead as a public health issue (CDC 1991; Graziano 1994).

We now know that even very small quantities of lead interfere irreversibly with neurological development in very young children. Thus, during the first six years of life, the time when growth of neural pathways in the brain responds most directly to external stimuli, children in leaded environments incur neurological damage they will carry for the rest of their lives (e.g., Rodier 1995). Recently, it has been shown that very young children who maintain blood-Pb concentrations as low as ~10 μg/dl suffer sufficient neurological damage during a crucial growth period to reduce academic and social performance for the rest of their lives (Needleman 1990).

Despite the fact that its toxicity has been understood for centuries, lead has been widely used in 20th-century American society as a primary ingredient of lead-acid storage batteries, as an agricultural pesticide, as a primary ingredient of type metal, as an ingredient of solder, in radiation shielding, in ammunition, as a gasoline additive, as an easily worked raw material in some crafts and hobbies, and as a pigment and mold inhibitor in exterior and interior paints (some paints have contained as much as 20 percent Pb by weight).

Lead is no longer used as a pesticide on food plants, and it is now almost fully eliminated from motor fuels in the United States. (Removal from our gasoline began in the 1970s, ironically because tetraethyl Pb interfered with the function of the catalytic converters devised to help high-performance engines meet the strictures of the Clean Air Act of 1970, not because lead had been implicated in general low-level poisoning of the American population. Lead is still added routinely to gasoline in other countries.) Lead has been illegal as an ingredient of solder since 1972 and as an ingredient in household paint since 1976. However, lead is still used in the manufacture and reconditioning of lead-acid storage batteries, now as in the past the largest consumer of the element; and it has not been replaced as a rust inhibitor in specialty paints applied to exposed steel structures (e.g., bridges). Lead survives both in paint and in solder in millions of older homes in the United States, and is bound to soil particles at waste-disposal sites; in the vicinity of metal-smelting facilities, where lead may have been the primary or even a secondary metal processed; adjacent to roadways that carried large volumes of traffic combusting leaded fuel; and adjacent to structures painted with lead-based paints.

Young children may ingest lead in water that has lain in contact with lead-bearing solder long enough to reach chemical equilibrium; by chewing on surfaces painted with lead paints (even if such paint has been covered by later layers of lead-free paint); by placing in their mouths playthings that have lain in dust or dirt contaminated by flakes of lead-bearing paint that have fallen from walls; by sucking fingers so contaminated; and by eating with their hands after playing in contaminated interior dust or yard dirt. Children who chew directly on wood surfaces painted with lead-based paints soon discover, as the Romans did, that the salts of Pb taste sweet. Once children have made that discovery, it becomes difficult to break them of the habit of chewing on surfaces painted with lead-based paint. Older children and adults, by virtue of avoiding most such behaviors, are much less at risk, and are beyond the age when they are likely to suffer irreversibly from small concentrations of Pb.

In the city of Philadelphia alone, some 500,000 homes are estimated to contain lead paint on deteriorating surfaces. The cost of mechanical abatement of interior lead-based paint is currently about $15,000/house, or $6 billion to remove lead paint from only the interior surfaces of all affected houses in Philadelphia (Richard Tobin and Carla Campbell, personal communications, 1997); several studies, furthermore, have shown that careless abatement may actually increase exposure to environmental lead by converting much of the removed paint to interior dust that then adheres to freshly cleaned surfaces, to be picked up by sticky little hands.

Lead-based paints were also used on exterior surfaces. The tendency of lead-based paints to "chalk," to shed fine dust more or less continually after drying, enabled rain periodically to "clean" painted surfaces. Thus, lead-based white paints were touted for their capacity to remain white long after nonleaded white paint would have discolored. The dust shed by surfaces painted with lead-based paint is as high in Pb as is the paint; thus, the dust that falls or is washed from an exterior painted surface accumulates near the base of the painted wall. Children playing against the base of an exterior wall from which lead-based paint is flaking play in an environment very high in Pb. Most cities in which records of childhood blood-Pb levels are kept have reported statistically significant increases in blood Pb in young children during the months of July and August. This effect has been attributed to the fact that windows are kept open in summer, allowing exterior dust to enter a house, and to the fact that children play outdoors more in summer than in other seasons, and thus are directly exposed to exterior lead-based paint and carry more of it into their houses on their feet.

The exposure of toddlers to environmental lead is higher in inner-city neighborhoods than in suburban neighborhoods because the houses are closer together and typically are older than in the suburbs; the absence of foundation plantings around city homes allows children to play directly adjacent to walls shedding lead-bearing paint flakes and dust; standards of neighborhood and household cleanliness are often lower in urban than in suburban environments; and the high incidence of single-parent families in urban environments leads to a higher incidence of toddlers left unattended for long periods of time. The two primary indicators of childhood lead poisoning are (1) residence in a house built before 1960 and (2) living at or below the poverty level. Because of the high concentration of minority populations in economically depressed older urban cores, lead toxicity disproportionately affects African-American toddlers. And, as blood-Pb data continue to accumulate as state and city health authorities put in place systematic programs of environmental-lead assessment, it has become apparent that the incidence of subclinical lead poisoning (at levels >10µg/dl but below levels at which symptoms are apparent) is overwhelmingly high among minority populations in low-income urban cores. The lifelong impact of early-childhood exposure to lead on those children and on those communities is difficult to quantify, but its contemplation has led a generation of public health practitioners to agree that low-level lead poisoning is the single greatest environmental hazard that urban children face today, and that that hazard disproportionately threatens African-American children.

Despite this realization, agencies that regulate environmental conditions and monitor public health have not been able to mobilize the enormous resources that will be required to remove lead-based paints from the millions of homes in the United States where that material remains, often buried under layers of lead-free paint applied later. The cost of removing all residual lead from painted surfaces in decaying urban cores is so high that few students of the problem express confidence that that risk will soon be eliminated or even significantly reduced. The cost of abatement is enormous, and those most at risk have not been active players in the political arena.

Programs in Academically Based Community Service at the University of Pennsylvania

The University of Pennsylvania traces its roots to Benjamin Franklin, who in 1740 founded a college in Philadelphia dedicated to educating young men via an educational system in which theory would be put to practical use. We must assume that early exercises in application of theory to practice took place in Philadelphia, in Franklin's time the political, industrial, and cultural center of the 13 colonies and the first capital city of the emerging confederation that was to become the United States of America. The University of Pennsylvania moved from the center of Philadelphia to the then pastures west of the Schuylkill River in 1867, but was engulfed again by West Philadelphia as the city continued to expand. By the early 20th century, Penn was once again an urban campus, but surrounded by homes of factory workers rather than by the factories in which they worked. As the university grew, programs with strong urban foci developed in all its 12 schools. In 1962, when the university was offered a large and attractive site in rural Valley Forge to which to move, ostensibly to rescue Penn students from both the distractions and hazards of life in a decaying urban core, the university declined, and acknowledged that its destiny was inextricably linked to that of the city of Philadelphia.

Many programs from many schools at Penn have addressed physical and/or social problems of inner-city life, but efforts to draw those programs together to enhance their visibility and effectiveness were not successful until the university established a partnership with a number of West Philadelphia social service organizations in 1985, and the West Philadelphia Improvement Corps (WEPIC) was born. Under its director, Ira Harkavy, WEPIC has become a year-round program that engages some 5,000 children, their parents, community members, and Penn students in educational and cultural programs, recreation, job training, community improvement, and service activities. WEPIC seeks to create comprehensive, university-assisted community schools that will serve as social, service-delivery, and educational hubs for the communities that surround them. WEPIC activities are coordinated by the West Philadelphia Partnership, a mediating, nonprofit, community-based organization comprising a broad spectrum of institutions, neighborhood organizations, and community leaders, who work in conjunction with the Greater Philadelphia Urban Affairs Coalition and the School District of Philadelphia.[2]

Since 1985, WEPIC has facilitated the development of many programs that bring the expertise of Penn faculty and students to bear on problems of the university's immediate West Philadelphia neighborhood. WEPIC has engaged thousands of Penn students in programs in which they share time and expertise with students and teachers in 13 West Philadelphia schools and deliver a variety of services to the neighborhoods served by those schools. In recent years, those programs have been linked to courses, primarily undergraduate, in which Penn students have made the environment and problems of West Philadelphia neighborhoods the focus of academic study and research (see Benson and Harkavy 1991; Harkavy and Puckett 1994).

ENVS 404

The undergraduate major in environmental studies at the University of Pennsylvania, in place since 1971, has sponsored many undergraduate research projects that addressed aspects of the urban environment, but it did not participate directly in WEPIC events until the summer of 1994, when we engaged several students in planning an undergraduate course on the urban environment, which became ENVS 404, The Urban Environment-West Philadelphia in Spring 1995.

In that course, we planned to engage middle school children from the fifth through eighth grades of the Shaw Middle School, a mile west of the university in West Philadelphia, in a program of environmental instruction and focused research. Shaw was then in the process of organizing its 800 students into four "learning communities" of some 200 children each. One such community adopted the name "Science Alliance," and proceeded to develop environmental studies as the integrating theme for its entire curriculum. Penn students were already engaged in assisting Shaw teachers in bringing enrichment to that curriculum.

In planning ENVS 404, we resolved to engage Shaw children in the assessment of an environmental problem of immediate interest to them and their families, while we encouraged the Penn students to place that problem in the larger context of the environmental history of cities in general and of Philadelphia in particular. We chose to address what is widely recognized to be the major environmental problem facing urban children in the United States today: exposure of young children to environmental lead still in place on the interior and exterior walls of houses, and resident in yard and street dirt and in dust from household interiors.

We set up ENVS 404 as a long-term experiment to see whether focused environmental education, leading to modification of early-childhood behavior, might represent a more cost-effective strategy to reduce early-childhood exposure to environmental lead than mechanical abatement of lead-based paint from household interiors has proven to be. The control for our experiment would be the continuing program of blood-Pb assessment carried out by the Philadelphia Department of Health in all neighborhoods in the city, including that served by the Shaw Middle School.

We chose the Shaw Middle School because WEPIC was already well established there, and because Shaw's principal, Al Bichner, was enthusiastic about the pervasive presence of Penn students in the curriculum of the school and in the lives of the Shaw children. We subsequently learned that the Shaw community lies in the center of that part of Philadelphia where random blood-Pb testing has repeatedly yielded the highest incidence of children with elevated blood Pb in the city. Fully 40 percent of children under six years of age in the Shaw neighborhood have tested higher than 10 µg/dl for blood Pb; some 8 percent have shown blood-Pb levels higher than 20 µg/dl (Richard Tobin and Carla Campbell, personal communications, 1997).

ENVS 404 was designed to provide comprehensive education for families in the Shaw neighborhood about the nature and risk of environmental lead by using their middle school children as sample collectors, data assessors, secondary teachers, and neighborhood advocates. If our program were successful, we hoped to see the Shaw neighborhood emerge as an island of low childhood blood Pb while the city continues to collect and archive blood-Pb data.

The Format of ENVS 404

In January 1995, we enrolled 21 students in the first iteration of ENVS 404. We began the term with an intensive study of the physics, chemistry, technology, toxicology, and public health threat of the element Pb. As a class, we identified those reservoirs of environmental lead that posed the greatest threat to young children in the Shaw neighborhood. We developed a series of sampling protocols and detailed sampling instructions whereby middle school participants could be entrusted with collecting and packaging samples from those reservoirs in and adjacent to their homes: interior paint, interior dust, yard dirt, and street dirt. In addition, we hoped to acquire shed deciduous teeth from Shaw children and their younger siblings and neighbors, from which we could determine the integrated exposure to environmental lead of those children who had shed the teeth.

We also recognized the need to collect basic information about the households in which the children lived. We divided the Penn class into four groups: (1) Questionnaire and Brochure, (2) Sampling, (3) Pb Analysis, (4) Data-Plotting. Not all groups were of equal size, and students were free to participate in more than a single group.

Students in Group 1 developed a questionnaire designed to provide vital information about each of the households from which samples would be collected: location of household, number and ages of residents, professions of employed household members, years of residence at the current address, age of house (all were built before 1960), years elapsed since the interior of the house was last painted (most had not been painted in the memory of current residents), history of lead testing of household members, etc. Group 1 visited the school, distributed the questionnaires, and returned a few days later to collect them.

Students in Group 2 visited the Shaw Middle School on a regular basis to explain the program to teachers and schoolchildren, to educate the children about lead during more or less formal classroom sessions, and to instruct the children in sample-collecting protocol and scientific record keeping. These lessons were repeated as often and in as much detail as seemed necessary. Students in Group 2 also picked up the samples as they were returned to the school.

Students in Group 3 received the samples and analyzed them for Pb on the X ray fluorescence (XRF) apparatus set up in the laboratories of Penn's Institute for Environmental Studies.

Students in Group 4 received the results from Group 3 and plotted those results on a modified Geographic Information System (GIS), simple enough to be manipulated by the schoolchildren within the limited capacity of the computers used in Shaw's Science Alliance learning community. This exercise formed the basis of a series of lessons in geography and map making that were integrated into the environmental curriculum of Science Alliance.

As data were compiled and plotted, students in Group 1 drafted, edited, and reproduced a brochure advising residents of households in the Shaw neighborhood how to protect children most at risk — preschool toddlers — from environmental lead known to be widely distributed throughout their neighborhood. The brochures were handed out in the classes of Science Alliance participants, who were urged to share the contents of the brochure with their families and neighbors and to participate actively in helping their younger siblings and neighbors to change behaviors that brought them into contact with residual environmental lead.

At the end of the term, each group wrote a comprehensive report on its share of the project. These reports were then compiled into a single document that was distributed to interested people at Penn, in WEPIC, in the school district, and within the EPA and the Pennsylvania Department of Environmental Protection.[3]

Problems With ENVS 404

While ENVS 404 is straightforward in concept, it has been beset with problems of effective implementation. Of course, the contemplation of each such problem and the efforts undertaken to address it served as essential aspects of the education of the Penn student participants. The problems we faced can be summarized as follows:

1. Despite the fact that they were only a few years older, the Penn students were quite unprepared for the limited attention span of the middle school students with whom they worked. Several Penn students made the observation that the schoolchildren who proved most difficult to work with displayed many of the effects of low-level lead poisoning, and therefore probably came from households where the risk of lead poisoning to younger siblings was high.

In addition, most Penn students, by virtue of the academic selection process they had survived, were drawn from school environments dramatically different from the one they encountered the first day they entered the Shaw Middle School. After the first shock, however, most of the Penn students submerged themselves in the task at hand, somehow learned to lower their expectations, and experienced firsthand why childhood lead poisoning and other problems of inner-city communities have proved to be so intractable.

2. Return of both questionnaires and samples was disappointingly low. In particular, we received so few teeth that the samples we had offered no statistical significance. Efforts to improve the sample return rate included multiple redistributions of sample bags, incorporation of the sampling exercise in classroom activities, pleading, cajoling, and a variety of reward structures (e.g., pizza parties for the classes that returned the most samples).

3. The time lag between collecting samples and reporting results was too long. Many of the children had forgotten about the sampling exercise by the

time they saw the data plotted on maps of their neighborhood.

4. The academic schedule of the University of Pennsylvania was not in synchrony with that of the School District of Philadelphia. The spring semester at Penn began two weeks after the Shaw children had returned to school, and ended long before the Shaw school year was over. Many samples that were returned to Shaw after the Penn students had left Philadelphia for the summer were analyzed by Penn student summer employees, but those data were not integrated into the semester's exercise at Shaw.

Successes of ENVS 404

Despite the problems identified above, ENVS 404 has made some important contributions to public health and environmental awareness in the Shaw community, and it has greatly expanded awareness of the nature of urban environmental problems among Penn student participants.

1. We learned, to nobody's surprise, that environmental lead is widely distributed in the Shaw neighborhood. Lead is present in high concentrations in paint chips collected from interior surfaces, in yard dirt collected from places where small children routinely play, and in dirt from the edges of curbs in front of houses. Interior dust, most often collected from the bags of vacuum cleaners, showed lower concentrations of lead. Of the few teeth that were collected, several showed evidence of long-term exposure to lead; those data were reported to the Department of Health of the City of Philadelphia. We did not collect paint directly from exterior painted surfaces, nor did we undertake a comprehensive program of water sampling in the neighborhood, although appropriate precautions in the use of tap water delivered via old plumbing were included in the brochure.

2. Hundreds of middle school children received intensive and repetitive instruction about the risk of lead poisoning in urban environments. These children carried the message so received home to their households and neighborhoods, within which the lead-avoidance message was widely disseminated. We think that such a message, carried by a child who has worked with the problem as part of a middle school curriculum, is likely to be more effective than a similar message couched in adult language and stuffed unsolicited into mailboxes in the Shaw neighborhood.

3. A cohort of middle school teachers has incorporated instruction in lead avoidance into a middle school science curriculum.

4. A group of well-educated students at Penn have been introduced, via an intensive seminar, to a major environmental problem that had before their participation in ENVS 404 been unknown to many of them, despite their well-developed interest in environmental issues.

The success of the first offering of ENVS 404 attracted modest EPA support for 1995 and 1996, thanks to which we extended the program to the Turner Middle School, also in West Philadelphia, and collected a suite of samples from the suburban Strath Haven Middle School, in Delaware County, Pennsylvania. (In the Strath Haven exercise, 100 percent of distributed sample bags were returned!) A major grant from the Kellogg Foundation, awarded in 1996 to support a variety of WEPIC activities, enabled us to purchase a field XRF instrument and to support many aspects of our in-class activities. ENVS 404 also received programmatic support from a HUD grant to the office at Penn that administers WEPIC programs — the Center for Community Partnerships. A grant from the Commonwealth of Pennsylvania has enabled WEPIC to build a modern GIS computer lab in the Shaw school, to be used in ENVS 404 and in other WEPIC-sponsored programs.

Given these successes, we intend to repeat this exercise each spring term for the foreseeable future, hoping to show, by documenting reduced blood-Pb concentrations in young children in the Shaw community, that our educational campaign has been effective. We will modify the program as conditions warrant; in 1996, for example, we were able to bring the field XRF apparatus directly into the classrooms and report preliminary lead concentrations of samples while the sample collectors watched.

Conclusions

ENVS 404 at the University of Pennsylvania has documented comprehensively the magnitude of the risk of environmental lead for a selected neighborhood in a part of West Philadelphia where reports indicated childhood blood-Pb concentrations were alarmingly high. We have set in place a program to assess that problem. We have reached a very large number of neighborhood residents with a simple message, carried by schoolchildren at the Shaw Middle School, that we hope will enable them to modify the behavior of young children in a way that will reduce their exposure to environmental lead. We have acquainted a group of highly motivated Penn undergraduates with an urban environmental and public health problem of alarming magnitude. As our program continues, we hope to be able to demonstrate that focused education, designed to modify childhood behavior, is a more cost-effective strategy to reduce the unacceptably high incidence of childhood lead poisoning than mechanical abatement of affected households has proven to be.

As the success of our efforts becomes apparent, we hope to introduce this program to other Philadelphia neighborhoods, and to other cities.

Notes

1. Michelle Belsley, Jennifer Cheng, Abby Close, Scott Cohen, Susane Colasanti, Christian Coli, Alan Danzig, Ralph Darmo, Michel Davies, Melissa Donald, Nijmie Dzurinko, Jacque-

line Eppolito, Ethan Fox, Mike Gerstner, Christi Gubser, Matthew Guerrieri, Greg Horowitz, Julie Huang, Ali Husain, Scott Ignall, Mike Isenberg, Jon Joseph, Sue Kim, Ethan Klein, Paul Lantieri, Alex Levine, Doug Levy, Nancy Loh, Christopher Magarian, Kristen McArdle, Susan Mermelstein, Alex Millard, Evelyn O'Donohue, Laura Paladino, Lynn Peterson, Christy Plumer, Laura Ross, Suzanna Roth, Dana Royer, Jonathan Seeg, Nirav Shah, Lisa Shluger, Matthew Shuba, Rebecca Skiles, Maria Stein, Monica Stein, Shivani Tibrewala, Josh Tull, Michael Turner, Jen Van Ness, Laura Viggiano, RuthAnne Visnauskas, Ilene Wong, Derek Woo.

2. More information on WEPIC can be obtained from Joann Weeks: *weeks@pobox.upenn.edu.*

3. Copies of final reports submitted to EPA for 1995, 1996, and 1997 are available from the authors.

References

Benson, Lee, and Ira Harkavy. (1991). "Progressing Beyond the Welfare State." *Universities and Community Schools* 2(1-2): 2-28.

Centers for Disease Control. (October 1991). "Preventing Lead Poisoning in Young Children." Atlanta, GA: CDC.

Eisinger, J. (July 1996). "Sweet Poison." *Natural History*: 48-53.

Franklin, B. (1786). The famous Franklin letter on lead poisoning: Philadelphia Department of Public Health.

Gilfillan, S.C. (1965). "Lead Poisoning and the Fall of Rome." *Journal of Occupational Medicine* 7: 53-60.

Graziano, Joseph. (1994). "Validity of Lead Exposure in Diagnosis and Surveillance." *Clinical Chemistry* 40: 1387-1390.

Harkavy, Ira, and John L. Puckett. (September 1994). "Lessons From Hull House for the Contemporary University." *Social Service Review*: 299-321.

Murozumi, N.T., J. Chow, and C. Patterson. (1969). "Chemical Concentrations of Pollutant Lead Aerosols, Terrestrial Dust, and Sea Salts in Greenland and Antarctic Snow Strata." *Geochimica et Cosmochimica Acta* 33: 1247-1294.

Needleman, H.L. (1990). "The Long Term Effects of Exposure to Low Doses of Lead in Childhood." *New England Journal of Medicine* 232: 83-88.

Rodier, Patricia M. (1995). "Developing Brain as a Target of Toxicity." *Environmental Health Perspectives* 103(Suppl. 6): 73-76.

Shapiro, I.M., A. Burke, G. Mitchell, and P. Bloch. (1978). "X-Ray Fluorescence Analysis of Lead in Teeth of Urban Children in Situ: Correlation Between the Tooth Lead Level and the Concentration of Blood Lead and Free Erythroporphyrins." *Environmental Research* 17: 46-52.

Zonies, David. (1997). "Lead Disease and Social Deviance in a 19th-Century Prison: X-Ray Fluorescence Analysis of Skeletal Lead Burden as an Indicator of Health Status." M.S. Thesis. University of Pennsylvania, Department of Anthropology.

Connecting the Classroom and the Community:
A Southern California Experience

by Nan Jenks-Jay

Welcome to the Southern California experience, a dichotomy of the best and the worst the environment can offer. Here students can easily apply their textbook learning to reality by going beyond the perimeter of campus into the community and experiencing a comprehensive environmental education.

The University of Redlands's Environmental Studies program has a particularly advantageous location that allows it to serve as an ideal laboratory for students to explore real problems and progressive solutions. California is truly an environmental paradox. Green indices rank California as leading the way in environmental policy and legislation relating to air quality. Yet, the Los Angeles basin still has some of the worst air pollution in the country, although greatly improved from 10 years ago.

California ranks first in the nation for renewable energy production and is a leader globally with 80 percent of the wind power, 90 percent of the solar power, 95 percent of the geothermal, and 90 percent of the biomass energy produced in the world. An electric car manufacturer is located in Redlands, and a half-hour away, 3,000 wind turbines cover the mountain pass near Palm Springs, generating electricity for Edison's grid. In the nearby Mojave Desert, the mirrored parabolic troughs and solar thermal generating systems constitute the largest collection of solar-powered facilities in existence.

While the California desert is home to an impressive array of alternative energy sources, it has also been the unfortunate recipient of tons of hazardous and solid waste. California's municipal solid waste record is an abysmal 49th in the nation. Recycling programs have only recently been mandated, trailing years behind other states. Already, however, it is profitable to recycle and reconstitute construction waste and shredded U.S. currency, converting them into roofing materials.

Environmental justice issues are at a high level, with activist groups such as the Mothers of East LA bringing attention to the injustices borne by their neighborhood. Lead paint removal and programs to test children's blood levels are now being funded. However, minority farm worker safety still remains an issue, with more than 3,000 doctor-reported cases of worker poisonings annually and most cases still going unreported. Pushing production to its limits, California's agriculture uses 10 percent of all the pesticides in the world, ranking 49th in sustainable farming practices.

Water-related resources are a true phenomenon in California. Natural waterways have been converted to concrete channels, with 95 percent of the original wetlands destroyed, but now streambeds and riparian habitat are being restored. Northern California water diverted through aqueducts provides Southern Californians with drinking water and their golf courses, lawns, and agriculture with irrigation for thirsty crops such as cotton and rice being grown in the desert. Today, however, more water conservation and reclamation occurs in homes, industry, and in agriculture. Farmers have incentives to replace old irrigation systems and plant less-water-demanding crops in order to sell their water rights to growing urban areas. Most lakes in California are constructed reservoirs, with many such as the Salton Sea having high levels of salinity, chemicals, and bacteria from domestic waste and agricultural runoff. More than 60,000 waterbirds died at the Salton Sea recently. The University of Redlands has received a $1-million grant from the U.S. Environmental Protection Agency to study the bioregional and binational problems of this body. Still, this is just a drop in the bucket considering the vast array of water-related issues and innovations occurring in California.

Rapid population growth results in the equivalent of adding another San Francisco each year. Open space represents little more than land being converted to suburban development connected by massive highway systems. Growth management and land-use controls are slowly being implemented, lagging far behind other parts of the country. These and countless other situations are directly available to our students. Nearby field trips allow first-hand examination of a municipal, nonchemical, wastewater treatment facility and a successful green waste business, campus landscaping with native, drought-resistant plants (xeroscaping), and land banking initiatives that protect the coastal, sage scrub habitat of endangered species. This is the laboratory that our students explore and some of the issues with which they become involved.

The University of Redlands and Its Environmental Studies Program

The University of Redlands has long maintained an emphasis on developing citizenship in its students through service and on offering a curriculum that integrates theory and practice. As its mission statement indicates,

> Welcoming intellectually curious students of diverse religious, ethnic, national, socioeconomic backgrounds, the University seeks to develop responsible citizenship as part of a complete education. . . . Redlands blends liberal arts and professional programs, applied and theoretical study, traditional majors and self-designed contracts for graduation.

The institution's Environmental Studies program was founded on a philosophy that recognizes the value of students working on real environmental problems at the local level. The program supports the university's mission by building this philosophy into its design through a number of principles that reoccur and are reinforced throughout the program. These principles include values, practical experience, communication, sustainability, collaboration, innovation, and community. The goal of the program is to provide a unique educational experience for students that directly links theory to practice, connects the campus to the local community, and immerses students in the surrounding environment.

These broad goals are realized through a curriculum that is designed to transform rhetoric into reality by creating concrete ways for students to encounter these principles throughout their four years at the university. Environmental studies students become directly involved in the rich opportunities that the region offers through core requirements including the introductory course, the environmental design studio, an internship, and a senior capstone project or honors thesis.

The Introductory Environmental Studies Course

The introductory course resembles any topical survey course with one exception. By mid term, students begin working in teams to address environmental issues on campus. Because the university administration supports the concept of our becoming a green campus, the students have access to key individuals and valuable information for their projects. Still, students lack experience in group problem solving and working in teams. Therefore, it is important to expose them to new ways of thinking, working, and learning.

In papers written early in the course, students identify environmental issues on campus that concern them. They discuss readings about group dynamics, and short exercises force them out into the community to acquire information from a public source around which a hypothetical environmental problem and solution are created. Soon afterward, the class selects one of the concerns they have regarding the campus. Concerns that students have about the campus typically coincide with those of the university.

As a result of this shared interest, the institution provides an open forum for students to study and improve their own campus. Relevant individuals are consulted for permission to explore various topics and are brought on board as partners in the projects, providing guidance and information throughout. In this way, students in the introductory class have investigated and assisted with such things as composting green waste; redesigning an irrigation system; monitoring an invasive, introduced plant along the creek on campus; siting new bicycle facilities; replacing disposable cups with reusable mugs; upgrading the recycling program; and developing a wilderness connection initiative.

The Environmental Design Studio

The central core of the Environmental Studies program is the environmental design studio, which provides students with a series of hands-on courses to explore methods of environmental problem solving. The environmental design studio represents a concept, a sequence of courses, and a physical space.

The studio as a concept was developed as part of a three-year curricular project, supported by $140,000 from a Leadership Opportunity in Science and Humanities grant from the National Endowment for the Humanities, Fund for the Improvement of Postsecondary Education, and the National Science Foundation. The goal in developing the studio was in part to provide a framework for students to understand better and respond critically to the daunting environmental issues facing us today and, more important, to become creative problem solvers. The introductory studio uses prototypical and hypothetical examples to expose students to systems thinking as an interrelated network of physical, natural, social, and value issues; application of data; spatial literacy; and teamwork. At advanced levels of the design studio, students work in groups undertaking actual projects addressing environmental problems in the community and region. With the skilled guidance of faculty and outside partners, students begin to learn the limitations of data, the complexities of competing values, and the benefits of cross-disciplinary collaboration. They test out plausible scenarios, some of which fail but which ultimately help them direct their creative abilities toward recommending better solutions. Learning directly from hands-on experience, participating in a process, and contributing to a final product that benefits the region enable students to gain the confidence and insight to begin thinking of themselves as potential agents of change. The introductory and advanced environmental design studios allow the university to participate in improving the local environment while providing our students with the experience of addressing real problems through projects that have been brought into the curriculum.

The physical space, dedicated solely to the purposes of the introductory and advanced environmental design studios, contains common areas for group projects and individual student carrels. The site is equipped with maps, resource materials, supplies, computers, telephones, and amenities such as a refrigerator, microwave, and tape player and is conveniently located adjacent to the university's Geographic Information System (GIS) lab. Students are assigned keys for 24-hour access, enabling them to work collectively or independently when they are either inspired or have available time outside of scheduled class periods.

Introductory environmental design studios work on hypothetical projects such as transportation planning for the Los Angeles basin and a resource protection plan for high chaparral regions. Real projects undertaken by the advanced environmental design studios initially evolved from the faculty's knowledge of issues in the region. As the students' work developed credibility and received recognition, proposals for new projects began to come in from outside entities. Students have a hand in designing and scoping the project, as a way of acquiring ownership of it. They meet with the principal parties involved and reach agreement regarding the project goals. Contracts or agreements of commitment are developed. (Informal arrangements have proven to be unsatisfactory, as expectations and goals are less clear.) A realistic budget is established to provide necessary resources specific to the project. Students create a time line with checkpoints, deadlines, and dates of other commitments such as athletic commitments and papers for other courses.

They break into groups not larger then three and begin tackling the tasks they have identified. Regular progress reports serve as a way to discuss problems they are encountering and to share information with others who might need data that another group came across. Class meeting times provide an opportunity to discuss ways to approach problems, prepare for public meetings, and ensure equal group-member participation while advancing the goals of the projects. By the middle of the term, the groups, faculty, and partners evaluate the status of the effort as a reality check and decide whether to modify the project's scope or to shift its focus. Students prepare and deliver a group report to those involved and give a public presentation.

Students in the advanced environmental design studios have worked on cooperative projects with local governments, state agencies, and private groups to develop a comprehensive resource management plan (CRMP) for the lake region and city of Big Bear. They have also worked with the city of Redlands on a commuter bicycle route connecting the campus to downtown.

The most ambitious work undertaken by a design studio came about as a result of the work conducted for the CRMP project and involved a project with the U.S. Department of Agriculture's Forest Service. When the San Bernardino National Forest and mining companies having rights within the forest discovered a conflict between five carbonate plant species and extraction of the high-quality limestone on which these plants grow, the parties requested assistance from the advanced environmental design studio. Initially, students were asked to produce a GIS map identifying areas where the plants and mining were both likely to occur. The stakes were actually much higher than they first appeared. The Forest Service is charged by the Endangered Species Act with protecting 26 plant species that are endemic only to the San Bernardino Mountains of Southern California, five of which grow on limestone-rich soils. The mining companies, on the other hand, were prepared to protect their rights, granted under the Mining Act of 1874. Annually, they extract 3.5 million tons of limestone, valued at $175 million, from Forest Service land in the San Bernardino Mountains.

Eventually, the scope of the project was enlarged, and it was divided into several stages to accommodate study of the 156,000-acre area identified as critical. Eliminating action in the courts that would have pitted two landmark laws against each other, this project led to a public/private partnership involving government, education, and industry. A total of 104 maps were produced, representing aspects and features of the area in question, with data provided by the Forest Service and the companies in addition to data from the students' own mapping of habitat with global positioning systems (GPS). Meetings hosted by the students brought the parties together to discuss the maps, to question the data, and to articulate concerns and interests. As the process continued, information became more available, accuracy improved, communication increased, and respect grew for opposing positions. Only once, early in the process, did a meeting require faculty intervention to restore civility.

A final analysis showed the high-priority mining and plant-protection areas were less in conflict then originally believed. Early assumptions had been speculative and lacked the vast amount of information that was compiled to generate a database and GIS maps. This was a project from which all benefitted, with a mutual agreement to accept the students' findings and the conservation plan they recommended for plants in conflict areas. The students' work was highly praised by the Forest Service and the mining representatives. A letter received from Vice President Al Gore stated:

> The agreement between the San Bernardino National Forest and mining companies represents an important innovative contribution to the process of resolving conflicts using partnerships. I commend the University of Redlands students for their work on this project. . . . As I hope all concerned learned in this experience, good information, good science, and reasoned dialogue avoid needless conflict.

The Environmental Justice Course

The Environmental Justice course, team taught by the directors of Redlands's Environmental Studies and Race and Ethnic Studies programs, provides another opportunity for students to become involved directly in real issues. The first two-thirds of the course focuses on the theory and history of race and environmentalism and develops a foundation of knowledge regarding the field of environmental justice. The last third of the course is dedicated to actual projects. The *Los Angeles Times* regularly features stories that focus on this area of concern, including the proposed siting of a hazardous waste facility in Ward Valley, on Native American lands near the California/Arizona border; the Mothers of East LA uniting against poor air quality in their neighborhood; and illness among farm workers, from exposure to fungicides applied to strawberries by inadequately protected Latino farm workers. However, the students have been eager to look into issues closer to home, and so have developed their own group projects in the local community. Several collected information for listed sites of hazardous spills, contaminated water plumes, current and former industries that handled toxic materials, or industries that had permits to release polluted air emissions or water discharges. Representing the information in a GIS map showed a disproportionate number of toxic sources were located in predominantly lower-income and minority neighborhoods.

Another group created a profile of a battery factory located in a poor Latino neighborhood to see whether the company was being a good neighbor. The project was suggested by a student who, for her university community service, worked in a program for at-risk kids from this neighborhood. The minority students in the course went straight into the neighborhood with ease, asking questions of residents and company officials. Hope that the company would have a clean record and be a conscientious neighbor disappeared when company officials lied to students about a previous fire and hazardous spill on-site. During the interview, it became clear that interest in the surrounding neighborhood was outside the company officials' concerns. Meanwhile, other students researched the batteries this company manufactured, the ingredients and by-products, their permits, and the poor environmental track record of the parent company. Since neighborhood houses are so close to the factory and the streets are very narrow, the students recommended that the company work with neighbors to develop a plan in the event of an emergency. Students recommended that warning signs in Spanish be posted next to those already posted in English. They informed managers of housing projects and neighbors about potential dangers in the event of an accident, alerted them to note adverse health effects on nearby residents, and provided the locations of health services. The company was encouraged to be a more responsible neighbor and the residents to be more conscious of the potential hazards in the immediate vicinity as a proactive way to avoid incidents and to recognize instances of environmental injustice that might exist or could be addressed.

The University Internship Program

Student internships have been available since 1984 through the university's well-organized Community Service Learning (CSL) program. Its mission states that

> [CSL] will foster partnerships between community agencies and the University of Redlands to match student, staff, and faculty in problem-solving efforts and in promoting social awareness for the common good. By educating both the head and the heart through service-learning courses, volunteer outreach, internships, and work study employment, CSL will enable university members to serve as agents of change and help seize opportunities in building healthier, stronger communities worldwide. By embracing and nurturing the volunteer spirit and service-learning curriculum, CSL will support, recognize, and promote the educational benefits for learning through service within higher education.

To achieve its goals, a CSL course is offered that includes an 80-hour unpaid internship with nonprofit groups in the community. Students attend classes on campus that help identify the educational objectives as well as the responsibilities of their positions. A supervisor provides an intern evaluation at the end, and the student-intern prepares a written paper. Reviewing journals kept during the month enables students to reflect on their internships and identify ways to transfer parts of their experience back to campus and the classroom. All students are required to participate in a CSL course prior to graduation. The CSL program, administered by the Dean of Students Office, has collaborated with the Environmental Studies program by adding a host of environmental internships to the CSL's list of opportunities. For example, students now intern in environmental education with the U.S. Forest Service's innovative "Children's Forest" in the San Bernardino Mountains and help develop watershed programs for schools with the County Resource Conservation District. The CSL is but one way to meet the Environmental Studies program's goal for students to connect with and benefit from working within the community.

Environmental Studies Internships

Students may fulfill the Environmental Studies program's internship requirement either by participating in the university's CSL course or through other environmental internships during the school year or summer. Three examples follow that demonstrate how different internships have connected students to communities and grown into even greater learning opportunities.

A student double-majoring in environmental studies and economics, who had worked on the Forest Service/mining carbonate plant species project in the advanced environmental design studio, acquired a summer internship in Washington State with Shore Trust Trading Group, an affiliate of Chicago's Shorebank Corporation and a subsidiary of Ecotrust, a nonprofit organization in Portland, Oregon, that believes "healthy communities and healthy ecosystems can best be fostered by releasing the energies and creativity of local people." Where better for a student to intern than under the tutelage of such a progressive organization, one that strives to improve environmental and economic sustainability within local communities? At the end of the summer, the student received a bonus check and a strong letter of recommendation. Work continued on the project back on campus as an honors thesis.

Another student obtained a summer internship with the Bicycle Federation of America, in Washington, DC, from her involvement in the commuter bikeway project undertaken by the advanced environmental design studio. Not having any internships, the Federation created one for her after seeing her background. Her primary task was to review bicycle transportation plans from cities throughout the United States. She quickly earned the respect of her coworkers and superiors, who entrusted her with the company vehicle for appointments around Washington, a folding bicycle hanging in the supply closet. Following the summer, she incorporated aspects of her internship into a senior capstone project for Redlands's cycling initiative.

A student established a new internship with the Environmental Systems Research Institute (ESRI) in Redlands, producer of GIS computer mapping software (ARCINFO). The internship involved assisting the director of conservation services, working with more than 2,000 nonprofit environmental organizations around the globe, connecting them with grants for funding and technical assistance. This student was later hired by ESRI.

Senior Capstone Projects and Honors Theses

Environmental majors are required to undertake either a senior capstone project or an honors research/project in which they assemble a team to work with. By the time these students are seniors, they have been engaged in a number of collaborative efforts working on real projects, attempting to improve the environmental condition on campus and in the greater community, from their first introductory class to their internships. They are able to draw upon their past experiences and build upon their successes with confidence when designing their senior projects and theses. Many projects evolve from earlier coursework and internships. All share the common threads or principles that are woven into the program's curriculum as an evolving theme in a student's education.

A project recommended by a faculty member involved producing for a local land conservancy an open-space map, with an analysis of where future development and continued conservation efforts should occur. In consultation with members of the conservancy, the student acquired data to produce a GIS map and used computer modeling to assess suitability. She gave two presentations of her final work: to her honors committee, which granted her honors, and to the conservancy, which gratefully accepted her study and invited her to join its board of directors.

The student whose internship was with the Bicycle Federation of America proposed as a senior capstone project to develop a street improvement program for the Redlands community, which the city council approved. The team she assembled included the director of public works and faculty, students, and citizen cyclists. She also used her internship contacts for assistance. The program she developed was fully implemented by the city and is working well. Following graduation, she worked with the Bicycle Commuter Coalition and intends to pursue graduate studies in planning, focusing on alternative transportation issues.

The student who worked with Shore Trust Trading Group demonstrated how experiences from an internship can be integrated back on campus and influence the design of an honors thesis. This senior continued his summer research as an ambitious honors thesis entitled "Non-Timber Forest Product Extraction and Markets in the Northwest," a copy of which Shore Trust received. This student went on to graduate school in resource economics.

What Has Worked and What Has Not

Project topics are identified and selected through several routes. Faculty members recommend topics, as with the conservancy land-use map and plan. The university, local community, and agencies within the region identify issues that cannot otherwise be pursued due to limited funding and resources. These often make ideal student projects; e.g., the recycling upgrade, composting, irrigation, bicycle routes for the city, and the Forest Service/mining carbonate plant species projects. Students also initiate their own projects such as their profiling the battery factory in the Environmental Justice course. Successful projects result in a constant flow of proposals from outside entities, and great care is taken to match a student's ability, background, and interests with the partnering group's expectations. The goal is for projects to be challenging educational experiences for students, which means they must have the latitude to fail at some things and learn from those mistakes. The partners must understand this fact at the outset or else will be disappointed. It is important for faculty to resist becoming a mini consulting service, as students' experiences in such instances have been less positive. Larger, more demanding projects can be broken into phases, with parts handled in the environmental design studios or pursued as honors work or internships. A delicate balance must be struck in education with service to achieve a valuable student learning experience with positive outcomes for the greater community.

Partnerships need not be highly structured, although large, complex projects involving funding should have an actual contract. Most can be formalized with a brief letter of agreement stating what parties understand as expectations, roles, deadlines, and desired final products. We have found that projects without any form of agreement have been less successful, due to misunderstandings and missed opportunities, and fall short of being fully embraced or implemented by the partner afterward. Projects should have points throughout the process that serve as reality checks. Modifications that significantly alter a project should include the partner's input. A tactic that has worked successfully in providing projects for students in following semesters is recommending that parts left undone due to time constraints become another phase undertaken through future environmental design studios or senior capstone projects.

Students require guidance to begin group projects. Readings and exercises expose them to group dynamics and working outside the classroom with varied types of information and diverse populations. Small, successful projects on campus followed by internships often build the confidence and knowledge required for students to develop and undertake more-comprehensive, advanced environmental design studio and thesis projects. Having students assess the demands on their time from other courses, athletics, jobs, and other commitments is a real test of their ability to understand time management in a setting not unlike the real world. The simplest way for students to learn to recognize limitations and expectations is for them each to create a personal time line once a project's time line has been established for the semester. A student can then agree to, say, contribute more at the beginning knowing he or she is likely to be away for a national athletic competition at the end of the term.

There is little about project-related courses that resembles traditionally structured courses. Faculty who orchestrate project courses act more as facilitators. These courses are extremely demanding on students and faculty alike. Much is unpredictable. As many things go wrong as go right. The questions on standard institutional course evaluation forms do not begin to match these kinds of learning experiences, and are therefore quite inadequate. Students frequently begin to comprehend the value of their experience only after it is over. Therefore, reflection should be incorporated at the end of projects and internships to assess the experience fully.

Student internships can be formal programs or be self-initiated. Many students find it very rewarding to approach an organization with a compelling request that enables them to work on something about which they are passionate. Both opportunities provide unique and valuable learning experiences that can be integrated into courses back on campus. Formal internships may require evaluations at the conclusion, but we suggest that at the end of self-initiated internships that students request letters of recommendation to go into their portfolios for graduate schools and future employers.

Finally, a few words on assessment are in order. Although there has been up until now no formal assessment of the before-and-after knowledge levels associated with internships and service-related opportunities nor any formal evaluation of partnership success, student reflections provide compelling arguments for continuing these opportunities. Students and alumni indicate that these were some of the most beneficial learning experiences they had during their undergraduate education. Many have indicated that they subsequently are more interested and capable of becoming involved with the communities in which they later find themselves. This alone signifies success. If we as educators can connect students in beneficial ways to a community during their college years, which later enables them to contribute to improving the quality of their own home communities over time, then our work has been well done.

An Experiment in Environmental Service-Learning

by Calvin F. Exoo

While a number of academic departments at St. Lawrence University have a history of offering credit-bearing internships, there was no university service-learning program until the fall of 1995. In that year, responding to a faculty initiative, the university created the position of director of service-learning. This was to be a member of the faculty, given a one-third reduction in teaching load to build a program. The director's mandate was simple: expand the number of service-learning opportunities for students and ensure their academic integrity.

That was easier said than done. The main problem was recruiting faculty. Either of two problems could disqualify a colleague from being involved: lack of interest or lack of time. Unfortunately, those faculty who scored highest on the interest axis tended to score the lowest on time. This was not just a coincidence. Several other interdisciplinary pedagogical innovations (residential colleges, writing across the curriculum, etc.) had gotten to the dance before service-learning, and had filled up the dance cards of those faculty members open to innovation.

The question, then, was how to involve faculty without demanding much of their time. The answer we devised asked faculty to be not a house for service-learning but a Lincoln log (a piece of a larger structure). The strategy we devised is, in most respects, not novel. We began offering a nondepartmental service-learning course, ND200. It has a fieldwork/internship requirement (eight hours per week on-site) and a writing component (a scholarly journal and a research paper on a subject related to the fieldwork). The director supervises those aspects of the course.

The third leg of the course is a series of reflection workshops, and it is here that we ask other faculty to participate. Each semester, the director and five other faculty members each offers one workshop (some preassigned reading and a two-hour seminar on a subject likely to have resonance with students doing fieldwork). Members of the workshop team also attend one another's sessions.

The irony of this resolution is that our weakness became a strength. The lack of time available from interested faculty forced us to ask for a little from a lot. Already, 17 faculty members from 12 different departments have participated. Most of them, of course, leave the workshops with an enhanced understanding and appreciation of service-learning and a willingness to recommend the course to students and to colleagues. In retrospect, it seems that we stumbled onto an ideal way to build a program.

ND200B: Environmental Internships

In Spring 1996, we began planning a second section of ND200, one designed specifically for environmental placements. We did so for two reasons: First, relatively few of the students or faculty being recruited for ND200 were from the sciences. We wanted to increase our profile in that division, and we thought an environmental internship course might help.

Second, most of our field placements at that time were in human services agencies; only a few were in the environmental area. For that reason, most of the workshops were planned with human service interns in mind and sometimes didn't resonate with the environmental interns, whom we felt would be better served by a workshop series of their own.

The course, Environmental Internships, ND200B, debuted in Spring 1997. Six workshop presenters included an environmental economist, a specialist in the literature of the outdoors, an environmental psychologist, a geologist, the director of our writing center, and a member of the Environmental Studies department. The topics (and readings assigned) were:

• Sustainability (R. Solow, "Sustainability: An Economist's Perspective")

• Environmental Ethics & Social Equity (M. Renner, "Jobs in a Sustainable Economy")

• The Right Word Is Worth 1,000 Pictures: Writing Effectively About Your Experiences (no reading)

• Sense of Peace and Other Affective & Cognitive Ties to the Environments (I. Altman and S. Low, "Community Attachment")

• A Native-American Perspective on Environmental Issues (L. Hogan, *Solar Storms*)

• Sustainability: A Third-World Case Study (J. Ives and B. Messerli, "Introduction," *The Himalayan Dilemma: Reconciling Development and Conservation*)

Because we wanted to make a good first impression on our agencies, we imposed a minimum GPA prerequisite of 2.8 and permission of the instructor for admission to the course. Later, as we read over the evaluations of our very satisfied field supervisors, we were happy we had done so. Furthermore, we did in fact attract the science majors we were after. Of our 20 students, 16 were natural science majors (most of them in biology); 14 of them were combined majors, all with environmental studies.

Each student was required to confer with the internship coordinator about internship possibilities. From there, students were encouraged to take the lead and follow their bliss: to contact internship sites they were interested in, ask for more information, present their credentials, and, if all parties were agreeable, finalize the arrangements. We gave students this autonomy and responsibility as a way of introducing them to what we hoped would be an outcome of the internship experience: a lesson in initiative and a sense of accomplishment. The students worked in such agencies as the State Department of Environmental Conservation; local nature centers; the Environment Division at Akwesasne, a nearby Mohawk reservation; the U.S. Geological Survey; the County Planning Office; and a local citizens group active on environmental issues.

One difference between ND200B and the first section (ND200A) involved the research project. The environmental internship course was partly funded by a SEAMS grant from Campus Compact. Under its terms, students were required to present lessons on "sustainable communities and resource preservation in low-income areas" to area high school students. Accordingly, the research project became a research and presentation project.

A chronic problem in service-learning is how to grade students when so much of their performance is not directly observed by the campus instructor. In the next section, I will discuss our commitment to fully integrating the fieldwork with an academic experience. That goal helped solve our grading problem. It meant that in addition to field supervisors evaluating students (on work not directly observed by an instructor), we were able to grade the students on the following directly observable work: (1) their journal describing and reflecting on the fieldwork (considered together with the field supervisor's evaluation, 40 percent of the course grade); (2) their research, lesson plan, and presentation (lesson plans graded by an on-campus instructor, class presentation by our cooperating high school teachers, 30 percent); (3) their written responses to each week's reading, together with classroom participation (30 percent).[1]

Did It Work?

The Workshops

The goal of our workshops was to offer readings and discussions that would help students conceptualize their internship experiences. This, of course, is a perennial challenge in service-learning. Indeed, it may be the most important challenge. In our case, the challenge was even greater because our students were working in a variety of different agencies. Hence, a focused workshop on, for example, environmental problems at Akwesasne would have clear relevance for the students working at that site and little relevance for the other students.

Course evaluations and journals indicated that two of our workshop sessions in particular were much appreciated by all the students. The first was a session on journaling. Journals, I would argue, are indispensable to service-learning. While the classroom offers students the chance to hear about others' experiences, and to share a few of their own, the journal is where the student can focus reflection on his or her particular experience and where the quality of that reflection can be evaluated and improved by an instructor.

All of our interns are required to keep journals, but most of them have had little experience doing so, and are a bit uncertain about what, in particular, the journal is supposed to be. In the ND200B session, our writing center director talked about the possible uses of journals, illustrating these uses through the work of environmental writers. The students especially appreciated that this was a hands-on session, one in which they learned by doing. They were asked to look at several scenes and describe them. These exercises were used to illustrate the joy of writing; of "showing," not just "telling"; of seeing what may not be visible at first glance; and of connecting the eye to the mind, and to the "right words" that will capture the image.

A second universally applauded workshop reviewed the spectrum of possible approaches to environmental ethics: the differences between mechanistic and holistic thinking, and among egocentrism, homocentrism, and ecocentrism. Again these approaches were illustrated through the work of various environmental philosopher-writers. The session gave all the students a chance to think about which approach predominated at their agency, and why. Even the environmental studies majors, for whom the material was a review of issues they'd met before, expressed appreciation for the refresher course, now that these issues were coming to life in conversations at their agency.

Tension in the Marriage of Thought and Practice

In all offerings of ND200, a "yin and yang" has arisen between the faculty and students: Consistently, the faculty emphasize theories and concepts; consistently, the students appreciate it when the talk turns to their experiences. Because the faculty have designed the workshops, their yin has trumped the students' yang in that setting. Currently, the classroom is mostly concepts; practice holds sway in the field and in the journal.

Recently, however, we've been re-imagining the classroom, wondering whether we couldn't achieve a better balance of thought and practice within that setting. Hence, we have developed a new plan. After two or three of the usual "guided" workshops, we will try a couple of "unguided" workshops. In these, there will be no faculty presenter and no agenda-setting readings. Instead, students will be asked to come prepared to tell the group about their internship. The group, including the instructor, will be responsible for trying to understand those experiences in a scholarly way.

One immediately apparent disadvantage of this approach is that the instructor will not be able to prepare for all the possible experiences, issues, and questions that might arise — and then might not know the answers. But is that a disadvantage or an advantage? Faculty would be transformed from what seem to be omniscient fonts of wisdom into mere fellow searchers in a now-larger circle of searchers. Students would be as responsible as faculty for finding answers to the questions that arise.

The following scenario that arose in a student's journal is the kind of topic that didn't make it into the classroom this semester, but might make it into the re-imagined classroom:

> The student is working at Akwesasne. She attends a meeting of tribe members, staff from the tribe's Environment Division, and representatives from the nearby Alcoa plant. She notices that the well-trained Environment Division staff speak in the technical language taught to environmental scientists for the purpose of "cleaning up messes." Other tribe members speak a broader language, of land and water and people. This is a language, the student thinks, more conducive to thinking about the kind of systemic change really needed to address the eco-crisis at Akwesasne. She asks, "Does our specialized training narrow our thinking?" The broader theoretical question might be: Is the training of what Gramsci called "organic intellectuals" always designed to perpetuate, or at least not to threaten, the status quo?

This is certainly not a better or more important question than the ones currently raised by faculty. But the fact that it arose out of a student's own experiences might make it seem more pressing and interesting to students.

The Research Presentations

The requirement that students present lessons on sustainability and resource preservation in area middle and high schools was a condition of the grant we received after students had signed up for this course. When they first heard of this requirement, there was some talk of dropping the class. The presentation seemed to be extra work, added to an already-demanding syllabus. (We call ND200 "the toughest course you'll ever love.") And, they would later admit, the students were anxious about public speaking.

But once again, what initially seemed to be a handicap would turn out to be a strength. The students' journals consistently pointed to three benefits of presenting these lessons: First, they came away with an enhanced appreciation of the teaching job we do ("I never knew how hard this is. You make it look so easy!").

Second, it provided a rite of passage. For most of them, the ordeal became a triumph. The following journal entry is from a member of a team of three students who set themselves an ambitious task (too ambitious, they often thought as they prepared for it): They brought a local middle school class to a wilderness lodge for a day and a half of lessons and activities:

> I must admit, I didn't think we would be able to pull it off. I was a bit scared when the students showed up and Ms. *** said, "They are all yours." It was remarkable how smoothly things went. At the beginning, I felt we did not have enough planned to fill the time, but the day and a half went by very quickly. . . . The best part of the trip was that our primary focus was the education, not crowd control, which was extremely nice. . . . Before I knew it, the day was over and I was back on campus. It was a great opportunity to be able to teach middle school students outside.

A final benefit came from our students' interaction with the high school students. Our grant mandated that this interaction be with residents of "low-income communities." St. Lawrence County fits that bill, and a couple of others as well: It is also rural, and isolated by many miles from any cities. Our students' image of their indigenous neighbors can easily slip into the stereotype of the ignorant yokel, happily accepting the devil's bargain of clear-cutting and strip-mining in exchange for jobs and weekends spent blasting the local wildlife into oblivion. As one student put it, "We call them 'townies,' 'hicks,' and 'North Country folk,' never really knowing the dynamics of their day-to-day lives." For that reason, the interactions came as a very pleasant surprise to our students.

> On Wednesday, we went to Colton-Pierrepont to give our lesson on deer herd management. Our only concern was that the class would be unwilling to participate, as most high school classes are in an unfamiliar setting. Their participation would be vital to the success of our lesson plan as we had structured it. These concerns were quickly forgotten as the majority of the class felt comfortable speaking about the topic. Deer hunting and the management of deer are important to the lives of many individuals in the North Country, as was clearly represented by the interests and participation of the students. Ironically, many of the students knew more about deer management than I had known before researching the field. *** and I were rather pleased with our audience's reception to our lesson.

The Internships: Uses and Gratifications

Encountering Nature. For some of our students, the importance of the internship was not just on-site nature lessons offered by field supervisors, but the outdoor experience itself: the chance to see parts of the North Country wilderness that they otherwise would not have seen, or just to be outdoors at all, communing with the timeless serenity of marshes and the power of cold rivers.

*** and I finished the Dead Creek trail today. We entered from the other side and connected the trail that *** and I had started previously. Dead Creek really is a beautiful spot. Nothing dead about it. Everything is full of life. It's truly a spiritual place. The GPS unit was weird. It went down for 1½ hours. We still were able to get the trail, but it was kind of annoying. Wondering if the area wanted to be mapped in the first place. Good place.

Encountering Diversity. Because our faculty and student body are not very diverse, an important goal of our service-learning program has been to engage the human diversity in our area. That, of course, is easier to do in human service internships, where the "clients" students work with tend to be from very different walks of life. In our environmental internships, the "clients" were, in one case, the ducks for whom students installed wood-duck boxes; and our field supervisors are, for the most part, college-educated, middle-class white people.

But in at least one case, our students did have a chance to encounter a culture that has been set apart, and to think about its relationship to the dominant culture.

The Reynolds quarterly meeting wasn't far from what I thought it would be. Three men from Reynolds came over to the Reservation armed with overheads, progress reports, and assurances. . . .

Right now Reynolds is in the process of designing and installing a new fume system to collect the ambient fumes from the bag house. At present these fumes are allowed to leave the building without any sort of scrubbing, via air vents in the roof of the bag house. . . .

Reynolds began to plan for this new installation because it was anticipating new regulations to be implemented by EPA by the year 1998. Now that it appears that EPA is not on schedule (surprise, surprise) Reynolds wants to stop any further work on this new system. Needless to say, the concerned Mohawk citizens who live downwind from Reynolds would like [the company] to install the fume system anyway. This is the point of contention. . . .

From what I gathered, previous meetings had gone well because Reynolds had previously been working toward installation of the new system. Now that [the company] seemed to be backing down, the Mohawk members of this committee were pretty annoyed and began to question the probable effectiveness of the fume system itself even if it were to be installed. . . .

Considering the adverse health and environmental effects suffered by the Mohawks, they were overly patient and understanding. The only Mohawk representative at the meeting who was really pushing the Reynolds spokespeople for answers was ***. *** is a work of art. Probably in *her 70s, she is totally uninhibited about what she says, regardless of whether she knows anything about the "science" of the issue. I feel that *** represents what has been lost in the ever-narrowing specialization that has swept through every level of education, especially higher education.*

In general, the chance to encounter human diversity arose more often in work with citizens groups than with bureaucratic agencies, and we are currently working to develop more internships with the former.

The Idea of Service. Another of our program's objectives has been to use students' service to the community as an opportunity to discuss such things as citizenship and obligation. In these conversations, the students consistently stake out a moral "middle ground" for themselves. On one hand, they firmly reject the notion that the pursuit only of self-interest is a tenable moral position. (Ayn Rand's vision of a society made up only of strong, self-reliant individuals is "la-la land," as one student put it.) On the other hand, they are also unpersuaded that there is a "categorical imperative," a moral sensibility apart from and having priority over the physical sensibility, whose dictates must be followed despite the objections of the physical (Paton 1965: 134-135). For our students, "doing good" and "feeling good" about doing good are constant companions, and they have no qualms about saying that they do the former in large part to feel the latter.[2]

For the environmental interns, themes of doing good and feeling good arose most often at those agencies with limited resources and a mission the students approved of:

> *I plan to go in for my last visit [to the reservation] on this day. I feel I've gotten a lot out of this internship, partly because I was able to help out a bit for some truly wonderful people who deserve better than what has been done to them. I really enjoyed myself and am grateful that this internship gave me the opportunity to acquire this experience.*

> *While working on the four boxes we actually saw our first pair of wood ducks. They were swimming and flying together. It appeared that they were mates. It is amazing how quickly these birds return and start mating. It was nice to see the pair of ducks, for whom we have done so much work.*

Internships and Ethos: The COPS Problem. A media critic has asked a question about "reality TV" cop shows that seems analogous to a question we might ask about our internships. On the show *COPS*, viewers accompany earnest, likable young police officers and hear them explain their job to us. There are bad guys out there, we are told, who represent a threat to police and public alike, and the peace officers who do nightly battle with these bad guys should not be handcuffed by naive claims on behalf of the "rights" of these wrongdoers. Is it not likely, the media critic asks, that audiences will find this point of view persuasive, uncountered as it is by other, also reasonable perspectives (Exoo 1994: 240)? The analogous question about our interns is: Are they not likely to adopt their agency's point of view, as they accompany their earnest, likable field supervisors and hear them explain the importance of what they're doing?

One answer media studies has given to the former question is, "Maybe." The school of British cultural studies has argued that, yes, the media (or in our case, the agency) has its message. But audiences have their predispositions, and depending on what those are, their "decoding" of the media's "preferred meaning" may be "cooperative, negotiated, or oppositional" (Fiske 1993: 64).

I close with selections from two students' journals. Both worked for the same agency, but responded very differently to its message.

> [DEC field supervisor] said that environmentalists do criticize the DEC, and I believe this is also true. Some people feel we should leave nature alone, and let it fix itself. I don't want to get into an ethical debate, but I believe the DEC manages and protects state-owned properties for the best interests of the public. They do a good job, too.

> As soon as I set foot out of the truck I felt the tension of the day release from my body. I looked around at long thin naked trees dusted on the south side with the fresh snow. There was a sense of peace with the trees, the land, and the snow. *** started to mark the trees with the bright blue paint from his well-worn can. When we were done with the 3-plus acres we could look around at what we had accomplished. A plot speckled with the blue blood of deoxygenated death; I felt sickened. But this is work with the state.

Summary: What Is It About Service-Learning . . . ?

Students have consistently rated our service-learning courses higher than the university average for upper-division courses. That has held true for the environmental internship course. That a large number of different faculty have rotated through these internships suggests that it is not a particular group of faculty that makes the students' experience a good one.

What these high ratings *do* mean is open to speculation. They might simply mean that students like getting course credit for a class that requires less reading and seat time than the average class. But based on what students say in their course evaluations and journals, we might draw a less-cynical conclusion. As we've seen, students appreciate several aspects of the service-learning experience that are not ordinarily afforded by other classes:

• **Lived conceptualization.** Of course, conceptualization goes on in nearly all college classes; but if the service-learning classroom is used well, the conceptualization that occurs there is about experiences the students are living through.

• **Sense of accomplishment.** Even the students who have been successful in the classroom may have doubts about their ability to meet challenges in the "real world" (as they call it),[3] where a variety of untested skills will be needed. When they do meet these challenges, it is, not surprisingly, an even more gratifying experience than succeeding in one more ordinary course would be.

• **Encountering diversity.** One of our students put it this way: "When the people you are surrounded by are worried about what dress to buy for their formal or what kind of beer they are going to buy on Friday night, you forget that there are people in the world with real problems. That is why I feel that community service is an important part of this educational setting."

• **Encountering nature.** The importance of this to our environmental interns emerged from the journals of those who did — and those few who did not do — their fieldwork outdoors. As one who did not noted: "Other students are having fun prancing around on snowshoes, teaching kids about trees, and I'm in a little office with three humming overhead lights throwing out a dull yellow artificial light. I might go crazy!"

• **Encountering service.** Again, while our students are reluctant to accept the notion that we have a categorical obligation to perform service, they still enjoy performing service, and we'll settle for that. For some of them, this is a taste acquired while they are doing their internships. In other words, as the French say, "The appetite comes with the eating." I'm referring in particular to those students who begin work with an agency for course credit, but go back the next semester just to encounter the sense of accomplishment, the diversity, the wilderness, and the good feeling of service again.

Notes

1. In the first two semesters of ND200B, each of the three components was a third of the total grade. We increased the weight of component 1 to 40 percent in response to the students' sense that this is where a plurality of their time and effort goes. At the same time, we moved the directly observable journal from component 2 (written work) to supplement the indirectly observed fieldwork.

2. The psychologists at our workshops tell me that this is a "normal" and "healthy" attitude toward obligation. Simone Weil, whose ideals of self-abnegation we sometimes discuss in the workshops because of my own admiration of her life and work,

was an "emotionally unhealthy" person, the psychologists tell us.

3. A false dichotomy, I tell them. In response to the suggestion that a university is somehow unreal or impractical, no less than an advocate of experiential learning than Kurt Lewin replied, "There is nothing so practical as a good theory" (as quoted in Kolb 1984: 36).

References

Exoo, C.F. (1994). *The Politics of the Mass Media*. New York, NY: West.

Fiske, J. (1993). *Television Culture*. New York, NY: Routledge.

Kolb, D. (1984). *Experiential Learning*. Englewood Cliffs, NJ: Prentice-Hall.

Paton, H.J. (1965). *The Categorical Imperative: A Study in Kant's Moral Philosophy*. London: Hutchinson.

Service-Learning in Environmental Studies at the University of Vermont Through a Senior Capstone Course on Environmental Problem Solving and Consulting

by Thomas R. Hudspeth

Since 1992, majors and minors in environmental studies at the University of Vermont (UVM) have provided valuable problem solving and consulting to local and state government agencies, environmental nongovernmental organizations, and even for-profit businesses in the community. The service-learning associated with these partnerships or collaborative arrangements takes place through a required senior capstone course, ENVS 204: Senior Seminar.

The UVM Environmental Program is a university-wide, interdisciplinary program that, since 1972, has offered bachelor's degrees in environmental studies to students enrolled through UVM's College of Arts and Sciences, School of Natural Resources, College of Agriculture and Life Sciences, and College of Education and Social Services. The major in environmental studies is a self-designed major, and requires a senior thesis or project. The Environmental Program also offers a minor in environmental studies to students enrolled in the College of Arts and Sciences. In recent years, the Environmental Program has been graduating approximately 80 majors and 20 minors in environmental studies each year.

ENVS 204: Senior Seminar in Environmental Studies is the culminating course in environmental studies for majors and minors in the Environmental Program. It seeks to serve as the capstone for the student's undergraduate major or minor, synthesizing and tying together many of the courses and experiences at UVM, and as a launching platform into graduate school, jobs, travel, and continued learning beyond college.

Past foci of ENVS 204 have included environmental impact assessment; environmental risk assessment; citizen participation and public involvement in environmental planning and decision making; utopian visioning and creating alternative visions; green heroes and heroines; creating environmentally sustainable communities; and maps for travelers in the 21st century.

In preparation for the Environmental Program's 20th-anniversary celebration in 1992, questionnaires were mailed to alums. One of the questions asked: "Is there any course or experience you wish had been available to you while you were a student at UVM which was not?" Another asked: "Is there anything we could have done to better prepare you for your present position?" Many alums (especially those working for environmental consulting firms) stated that they would have liked a skills-oriented course that linked them to real-world clients solving real-world environmental problems. Some said they wished the Environmental Program had placed greater emphasis on teamwork in its classes. Several alums said they personally had received such experiences through internships or as part of their senior thesis or project in environmental studies, but felt such experiences should be incorporated into a required core course for all environmental studies majors and minors.

Building on the alums' recommendations and my own assessment of what was needed, I revised ENVS 204 between 1992 and 1996 to focus on environmental problem solving and consulting. This revised course is documented in the edited version of its course description *opposite*.

Class Format

Conducting the course as a seminar (after all, it is the Senior *Seminar*) with active participation by all class members is not that difficult when there are 12 or even 30 students enrolled. However, it is quite challenging when there are 67 or 96 students enrolled!

Environmental Problem-Solving and Consulting was offered once a year until 1996 as the sole ENVS 204. Since then, multiple sections of ENVS 204: Senior Seminar have been offered, with foci other than environmental problem solving and consulting, and with no section exceeding 30 in enrollment. The number of participants has ranged from 12 to 96 (12, 30, 56, 67, 67, and 96). On one of the occasions when there were 67 students, I cotaught the course with the director of the Field Naturalist master's program and his assistant; on all other occasions, I taught the course by myself, with a teaching assistant helping out when there were 96 students. Even when class size was large, I sought to involve students actively through use of a variety of creative teaching methodologies, including debate, point-counterpoint, panel discussion, role-playing, skit, game, simulation, etc.

Readings

The first semester I offered Environmental Problem-Solving and Consulting, I required the students to buy and read all three books in their entirety. In course evaluations at the end of that semester, students said they felt overwhelmed by the sheer number of different techniques; they noted that there was a bit of overlap among the three books; and they resented the expense of Van Gundy's book. They suggested that I make the three books available on reserve in the library, but not require students to

COURSE DESCRIPTION

ENVS 204:
ENVIRONMENTAL PROBLEM-SOLVING AND CONSULTING

I. CONTEXT

In ENVS 204, you go beyond identifying environmental problems to actually focusing on solutions. This takes two forms: (1) Who: becoming familiar with, learning from, and celebrating individuals and groups who have themselves achieved success at solving environmental problems, and who are thus role models or examples for others to follow or emulate, and (2) How: as part of a 3-5 person interdisciplinary consulting group/team/task force, applying problem-solving skills to real-world environmental problems and thereby helping a real client in need.

     College seniors examining global environmental issues are often overwhelmed by the enormity of the problems and feel that the issues are so complex that there is little or nothing they can do about them. I seek to overcome these feelings of lack of control, despair, paralysis, apathy, inaction, doom and gloom, confusion, powerlessness, and helplessness by having you think globally and act locally. Action at the local level is often the first step toward a solution to global environmental issues. This course attempts to empower you to make a difference, to do something about the global environmental problems, by acting at the local level...but only after you have first focused on where you want to be as an individual and member of society and how you want to get there. To that end, we examine change strategies for creating sustainable communities, for bridging the gap between our utopian visions and the harsh present-day environmental realities, for getting from where we are to where we would like to be.

II. OBJECTIVES

(1) Become familiar with and employ interdisciplinary group problem-solving skills in solving a real-world environmental problem for a real client.
(2) Employ "Writing Across the Curriculum" approaches to improve thinking and writing skills and powers of reflection.
(3) Gain insights and advice and suggestions from interesting guest speakers.
(4) Gain exposure to cutting edge ideas in Environmental Studies through reading and discussing and writing about stimulating books.
(5) Apply the subject matter of this course to your personal life, to your own future.

III. RATIONALE

Explanation of the rationale behind the various elements emphasized in this course gives you a better understanding for why it is designed and carried out as it is.

     Why problem-solving? You'll be doing it plenty once you leave here, and the better prepared you are to do it, the better off you'll be. In the past, I have found that successfully solving problems has empowered students and enhanced their sense of self-confidence and personal efficacy.

     Why groups? Increasingly, the *modus operandi* of environmental practitioners is as part of cooperative interdisciplinary problem-solving teams, yet most of your education has probably emphasized atomistic, individual, competitive efforts. Groups can provide a sense of belonging and intimacy, of being part of a learning community.

     Why real clients? They need all the help they can get. They will be a lot like real clients you might have if you go to work for a consulting firm once you get out of UVM. Your college education should give you not only knowledge and skills for creating desirable futures, but also motivation and inspiration to contribute, to give back to society, when you get out of college. In the past, several students have found their contacts with clients have led directly to part or full-time employment after graduation.

Why a limited scope to your term project? It is important to experience success when first seeking to create desirable futures, in order to gain sufficient confidence to continue and expand your efforts. To enjoy success in a very limited time span--about three months--it is essential to reduce the scope of your term project to a manageable level.

IV. NATURE OF THE LEARNING EXPERIENCE

A. CLASS FORMAT:

The course is conducted as a seminar. Groups discussion of the readings and assignments constitutes the structure for most of the class discussions, although there are occasionally lectures, guest speaker presentations, individual and group presentations, etc., as well. Active participation by all class members (including raising questions related to reading assignments) is essential for the class to be a success.

B. READINGS:

To derive maximum benefit from the course, it is essential that you: (1) complete the assigned readings in advance of class; and (2) allow time for reflecting on what you read (journal entries will help in this regard). Some readings on reserve in the library or available as photocopied handouts offer advice and numerous problem-solving techniques to assist your consulting group:

Bransford, John D., and Barry S. Stein, *The Ideal Problem Solver: A Guide for Improving Thinking, Learning, and Creativity* (Freeman, 1984).

Committee on the Application of Ecological Theory to Environmental Problems, Commission on Life Sciences, National Research Council, *Ecological Knowledge and Environmental Problem Solving* (National Academy Press, 1986).

Van Gundy, Arthur B., *Techniques of Structured Problem Solving* (Van Nostrand Reinhold, 1988).

Other readings, available at the bookstore, do not explicitly address environmental problem-solving and consulting, but expose you to cutting edge ideas in Environmental Studies. In the past, students have appreciated the opportunity to read and discuss stimulating books while working on their projects.

C. JOURNAL:

Specific journal-writing exercises are given in class and as homework assignments. They relate to the group project, the readings, the guest speakers. They are intended to help you process and incorporate your own ideas and to reflect on the ideas of others.

D. GUEST SPEAKERS:

Each semester, I invite about six UVM Environmental Program alumni/ae, environmental professionals, environmental activists, UVM faculty, community members, and other guest speakers to come into the class to talk about what they are doing and how they got where they are now, and to offer advice (What would they do differently if they could do it all over again?; if only they knew then what they do now, etc.). You may wish to consider their presentations as case studies, as the speakers tell about real environmental problems they are dealing with at the time, the problem- solving strategies they employ(ed), and the outcomes. In the past, such guest speakers have served as role models or exemplars for the students to follow or emulate. Students felt they learned much from those who had gone before them, both from their successes and their "failures" (learning opportunities); they appreciated the inspiration, encouragement, and fresh ideas these guest speakers provided.

E. GROUP PROJECT IN ENVIRONMENTAL PROBLEM-SOLVING AND CONSULTING:

The project provides a real-world opportunity to apply problem-solving skills to a complex (higher-order) environmental problem by a deadline--thereby gaining a better understanding of that issue--and to help a real client (agency or organization or business) in need. This hands-on, learn-by-doing project will hopefully strengthen all four skills involved in effective problem-solving (creative thinking, critical thinking, intelligible management, and good communication) and will help you integrate them with better results.

Problem-solving techniques are presented in class and readings--by the instructor, guest speakers, and student teams; in addition, in class you are presented with hypothetical situations in which you apply what you are learning about problem- solving. The techniques are drawn from the military, big business, and the environmental field; and from such academic disciplines as Engineering, Environmental Science, and Parapsychology. Beyond techniques normally thought of as problem- solving, I also include skills I learned once I was on the job--either as a university professor or as a consultant, and that I wish some one had taught me in college or graduate school. Some of those (e.g., working in groups, facilitating effective meetings, problem identification and definition, management skills, organizational skills, time management, writing a group document, making oral presentations) are offered every semester; others, as they are needed by groups to complete their projects.

Topics are chosen to provide relevant field experience and--most importantly--to be of real value to the community. As you apply techniques to your environmental problems as professional environmental consultants (interdisciplinary consulting groups/teams/task forces), I will emphasize process and approach--how you are doing what you are doing and why; and will offer a Generalized Methodology for Solving Environmental Problems for your consulting team to utilize (I believe that having a structure to fall back on and using a systematic approach actually allows you to be more creative in solving environmental problems). I will devote much class time to helping you with your project, and expect a high-quality, genuinely-useful, professional product--delivered on time. Members of each group share the same grade for their work. During the last two weeks of the class, each group makes an oral presentation to the rest of the class and to clients, and each member must participate in some way in that presentation. Clients and community members are invited to the presentations, and most clients come.

Criteria used in developing this project include:
- students have first-hand experience in higher-order problem-solving in an in-depth study
- 3-5 person group, where each person is a contributing member; the group works cooperatively, and each member experiences leading as well as being a good follower
- students interact with and provide a tangible benefit to "realworld" client in the community outside the university
- students orally present their findings to the rest of the class.

Some projects require as a prerequisite at least one of the group members to have taken a specific course (e.g., Environmental Education, Environmental Interpretation, Environmental Design, Environmental Economics, Environmental Policy, Environmental Law, Natural Resource Planning Theory and Techniques, etc.) to gain specific skills necessary to implement the task.

Several journal-writing exercises (most employing application of problem-solving techniques to your problem) help keep you on schedule. Do not miss deadlines. No exceptions and no negotiations. Materials turned in late will not be accepted!

Following is the time-frame, within a 15-week semester, used in addressing the environmental problem:

Week 1: identification of project topic and team members

Week 2: signed agreement form to client after initial consultation with and charging by client

Week 5: progress report

Week 6: presentation of "mock-up" of the desired final product to client and gaining feedback from client before actually collecting data

Week 11: completion of first draft of report

Week 13: completion of final, polished report; presentation of final, polished report to client; rehearsal of oral presentation.

Weeks 14 and 15: oral project presentations in class; critiques by fellow course participants and instructor(s); evaluation of process; evaluation by client.

F. "LIFE AFTER UVM" PAPER:
Devise a plan for your "life after UVM." The plan should emphasize your hopes and dreams and aspirations in the next ten years, but not be confined exclusively to that period.

Utilize as many problem-solving techniques as possible in devising your plan. Mention some of the approaches or techniques that you found most helpful.

Speculate on the differences (if any) between this plan and a plan you might have written without having ever taken this course in Environmental Problem-Solving.

The plan should be typed, of course. There is no specific page limit...but make the paper the length you feel is necessary to concisely state what you plan to do after you leave UVM.

G. GRADING:
Grades are based on:

Task	% of total grade
Active class participation	10
Journal	20
"Life after UVM" paper	15
Term project	
Final polished report	50
Oral presentation in class	5

TOTAL	100

purchase them; further, they suggested that I present *the most important* (but not all!) problem-solving techniques in class myself, using handouts and demonstrations. Since 1993, I have followed these recommendations.

In class discussions and journal-writing assignments, I have students draw parallels between these books and their group projects. In the one semester that I had all the readings relate exclusively to problem solving, students in their course evaluations complained that the course was not expansive enough . Since then, I have included about five such "expansive" books each semester. Books selected in recent years have included these:

• Durning, Alan, *How Much Is Enough?: The Consumer Society and the Future of the Earth* (Norton, 1992)

• Goldsmith, Edward, *The Way: An Ecological World-View* (Shambhala, 1993)

• Hawken, Paul, *The Ecology of Commerce: A Declaration of Sustainability* (Harper, 1994)

• Lappe, Frances Moore, and Paul Martin DuBois, *The Quickening of America: Rebuilding Our Nation, Remaking Our Lives* (Jossey-Bass, 1994)

• Meadows, Donella, *The Global Citizen* (Island, 1991)

• Orr, David, *Earth in Mind* (Island, 1994)

• Perrin, Noel, *Life With an Electric Car* (Sierra Club, 1994)

• Roszak, Theodore, *The Voice of the Earth: An Exploration of Ecopsychology* (Simon and Schuster, 1992)

• Wackernagel, Mathis, and William Rees, *Our Ecological Footprint* (New Society, 1996)

• Wallace, Aubrey, *Green Means* (KQED Books, 1994)

• Wilson, Edward O., *Naturalist* (Warner, 1994)

Journal

I've found that breaking down the term project process into numerous "bite size chunks" as journal entries has helped groups keep up and stay on task.

Guest Speakers

I make a point to include some UVM Environmental Program alumni/ae as guest speakers; I have found that students especially like to hear from folks who went through the same academic program they are currently majoring in (even though it has evolved considerably). Alums who have been guest speakers in the class in recent years have included these:

• land-use planning coordinator; writer; photographer; activist in Richmond Land Trust; former executive director of Vermont Natural Resources Council

• U.S. attorney of Burlington, VT.; former lawyer with Ralph Nader's group and with large Wall Street law firm

- president of Autumn Harp, in Bristol, VT; former environmental officer for Ben and Jerry's Ice Cream Company; former director of education for Shelburne Farms
- associate director of Vermont Youth Conservation Corps
- faculty member at Antioch New England Graduate School and facilitator for sustainable communities project in the Upper Valley of the Connecticut River
- environmental economist for National Wildlife Foundation
- environmental journalist and citizen-participation advocate; former editor of *Vermont Environmental Report*
- president of Solar Works (a photovoltaics company)
- children's travel book writer
- president of Outreach for Earth Stewardship; environmental educator; bird rehabilitator; ornithologist.

In addition, students are strongly encouraged (and sometimes even required) to attend and participate in presentations by guest speakers on the UVM campus and in the community. Such speakers in recent years have included Donella Meadows, Ralph Nader, John Todd, Frances Moore Lappe, Christopher Flavin, Winona LaDuke, Herbert Bormann, Helena Norberg-Hodge, Susan Meeker Lowry, David Suzuki, Bernard Sanders, Anita Roddick, David Orr, Norman Myers, Gary Snyder, Vandana Shiva, David Brower, David Foreman, Helen Caldecott, Joanna Macy, Paul Hawken, Patrick Noonan, Damian Randle, Kirkpatrick Sale, Helen Nearing, Robert Repetto, Bill McKibben, and April Smith.

Group Project

On one occasion, master's students in the Field Naturalist program in the Botany Department and in the School of Natural Resources took the course along with senior majors and minors in environmental studies, and the director of the Field Naturalist program and his assistant cotaught the course with me. On that occasion, graduate students were split up among the groups, with a grad student serving as project leader ("unpaid teaching assistant") for each group. The grad students also presented problem-solving techniques from Van Gundy's book during some of the classes. As might be expected, the quality of the final products was higher and the praise from clients more exalted on that occasion than others.

In the past, there have been some semesters when the topics to choose from were many and varied and relatively unrelated; on a couple of occasions, the choices were related by topic or geographical location. Project topics for student consulting teams in recent years have included these:

- community development projects on the Burlington waterfront

- a Lake Champlain Basin Science Center for the Burlington Waterfront
- sustainability projects in the Intervale
- achieving greater food and energy self-sufficiency in Chittenden County
- protecting Vermont wetlands
- alternatives to single-occupied vehicles for human transportation
- commuter rail system from Burlington to Waterbury, Montpelier, and Barre; and from Burlington to Shelburne, Vergennes, and Middlebury
- transportation between the UVM campus, downtown Burlington, and the Burlington waterfront
- bicycle path and trails and greenway development
- Lake Champlain shoreline protection and management
- managing aquatic nuisances in Lake Champlain
- streambank stabilization and erosion control
- water quality monitoring programs and watershed protection and management through associations
- alternative wastewater treatment systems (e.g., Living Machines)
- comprehensive land and resource management plans for Winooski Valley Park District sites, town parks, and Burlington's "Urban Reserve"
- household hazardous waste collection system
- backyard composting
- reducing resource consumption
- helping to improve the plight of the Abenakis in northwestern Vermont.

"Life After UVM" Paper

The course does not have a final exam per se. However, there is a final paper due during exam time.

On the course evaluations at the end of the semester, invariably this assignment receives mixed reviews: Some students love it and thank me for requiring them to do what they feel they should have done on their own but in a more systematic fashion . . . and a few students hate it and think it is a waste of time.

Industrial Areas and Natural Areas:
Service-Learning in Southeast Michigan

by Orin G. Gelderloos

Service-learning in the environmental programs at the University of Michigan-Dearborn encompasses a broad range of activities. These activities can be grouped into two categories: (1) service through the internship or "world of work" requirement in the environmental programs, and (2) service to the community through the programs in the environmental studies area.

The University of Michigan-Dearborn is one of three campuses of the University of Michigan (together with Ann Arbor and Flint). Our institution is a regional, commuter campus and serves students from the Detroit metropolitan area.

In developing the university's Environmental Studies and Environmental Science programs in the early 1970s, the concept of experiential learning played an important role because environmental issues are problems to be solved by working in a societal context. Thus, an experience in the world of work, preferably off-campus, was required.

Service-Learning Through Environmental Internships

The Environmental Studies program requires an off-campus experience in the world of work as part of the degree requirements. Although work experiences were embedded in the engineering and management curricula from their inception, the Environmental Studies program is the only program in the College of Arts, Sciences, and Letters to require such an experience.

Because an internship is not a traditional part of the college or university experience, and a service-learning assignment even less so, students commonly ask, "What does the internship involve?" Our standard response is that the internship is an opportunity to gain valuable experience by "trying out" a professional position before graduation and to make contacts in the environmental network.

A great deal of responsibility for arranging an internship rests with the student — similar to a search for a professional position. Thus, the students face related procedural and emotional challenges while they can ask for assistance from university and college faculty and staff and before they make costly mistakes. As the students approach their internships, I ask them to consider three questions:

1. What would I like to do when I graduate?

2. What organization does what I want to do?

3. Who in the organization makes the decisions about hiring?

Dealing with these three questions is a reality check for the students. Often students have only a vague understanding of the relationship between what they would like to do and who will pay them to do it. In our advising session I find it suitable to discuss the difference between three views of their professional activities; namely, *job, career,* and *calling.*

I suggest that it is relatively easy to get a *job,* which involves working under someone else's direction to acquire money so that one can enjoy one's life in nonwork hours, on evenings and weekends. Such positions can pay well and have good benefits, but the level of job satisfaction is often low.

A *career* allows a person to have a position of greater responsibility, to exercise authority over the work and activities of many people, set policy, and make executive decisions. Typically, a graduate who is bright, has good interpersonal skills, and is emotionally mature will steadily climb the organizational career ladder to higher positions. A career has prestige and power, but it often brings unexpected tensions and emotional turmoil with which the student or graduate may be unable to cope.

Accepting a *calling* may represent an alternative to a job or a career, because it provides a service to society and does not have the goal of income maximization. A calling is also consistent with service-learning experiences in that it contributes to and assists a community without the expectation of profit and individual gain. Persons who have accepted a calling range from Mother Teresa to the director of a regional watershed coalition.

Accepting a calling is a great challenge and involves many more complications than moving into a job or a career. The student faces a wide range of responsibilities and often has a limited financial safety net. Not only does a student have to contend with many financial and bureaucratic burdens, but he or she also has to explain and justify the decision to parents and spouses who have had different expectations for him or her for many years. Messages such as "You mean you have a college degree and you are doing what?" often put the student on the defensive.

Many of the opportunities available for environmental studies students require a strong sense of entrepreneurship. An entrepreneur is involved in "enterprise" which, by definition, is "a bold, difficult, dangerous, or important undertaking." Most people associate an entrepreneurial person with business and commercial ventures, because an entrepreneur accepts a risk for the sake of profit. Yet environmental studies students are probably required to exhibit more entrepreneurship, in the broad sense of the word, than do their counterparts in business and management, because the former accept a risk for the benefit of society and improvement of the quality of life while at the same time they are uncertain of a living salary and security in their positions.

Thus, participating in service-learning while in college is beneficial for the students in several respects. Not only are they able to learn skills not taught in classes or laboratories, to practice good work habits, and to address societal needs; but they also are able to learn what motivates and drives their employers to work in various positions and organizations. For example, one assignment in which several students have been involved is to assist the director of a recycling center who manages the facility from her house where she lives with her husband and six children — an experience seldom encountered in the corporate world of work.

Student Obligations and Responsibilities in the Environmental Internship

When the students have decided about the organizations with which they will be doing their internships, I provide the following information to them about their obligations and responsibilities:

During the environmental internship you must keep a "daily log," which consists of a chronological sequence of your activities; typically, an entry will include a statement of the duties of work performed each day of the internship. Simultaneously, you should record additional information about the internship in separate sections of the internship notebook. This information should attempt to evaluate your performance and learning experience by addressing questions such as:

1. Who are the people you have met (name, title, position, address and telephone number, educational background, and professional experience)? This information will be the basis of your professional "network."

2. What goals of the internship have you accomplished today?

3. What questions could you ask about this organization based on your experiences today, this week, this month?

4. What is your impression of the organization's goals and operating procedures?

5. What is your impression of the people with whom you work regarding (a) level of education, (b) professional attitude, (c) dedication and loyalty to the profession and organization, and (d) collegiality?

6. If you were in charge of the operation or organization, what changes would you make?

7. Based on this internship experience, do you wish to pursue a career with this organization or any similar organization?

At the end of the internship, you are required to submit a final report consisting of the following components: (1) the daily log, (2) a summary of the work performed over the duration of your internship (including questions 1 and 2 above), (3) a subjective statement expressing your opinions of your internship according to questions 3-7 above.

These materials must be submitted to the program adviser on the last day of the semester in which the student is registered, or two weeks after the internship is completed if the internship extends beyond the semester in which the student is registered.

By following this format, the students develop a habit of recording their activities on a daily basis (often required for consulting firms and laboratory positions) and systematically reflecting on their experiences and professional growth.

Students receive a grade of pass or fail for the internship unit. Typically, they receive three hours of credit for an internship (Env Studies 385: Internship in Environmental Topics) based on a total of 130 contact hours in a semester. The basis of this determination is that students should spend a day per week working within an organization for a semester (16 weeks) to have a meaningful experience. They may arrange their hours to suit their specific situations, such as working two 4-hour periods per week, or two 8-hour days per week if their internship is during one of the two 8-week summer sessions.

Example of a Service-Learning Project

For more than a year, several interns worked on the development of a salvage yard guide to be distributed by the Michigan Department of Environmental Quality (MDEQ). The impacts of salvage yards on groundwater and surface water can be severe, because of the diversity of materials that leak into the soil and run off the property. The students researched the kinds and quantities of materials collected in a salvage yard. These included oils, oil filters, antifreeze, CFCs, tires, gasoline, and batteries. They also reviewed the regulations for the use of underground storage tanks and storm water permits. They visited an environmentally friendly salvage yard to learn the proper methods of waste handling to prevent discharge into the environment.

Preparing the information for publication was an equally challenging experience. The students learned the proper procedures to follow in getting a document approved by a state agency, the lead time involved in each step of the project, and how to make arrangements for the printing of the brochure. Eventually, the students were pleased to receive permission from the administration at the University of Michigan-Dearborn to have the university's seal affixed to the brochure indicating cooperation between MDEQ and the university. The guide is now being distributed throughout the state of Michigan. Other interns are following up by making personal visits to salvage yards and speaking with the owners and operators to encourage them to pursue the practices detailed in the guide.

Examples of Service-Learning Internship Positions

Students in the Environmental Studies and Environmental Science programs have made significant contributions to many organizations in many locations in a wide variety of ways. In each case, the students served without salary or benefits, or received only a living allowance if they had to work away from their home. In some cases, the students worked full-time (particularly if they worked at a location away from the Detroit metropolitan area). Several students also worked with for-profit organizations. (Their experiences are not included in this report.)

Many students find fulfilling service-learning experiences with the Michigan Department of Environmental Quality or the Michigan Department of Natural Resources because one of our alumni serves as an employee in the MDEQ and coordinates the placement assignments. The students have been involved in a variety of activities:

- worked on many litigation projects for an assistant attorney general
- compared wetland permit statements of intent with the actual status of wetland mitigation
- conducted lake surveys and creel census.

Students also have worked with the South-East Michigan Council of Governments (SEMCOG) on several projects:

- used Geographic Information Systems data and TIGER files to compile reports on southeast Michigan for SEMCOG staff
- assisted the Rouge Project Public Information campaign and developed materials on the Rouge River for touch-screen informational kiosks.

In other projects, students:

- developed a trail guide and conducted public programs at a provincial park in Ontario
- developed an urban ecology exhibit for the Denver Museum of Natural History
- coordinated numerous activities for the Downriver Recycling Center, including organizing workshops, assisting with writing the newsletter, and coordinating the Healthy Garden Tours program
- developed a hazardous waste collection program for a county planning department
- evaluated and modified the annual Rouge River cleanup program of Friends of the Rouge
- worked on an environmental justice project in Cincinnati through the U.S. Environmental Protection Agency
- served as the chair for the executive committee of a county recycling

program and interfaced between the operational aspects of the recycling program and its board of directors, which involved review of employee performance, general business practices, contract agreements, and finances

- organized environmental education curriculum materials for Michigan United Conservation Clubs
- assisted the North American Indian Association by interviewing traditional people on First Nations' beliefs, attended pow-wows and other meetings to learn firsthand about changes in native cultures for the development of an outdoor education curriculum for First Nations.

Comments From Students About the Internship Experience

The final reports by the students about their internship experiences are always a pleasure to read. Their comments are forthright and candid. Here is a small sample.

From a student who worked for a not-for-profit community watershed organization:

> I think this experience has significantly enhanced my employment potential in many areas of the environmental field. The experience I have gained has opened many more possibilities than just a Bachelor's Degree can give. I'm so glad that an internship was a requirement for the Environmental Studies program.

From a student who worked as a legal assistant:

> To conclude, I cannot express how much I enjoyed my internship. The knowledge gained, the people with whom I interacted, the experience functioning as a legal assistant, and the exposure to current environmental issues are factors responsible for making this experience beneficial and positive. Working with such a wonderful person and the compliments from her gave me confidence to go forth and pursue my future in my field of interest as a legal assistant.

This student worked with an assistant attorney general for the State of Michigan. In other discussions with the student, she volunteered to me that this attorney could be making much more money working for a private law practice but chose instead to work as "public servant":

> I feel as though the purpose of an internship is to help me decide exactly what I want to do, and even more importantly what I know I do NOT want to do. Before I did this internship, I had thought seriously about attending law school. After working with a lawyer and with a law student I no longer

want to go to law school and I know for sure I do not want to be a lawyer (that would be absolutely horrible.) On a more positive note, I now feel that maybe I will get my master's in environmental engineering. Even though I know I would never want to be a lawyer, getting to know [my supervisor] has given me a much better perspective on lawyers in general, she is a very down-to-earth person and it has been a pleasure working with her. [She] gives lawyers a good name.

From a student who worked for an environmental engineer in a state agency, where he and another student learned that government employees are happy to be serving the citizens and can handle the pressures of the heavy workloads and the vagaries of political bureaucracies. The students learned a great deal about providing public service — both from their own work contribution and from their mentors:

Almost without exception, the people with whom I came into contact were friendly, diligent workers with a genuine concern for the environment. They were happy to talk to me despite the obvious burden of their workload and the demands on their time. Complaints by the public and by industries that state employees are slow, lazy or incompetent are completely unfounded and made by people ignorant of the type of work done by the MDNR and MDEQ. If anything, I found the employees to be overworked, with far too many sites to inspect and too much paperwork to review during the course of their week. Despite the lack of appreciation for their work, morale was high and no one seemed especially resentful or bitter as I would have thought.

From a student in a governmental agency:

I really enjoyed all the people I had the privilege to work with in this agency. K.S. was a young dedicated worker who always could find the humor in the worst situations. He showed me professionalism in the field and was always there to lend a hand. C.N. was the hardest worker in the office. I learned the most regarding permits and regulations from her. She taught me how to conduct myself when calling industries and how to "kill them with kindness" if they got irate. She was a workhorse who never seemed to catch up on her paperwork. E.P. was the comedian of the agency. I thought he has the most depressing job (checking complaints) and yet he never complained or showed any dislike towards it. He told me to always expect the unexpected on the job and in life. E.P. taught me to handle every complaint on a person-to-person basis and not to throw your authority around. Always try to work with the people (if you help them, they will help you.)

From a student who worked in a community not-for-profit recycling center:

> *Working for a nonprofit organization requires hard work and dedication. Money is always an issue for the life of the center and much time was focused on monetary issues. I have learned that there are not only generous people, but also cut-throat, greedy people in the environmental field. The concept of politics plays a major role. Learning how to deal with politics is a worthwhile skill to learn.*

These comments are typical samples of more than 100 service-learning projects. Through their reports, the students communicate about many intangibles that they have learned that complement their classroom and laboratory experiences.

Environmental Study on the Campus of the University of Michigan-Dearborn

The campus of the University of Michigan-Dearborn is located on the estate of Henry Ford (1865-1947), the founder of the Ford Motor Company. Some of the trees on the 300 acres of floodplain forest surrounding what was his private residence predate the Revolutionary War. Our records show that 60 percent of all the species of birds recorded in the state of Michigan have been observed on our campus.

In the 1960s, there was a proposal to develop this outstanding urban natural area. These controversial plans provided the impetus for the students at the university to become involved in the long-term process of preserving and maintaining this area by providing high-quality educational programs for the general public. In return, the students have received unparalleled educational experiences in learning and teaching ecology, natural history, and environmental issues on campus, as well as in developing their entrepreneurial and diplomatic skills.

The Environmental Studies program facilitates service-learning experiences for the students at UM-Dearborn by providing an interface between classroom and service. Because of the existence of an outstanding natural area on the campus, the Field Biology course has been taught there for more than three decades (a course syllabus is available upon request). This course, along with courses such as Ecology, Environmental Interpretation, and The Environment as an Educational Resource, provides an opportunity for university students to teach others.

The demand for field trips from schools and community groups is heavy. Students are involved in the design, planning, and implementation of a variety of educational experiences for children and adults. Because the Environmental Study Area hosts more than 8,000 learners from the community each year, university students have ample opportunity to reinforce their knowledge of the flora, fauna, and ecological processes, as well as to hone their teaching and communication skills. Thus, the students have recognized that they can learn while they serve.

The variety of experiences available for the students is vast. Throughout the season, they may lead field sessions on bird migration, wildflower/insect pollination adaptations, tracks in the snow, owl prowls at night, aquatic organisms, bats and flying squirrels, spiders, and fruits and seeds. Most of these topics require considerable investigation, organization, and planning beyond any information they may have learned in class. Thus, the exchange between the participant and the leader results in a mutual learning experience.

Although a student may begin this activity to fulfill a class project requirement, about 50 percent of these students continue their involvement through the remainder of their time at the university. We are also pleased that many of our alums continue to serve our programs with contributions of time and money or become involved as volunteers in their own communities with nature centers and ecology centers or as leaders of scout groups and such.

Several of our programs involve activities that promote more-intense, specialized learning experiences:

• The Dearborn Public Schools have a Winter Outdoor Ecology program for fourth-grade students. This program combines a history of Henry Ford and a tour of his home with the natural history of the estate. In addition, children develop their mathematical skills by measuring the heights of trees through triangulation. At the conclusion of the program, staff members have a debriefing session over hot chocolate and tea in my office. This session helps to plan strategies for improved learning in future sessions and builds camaraderie among the staff members.

• The forest is dominated by sugar maple trees. In February and March, many of the students are involved in the labor-intensive experience of leading a public program to tap these same trees tapped by Henry Ford, and then to collect and boil the sap to maple syrup. The students are also involved in arranging a pancake breakfast for more than 100 volunteers to learn strategies for culturing and nurturing volunteers in service projects.

• The city of Detroit has an unfortunate tradition of burning vacant houses on Devil's Night, the night before Halloween. To put a positive spin on Halloween and take attention away from this destructive activity, we developed for Devil's Night an "edutainment" program at our nature area that has been a sold-out event for many years. At the same time, this event has become a unique learning experience for the students. More than 60 volunteers are needed to execute this program of about 10 skits held at various locations throughout the forest. The students learn complexities of major event programming — from program announcement, to taking reservations, to holding brainstorming sessions for skit ideas, to interfacing with the university on logistics, to gathering materials for the skits, to actually performing the skits. Their efforts are richly rewarded through the positive responses visitors make in personal and written evaluations. The students feel that they have been able to have an impact on the children and their parents while providing an entertaining evening. In the process of developing this program, the students learn the importance of balance in an environmental message. In order to be successful, they have to provide information in an entertaining manner, which usually requires considerable thought about props and logistics. They may include an element of surprise in their program, but not shock. They should deal with contemporary issues, but will find their message counterproductive if it is viewed as an attempt at politicizing the audience or if it reflects partisan politics.

• For more than two decades, the university has provided space for a community organic garden, including Kinder Gardening for children ages 4-6 and Sprouts for children 7-10. In projects involving the garden, students learn a great deal about planning, organizational skills, public relations, conflict resolution, management procedures, and record keeping. They also add a great deal of creativity to these programs as they initiate ideas and implement educational strategies.

Public Information and Security

More than 30,000 people walk the trails in our Environmental Study Area each year. To enhance their experience, we attempt to make them feel welcome and provide information about current events in the area. At the same time it is important to provide a personal presence in the area, so that the visitors feel safe and that potential abusers of the area will be deterred. The students at the university provide an invaluable service by interfacing with the general public and preventing abuse to the area.

Working under the auspices of the Campus Safety Department and under guidelines developed by me in my role as director of the Environmental Study Area, students walk through the area during hours of high visitation. They must learn to be polite, hospitable, and congenial, yet they must also exercise judgment on when to be authoritative and firm, often having to make decisions on the spur of the moment.

Conclusions and Recommendations

Many of the lessons learned through service-learning experiences cannot be taught in the classroom. Service-learning helps students come to an understanding of the problems others have, an understanding they must have before they are able to propose solutions. In addition, they learn reliability, punctuality, respect, and how to best represent an agency or organization.

Based on my reflections on the service-learning activities in which our students have been involved for nearly three decades, I am extremely pleased with the results and have only a few "what I would do differently if I had it to do over again" recommendations:

• The internship experience could be improved by university faculty members or a staff person having greater involvement with the employers or supervisors. The amount of time involved in making site visits to arrange for internships and to inquire about student progress during the course of the internship significantly exceeds the amount of time available from the university for this activity. Even if this discrepancy could be corrected by assigning adequate teaching credit for the internship, another problem would still exist. The nature of the supervisory work internships require is different from the nature of traditional "professorial" activity, the major responsibility of a faculty member. As satisfying as it is to have students succeed in internships and service-learning projects, a faculty member has to shift mental gears from coursework and a scholarly mode to a managerial mode. Often the gears "clash," and neither activity is done as well as one could wish.

Furthermore, much of the legwork for internships could be done by a staff person. Staff assistance in managing internships and service-learning projects off-campus should seriously be considered. The staff person could be a recent graduate beginning to work in the field and using the internship coordinator position as a networking tool to find a permanent position. Or the position could be held by a retired person who wishes to assist students in finding appropriate positions.

• To provide a deeper and more meaningful internship experience, I would enhance the requirements of the final report by having the students write a reflection paper on how they obtained their internship. They should begin at the point when they first became aware that they were required to complete an internship for their degree, and recall some of the thoughts that then went through their mind. Perhaps they could answer questions such as: What range of experiences first came to your mind as you considered an internship? What factors were significant as you narrowed your choices? How important were the opinions of your classmates, adviser, parents, et al. in making your choice?

• Students in the environmental field are pioneers in many respects, both in their interdisciplinary academic program and in their search for a fulfilling position in the world of work. As stated earlier, they are entrepreneurs who are undertaking a bold, difficult, dangerous, and important enterprise. Thus, a number of questions arise that I believe should be discussed in higher education circles:

1. How can we in higher education develop and enhance a sense of entrepreneurship in our students?

2. Can we teach this quality and competency in our courses?

3. Does a theoretical basis exist for the "discipline" of entrepreneurship? If so, how do we explore it?

4. Should we encourage the career placement offices on our campuses to teach courses on entrepreneurship?

5. Should we hold national workshops for faculty to learn how to infuse this topic into our courses in much the same manner as we hold special workshops for critical thinking?

Service-learning during the acquisition of a college or university degree is an excellent way for students to become engaged citizens *and* to begin making the transition to lifelong learning through nonformal education.

ALLARM: A Case Study on the Power and the Challenge of Service in Undergraduate Science Education

by Candie C. Wilderman

Why Be ALLARMed?

The Alliance for Aquatic Resource Monitoring (ALLARM) is a statewide volunteer stream-monitoring organization, founded in 1987 by the Environmental Studies Department at Dickinson College, in Carlisle, Pennsylvania. ALLARM (originally called the Alliance for Acid Rain Monitoring) grew out of a concern of a local state representative that the public was inadequately informed about the impacts of acid deposition in the state. In his effort to introduce an Acid Deposition Control Bill in the legislature, he suggested to a group of scientists that a program be started in which volunteers could monitor streams and see the effects themselves. Intrigued by the prospect of a scientifically empowered public and hopeful that applying academic work to help solve human problems would motivate students, the Environmental Studies Department at Dickinson agreed to start such a group on an experimental basis.

Over the past decade, ALLARM has grown to include an army of more than 500 volunteers who are monitoring streams in Pennsylvania for environmental impact from human activities. Interest in monitoring has continued to be strong, as people express increasing disillusionment with the traditional political paths for change and view contributing to an environmental database as an alternative way to help solve human problems. Under the guidance of a grass-roots board of directors, ALLARM is staffed entirely by Dickinson College faculty, support staff, and students. Students are responsible for volunteer recruitment and training, development of laboratory and field protocols, maintenance of a quality control/quality assurance program, publicity, training workshops, community presentations, fundraising, office management, data management, data analysis, and data interpretation. Students also staff a youth education arm of ALLARM called SMART (Students Monitoring Aquatic Resources Together), which includes more than 50 youth or school groups from kindergarten through high school.

Created originally with public education as its primary goal, ALLARM quickly expanded its focus as it began to appreciate more fully the value of the data being collected. We now have the largest database on stream acidity in Pennsylvania, with more than 30,000 data points from 550 streams in 61 counties of the Commonwealth. These data have been used by environmental groups, neighborhood groups, private businesses, environmental consulting firms, government agencies, and the scientific research community.

ALLARM managed to operate on a small annual budget of $10,000 during its early years, funded primarily by volunteer donations and small foundation grants, with in-kind contributions and small grants for student wages from Dickinson College. During the last five years, ALLARM has received grants from the Consortium for the Advancement of Private Higher Education (CAPHE) and the National Environmental Education Training Foundation (NEETF). Most recently, ALLARM has received environmental litigation monies from CBS, Inc. and a small grant from the Heinz Foundation. We continue to receive a portion of our student wages from the college, and computer support services, access to analytical equipment, and support personnel, as well as laboratory and office space.

ALLARM represents an excellent example of the mutual value of a strong partnership between an academic institution and its community. In recent years, ALLARM has redefined its focus from working with individual volunteers to assess the impact of acid deposition on streams to working with watershed groups on more widely integrated environmental problems. We have recently established a Technical Support Center for volunteer monitoring groups, providing sophisticated laboratory analysis of samples in our Community Aquatic Research Lab, technical support, and comprehensive educational services covering watershed definition and delineation, sampling design and sampling techniques, habitat assessment, macroinvertebrate community evaluation, chemical analysis, flow measurement analysis, data management, data analysis, data interpretation, and restoration and protection strategies. We have developed strong relationships with various state agencies involved in environmental assessment and protection and often act as a much-needed communication link between the public and public workers.

This unique collaboration of citizen groups and the academic institution has given both parties a credibility and power for direct action far beyond what either could achieve alone. The collaboration has brought previously disenfranchised laypersons into the discussion of environmental issues with a high level of credibility, changing the very meaning of public participation in Pennsylvania. And it has brought formerly "isolated" science curricula out of the traditional laboratory and into the forefront of action for political change in the Commonwealth.

But ALLARM's activities have also presented serious challenges for students, faculty, and community members as they struggle with issues of scientific uncertainty, quality control, defining the public interest and the responsible use of data for advocacy. This essay addresses both the achievements of ALLARM in its 10-year history as one model of service in undergraduate science education and the unsolved challenges we face as we perform science for advocacy in the public interest.

The Achievements

Empowerment of Students: Making Undergraduate Science Education Relevant

Working with community people toward the goal of "stockpiling the truth" instills in students an appreciation for the value and power of scientific information. We find that most Dickinson College students view undergraduate education (and especially undergraduate science education) as a simple extension of high school — intellectually stimulating, but rather self-serving and isolated from the challenges of solving human problems. It is no wonder that most students are disengaged from society's problems and self-absorbed in their daily process of meeting deadlines in required courses. Often students do not discover the practical value of their education until after they have graduated. Providing students with an opportunity to use their own education to train others in practical skills that can result in useful data sheds new light on the relevance of undergraduate education and motivates students to reach out to new courses and new standards of achievement. We have found that many ALLARM students discover new directions for their own coursework; experience a heightened sense of motivation for many of their academic activities; develop a high sense of accountability and honesty in their academic endeavors; experience increased peer respect for their activities; and are more attractive to future employers.

We have seen numerous examples over the years of students, as a result of their work experience with ALLARM, deciding to take courses that either were not required or were previously thought to be too intimidating. They report a heightened sense of motivation and focus in those courses. For example, the prospect of becoming involved in a year-long project with a grass-roots group from Lehigh County that is concerned about groundwater contaminated with synthetic organic compounds from a Superfund site has led several students to enroll in the much-dreaded organic chemistry course. Other students were involved in training teachers to sample aquatic macroinvertebrates in the SMART program and later enrolled in a course in invertebrate zoology to study the various taxa systematically and to improve their ability to answer questions and to train others. Students have taken courses in hydrology, Geographic Information Systems (GIS), quantitative methods in the social sciences, English composition, political science, and aquatic resource management as a result of their work with community activists. Many of our students now choose courses outside of their major: policy studies students enroll in chemistry courses, and environmental science majors take writing and political science courses. These students consistently demonstrate increased personal motivation, increased creativity, and higher personal standards for achievement in these courses, as long as they can see some connection between the course content and their work with community groups.

Naturally, not all students alter their course choices while they work for ALLARM, but many feel an increased motivation to understand more deeply the concepts that they are teaching to community people. If they need to be able to explain methodologies, rationales for design decisions, study results, and options for action, they must feel confident that they have a broad enough background to field questions and to challenge the most knowledgeable volunteers. They discover this necessity quite early in the process, and often their own mistakes and perceived blunders are the guiding light for their pursuit of more knowledge. Spending time with adults who are appreciative of any information that they might have also leads them to a heightened appreciation of their own educational opportunities. Many return from training workshops with more questions than answers and become eager, independent listeners and learners.

Furthermore, in conducting scientific analyses for ALLARM volunteers, students feel a heightened sense of accountability at almost all levels. When introductory students are testing samples collected by volunteers and are aware that the results will be returned to the volunteers for future action, the students' sense of honesty and responsibility for the accuracy of the results increases significantly. I have seen introductory students laboriously redo samples because replicates were too disparate (in their judgment) or because they might have made an error in technique. Upper-level students ask to do extra replicates and to increase the number of points on their calibration curves so that they can feel more confident of their results. In their efforts to produce accurate test results, students are introduced firsthand to concepts of variability in sampling and struggle with issues of acceptable margins of error. For example, ALLARM participants involved in our quality control program must decide whether volunteers pass or fail our quality control tests. At first it might appear that this is just a simple matter of matching results, but then issues of "how close is close?" emerge. In addition, students realize that some volunteers will become discouraged and drop out of the program should they fail quality control measures. Hence, the students must consider the practical consequences of their assessments of acceptable error. They also grow to understand that data used for different purposes should be subjected to different standards of quality control.

Relatedly, students involved in quality control projects often find that test kits and other equipment from different manufacturers vary considerably in their own quality, and that higher precision equipment is more expensive. Using sophisticated analytical equipment available in commercial laboratories is even more costly. Since community groups often have severe budgetary constraints, they simply cannot afford highly accurate test equipment and must be prepared to respond to criticism from the scientific elite who will question their credibility.

Suddenly science no longer appears to be a dry game of absolute numbers available to anyone willing to put forth the effort; instead, we find that high levels of accuracy may be a privilege of the wealthy or established. And even if students put forth their finest efforts to produce accurate, low-cost results, they may find a community group unwilling to utilize the data because of the possible political consequences. The laboratory takes on a creative, politicized, and often contentious ambiance.

Students involved in the ALLARM project have many opportunities to share their experiences with faculty and other students. They periodically make presentations at the department's weekly lunch seminars; their community presentations and workshops are often covered by local newspapers; and they may present results of projects related to ALLARM in other courses. Volunteers praise their participation at workshops; inquiries from other university students and invitations to speak at other college environmental club meetings are common. The presence of ALLARM made it possible for the third annual regional Volunteer Monitoring Conference to be held at Dickinson College in 1993, and two Pennsylvania Environmental Congress annual conferences to be held there in 1996 and 1997. All of these events give students excellent public speaking experience, increase their self-esteem, increase their prestige among their peers, and allow them to relate to their peers in a professional manner.

Work with ALLARM also provides our students with real work experience. For many student participants who demonstrate a broad understanding of community issues at interviews and whose work experience is unique and impressive, entry into the nonprofit sector after graduation has been relatively effortless. For example, our pioneering work using GIS for analysis and interpretation of citizen-collected data has led to numerous new connections within the state for our students. In recent years, graduates have landed jobs right after graduation with such groups as Environmental Action, The Nature Conservancy, PIRG, Clean Water Action, and The Chesapeake Bay Foundation.

Empowerment of Community Members – On the Path to Environmental Justice?

Just as students feel a new sense of empowerment from their ability to apply skills they have learned to help solve human problems, so do community members who are trained to become their own experts. Training laypersons to assess water quality in their local watersheds not only provides them with tools to become better advocates but also opens up previously closed doors for meaningful participation in the decision-making process. Citizen monitors can collect independent data that they can use either to corroborate or to challenge public agency data. This kind of dialogue ultimately leads to the mutual trust that is essential in efforts to solve environmental problems, but that is so sorely lacking in most communities. A citizenry empowered with understanding promotes timely reaction to real threats and averts overreaction to lower-risk situations; that is, empowerment of this kind allows a meaningful identification of priorities. In addition, volunteers who monitor streams on a regular basis develop a strong sense of relationship to place — a fundamental prerequisite to building stewardship.

Recently ALLARM students helped the Codorus Creek Monitoring Group (CCMG), from York County, Pennsylvania, testify against the renewal of an NPDES permit for P.H. Glatfelter, Inc., a large, local paper manufacturer. Students used GIS to plot the group's weekly data on water quality in Codorus Creek collected over the past eight years. The data clearly demonstrated a major impact on the dissolved oxygen in the creek downstream from the paper company's discharge pipes. At a key meeting, a map and graphs were presented for public comment, in an effort to ensure that more-stringent standards be established for the renewed permit. The CCMG was the only group to present technical data; and although its volunteers insisted that the ALLARM students take the lead in this presentation, the group now reports that its volunteers will feel more comfortable doing a similar presentation on their own in the future. Group members left the meeting feeling newly empowered to continue the excellent work that they have been doing.

Such an instance demonstrates clearly that possession of data alone will not necessarily ensure meaningful public participation, but that volunteer groups must be trained in data analysis, interpretation, and presentation, as well. Indeed, empowering laypersons with new skills and knowledge to assess their own problems helps depose the traditional way in which science is performed; that is, by a so-called "elite priesthood" of scientists, who have very little sense of the importance of public participation in the solving of community environmental problems.

Importance of an Interdisciplinary Approach – Curriculum Opportunities and Impacts

Experience has shown us that approaching human problems from traditional academic disciplinary perspectives often fails to promote meaningful discourse or solutions. Nonetheless, there is a long tradition in academia of natural scientists and social scientists each viewing the other as being peripheral to the solving of environmental problems. The existence of a service project such as ALLARM not only provides an opportunity for faculty and students to collaborate across traditional disciplinary and even divisional barriers but actually requires that they do so. There is no way that a project such as ALLARM can operate without the support of methodology and knowledge found in the social sciences, the natural sciences, and the humanities.

Many of the connections are initiated by the students themselves, and oftentimes they are not aware that in attempting to solve a problem they are using information and methodologies traditionally housed in separate spheres of learning. In this way, ALLARM reflects more accurately how the world operates outside of academia, and ALLARM's presence inside the walls of an academic institute makes it both unique and unifying.

An example of an ALLARM activity that continues to require collaboration and support from different disciplines and departments is the work of our new Community Aquatic Research Lab. This lab requires utilizing analytical equipment that is now operated by the Geology and the Chemistry Departments. We need the support of their faculty and technicians to train us to use the equipment properly, to schedule equipment use to avoid conflicts, to troubleshoot and repair instruments, and to help us interpret results. Reaching out to the Chemistry Department to use its gas chromatography/mass spectrophotometer to analyze volatile organic compounds in groundwater has led to submission of a joint proposal for a new instrument to meet the increased demand. The Community Aquatic Research Lab has also opened up opportunities for the involvement of chemistry and geology students in independent research projects, and consideration is now being given to teaching instrumentation in the introductory chemistry course by analyzing water samples collected by ALLARM volunteers.

Recently, Dickinson College saw the establishment of a new center, the Clarke Center, to promote the interdisciplinary study of contemporary problems. Although the center has been remarkably successful in establishing enrichment programs involving the social sciences and the humanities, it has had more difficulty involving the Science Division. This year ALLARM became an important link to the sciences. Our efforts to institute the Technical Support Center and the Community Aquatic Research Lab have inspired an ambitious Clarke Center proposal to establish at Dickinson a Center for Science in the Public Interest, using ALLARM as its centerpiece but involving all interested science departments.

Since ALLARM is itself a nonprofit, grass-roots environmental organization, there have been numerous occasions when social science programs have collaborated with it. For example, the semester project in a recent course on quantitative methods in the social sciences involved a study of voluntarism, using ALLARM members as survey participants. Student staff for ALLARM learned what motivates people to volunteer for the organization, what kinds of backgrounds its volunteers represent, and what techniques can help ensure that they stay committed for at least a year at a time. We have now integrated the results of this class project into our ongoing long-term planning for the organization.

Examples such as these suggest that there exist many opportunities for faculty to utilize the ALLARM project to move courses and course projects in new directions and to take advantage of opportunities for collaborative and interdisciplinary learning, teaching, and research. Unfortunately, having to rely on students and faculty from other departments can often be disappointing, since faculty naturally recruit the best students for their own projects. More important, it is often difficult to convince discipline-based science faculty that an interdisciplinary project is "real" science. Often it is students, not the faculty, who initiate a collaboration. But for the students who work as ALLARM staff members, the traditional walls between the natural sciences, the social sciences, and the humanities simply collapse in the face of their work's problem-centered focus. As a result, they emerge with a high level of interdisciplinary problem-solving skills and an openness to learning that will serve them well in their future careers.

The Challenges

Scientific Uncertainty – Can We Ever Know?

The issue of dealing with scientific uncertainty is especially acute when compiling and interpreting data collected by laypersons. The uncertainty that is related to field and laboratory methods can be controlled to some extent with strong quality control/quality assurance programs, but it can never be eliminated. Volunteer monitors are inexperienced, and ALLARM staff have often found that volunteers may consistently make errors due to lack of close supervision. More important, volunteer organizations usually have very limited budgets and can only afford to use lab and field methods that have rather large inherent margins of error. With a strong quality control/quality assurance program, the level of uncertainty can be measured and taken into account when decisions are made as to how the data are to be used. Not all data can be used for litigation or enforcement purposes, but most can be used for screening and targeting areas in need of further study. It is our contention that all data are valuable data as long as they are of known quality. Unfortunately, volunteers are often discouraged by comments from public agencies or other "experts" that the techniques they are using are not state-of-the-art and therefore are useless.

Another source of scientific uncertainty is related to the density of the sampling sites. As the number of sites increases, uncertainty will decrease. But the number of sites largely depends on the resources of the group and can be rather fixed. One of the most time-consuming tasks that we undertake when we begin to work with a volunteer monitoring group is designing a sampling protocol — the what, where, and when questions. We require that our watershed groups do a good deal of research prior to the sampling phase, including research on all permitted point dischargers, Toxic Release Inventory reports, the geology and hydrology of the watershed, stormwater management plans, and other relevant reports published in past years. They must delineate watershed boundaries and do a complete streamwalk of targeted and control areas. If resources are limited, volunteers are rarely eager to establish control sites, and often lose interest in sites that are showing no dramatic impact. Volunteers almost always need to monitor more sites than they can afford to, and decisions regarding the most important sites may lead to conflict within a group. It has been extremely educational for ALLARM student staff to be involved in this process. ALLARM students often report that they are surprised at how much effort needs to go into a sampling design; but this is a lesson worth learning, since all research is constrained by a limited budget and the sampling design is probably the single-most important determinant of the utility of the study. Most students, even if they are involved in independent study with faculty, rely largely on the faculty to make these initial decisions.

Perhaps the most insidious source of scientific uncertainty is that the scientific community simply does not have good data on the chronic effects of most chemicals on aquatic systems or on human health. This is especially the case when several chemicals are present, since the effects of interactions are virtually unknown. Also, the effects of certain toxins can depend on other parameters that were not measured and can vary from organism to organism. This data gap is unavoidable, and the problem it causes is independent of uncertainty related to field and lab methods. As a result, it is extremely difficult to propose responsible options for mitigation. At what levels should action take place? At what cost? Who should bear the burden of the cost? Who is bearing the burden of no action? How much certainty do we need to act? And most important, who should make these decisions?

Interpreting and Acting Responsibly – Can We Ever Act?

Although volunteers can be trained to be quite adept at monitoring, the art of interpretation requires even more experience. Volunteers do an excellent job of documenting trends and perceiving correlations, but they need help in putting the results into a larger context. Doing so often requires research on the part of the student staff; students report that this research is enjoyable because they know how important the results might be to a future action plan.

With regard to recommended options for action, considerations that go well beyond science dominate. Any plan for mitigation that might be suggested will be based on the perceived risk of no action. But risk assessment is a normative process and requires an in-depth understanding of context. Different members of a group may have different perceptions of the risks involved; some of these differences reflect personal worldviews, but most are based on positions vis-à-vis the costs and benefits of action and the time frame over which one is willing to weigh costs and benefits. Who represents the group, the community? Often, especially in so-called company towns, where most of the jobs and the economic well-being of the community are dependent on a single company or group of companies, an environmental activist group is considered "fringe." For whom are the benefits of an action plan intended and how do "we" make that decision? What is the ethical limit of the role students can play? Students quickly realize that solutions are not simple and that no matter what action is taken, some will benefit and some will have to bear a new cost. Students involved in this process will never again view science (and especially its application to human problems) as a set of dry facts.

Thus, producing a citizenry that is empowered with a database challenges students to:

• design quality control programs appropriate to the ways in which the data are to be utilized and within the budgetary constraints of the participants;

• construct sampling designs that will not bias outcomes, that will produce the most information for the effort expended, and that are within the budgetary constraints of the participants;

• help laypersons understand and act in the face of scientific uncertainty;

• help the community understand risk and mitigation options;

• use the data for advocacy in an ethical manner.

These challenges force students to reach into all disciplines for training, to listen to and learn from community members, and to appreciate the limitations and power of using scientific data for advocacy in the public interest.

The Future — What Lies Ahead?

A service project such as ALLARM cannot operate without a significant commitment of college resources. Such resources did not come immediately to ALLARM; for years we struggled with the challenge of gaining recognition and support among our colleagues. Initially, the college tolerated the project but would not consider faculty involvement as "scholarly activity" for the purpose of tenure and promotion decisions. Other science faculty viewed the data as questionable and the project as diverting science students from real scientific research. Nonetheless, the environmental studies faculty were strongly united in their commitment to the project, both for its outreach potential and for its ability to enhance the relevance of science education. As ALLARM grew in size and impact, the college and the faculty began to recognize its value in recruiting students to Dickinson, in attracting students to major in the sciences, in enhancing public relations, in developing the science curriculum, and in enhancing our ability to seek outside grants, especially for innovative curricula and student/faculty collaborative research projects. Support among the administration grew and the commitment of resources increased. During its 10th year of operation, ALLARM was able to hire a director, using outside monies and with the full support of the college. Hiring a director was the single-most important step ALLARM has taken thus far; students are now fully supervised, the efficiency and scope of our operations have dramatically increased, and there is a mechanism for future fundraising.

It is our hope that ALLARM will become the centerpiece of a larger college effort to promote science in the public interest, and that faculty involvement will increase as they discover the numerous opportunities both for collaboration across the disciplines and for curriculum enhancement. The ALLARM project also provides a possible model for other institutions, and its success demonstrates that service projects can provide a much-needed context for the undergraduate science curriculum. As the public clamors for more information regarding the environmental impacts of human activities, we have seen the demand for technical advice and support increase in the Commonwealth. ALLARM is one model capable of creating a mutually beneficial partnership between an academic institution and its community to work toward the education and empowerment of the public, thus ensuring the democratization of the decision-making process.

Environmental Service and Learning at John Carroll University:
Lessons From the Mather Project

by Mark Diffenderfer

In the spring of 1994, the environmental studies concentration at John Carroll University initiated an environmental education program in conjunction with the Steamship William G. Mather Museum and the Cleveland Public Schools. This interdisciplinary program was designed to introduce seventh grade students to the ecology of their region (i.e., the Cuyahoga watershed of Lake Erie) as well as to the social, political, and economic forces that have affected Lake Erie and the other Great Lakes. It is staffed by environmental studies faculty from the departments of Biology, Political Science, and Sociology, with volunteers drawn from many disciplines.

A colleague and I have already reported on the results of an assessment that was conducted in the first year of this program (see Diffenderfer and Earle 1996; forthcoming). At each school, a pretest and a posttest were administered to students who participated in the program as well as to a control group of students in the same grade who were not involved in the program. This assessment demonstrated that students who participated in the program increased their knowledge of the Great Lakes in general and Lake Erie in particular to a greater degree than did the control group.

This report will describe the initial design of this program with particular attention to the role of "volunteers" (i.e., students whose elective participation is not formally linked to credit-bearing course assignments) from John Carroll University's environmental studies concentration. I will also discuss how the program has evolved over the past few years in response to feedback from past programs. Finally, I will describe our plans for the future and discuss how we will continue to make service-learning a key component of this project.

I wish to acknowledge the efforts of the many people who have made this project possible: Dr. Dean Birch and Dr. Edwin Skoch, of John Carroll University; Ms. Lin Bartle, of the Steamship William G. Mather Museum; the teachers and staff of the Cleveland Public Schools; and the many volunteers from John Carroll University and the museum.

Community Service at John Carroll University

As a Jesuit liberal arts institution, John Carroll University stresses the importance of community service. Its mission statement emphasizes the use of
knowledge in the service of others. To advance the role of service at our institution, John Carroll created the position of director of community service,
which has been filled by Mark Falbo. Over the past couple of years, he has
devoted a great deal of time to increasing the number of service opportunities in the environmental area. There has long been an active student environmental group on campus, Student Advocates for the Environment (SAFE),
which has been running a recycling program and some environmental education programs. But over the past few years, Dr. Falbo and I have been
developing other possibilities for them. Students work with a variety of nonprofit organizations such as the Clean Air Conservancy (formerly Inhale), the
Earth Day Coalition, Shaker Lakes Nature Center, and SEED Ohio (Sustainable Energy for Economic Development); Clean-Land Ohio; and the Cuyahoga National Recreation Area. In the fall of 1997, Dr. Falbo began hiring a
work study student, whose specific responsibility is to coordinate environmental service.

Since then, two new programs have been implemented. The first is a trip
to Maine, where the university students work on various service projects for
two weeks in Acadia National Park. The second program, initiated in the fall
of 1997, is called Student Helpers and Advocates for a Renewed Earth
(SHARE). In this after-school program, student volunteers from John Carroll
University work with middle school students on an examination of satellite
images to analyze the impacts of urban sprawl.

We also assume that service is most valuable to the undergraduate volunteers if they are learning as they serve. Thus, Dr. Falbo has worked dili-
gently over the past few years to increase the number of courses that incorporate service-learning into their curriculum. Many of these courses count
for credit toward the environmental studies concentration, which has been
a strong supporter of service-learning. We see service projects as a valuable
way for our students to develop knowledge and skills that complement the
learning in the classroom. Currently, a new concentration in community service is being organized around courses that incorporate this principle. A few
brief examples from my own courses will illustrate this approach.

While not a part of the environmental studies concentration, Sociology
111, Introduction to Community Service, is elected by many environmental
studies students. This course discusses the various factors that have led to
a decline in our sense of community and suggests service as a means of ini-
tiating change. Those students who pursue environmental service learn to
expand their definition of community. They develop a greater sense of con-

nectedness to other species. They also discuss in a final paper how their service has promoted social and environmental justice.

Three other environmental courses also specifically incorporate service. Appalachian Regional Issues is a summer course that travels through Central Appalachia for two weeks examining social and environmental issues in the region. When it was first offered, students said that they would like the course to include a service component. In subsequent years, we have worked for a day with the Christian Appalachian Project. This gives students a sense of connectedness to the region, and many have said this day was one of the best parts of the course. In Energy and Society, students have developed an energy education program, which was presented at elementary schools in the area. Finally, a new course, Applied Environmental Sociology, has been developed to meet the needs expressed by many students for a greater understanding of how to implement change. In this course, they study how to change attitudes and behavior as well as social structures, while facilitating such change through environmental service in the surrounding community. Students can work with any of a variety of local nonprofits or they can develop their own environmental education programs. Students can work in groups to develop such a program, and there is a class project geared toward solving an environmental problem at John Carroll University (e.g., paper reduction on campus).

Indeed, many of our students seek additional opportunities to pursue environmental education. Such opportunities are provided through a program that we run each spring aboard the steamship *The William G. Mather.*

The Mather Project

Background

In 1991, the International Joint Commission recommended that the Great Lakes states and provinces incorporate the Great Lakes ecosystem as a priority topic in existing school curricula. In addition, the U.S. Environmental Protection Agency has argued that there is a need for special outreach programs that target minorities, the urban poor, and Native Americans. We have combined these two recommendations in an environmental education program that focuses on the Great Lakes and is geared primarily toward Cleveland inner-city students.

When we designed this program, we had several goals. First, we wanted a program that focused on ecology and the impact of population and industrial growth on the quality of the lake. But we also wanted to foster a sense of place and a knowledge of local resources. Furthermore, we wanted to instill in public school students an awareness of the social, political, and economic underpinnings of our environmental problems. We wanted them to learn about the role of federal, state, and local governmental organizations in protecting the lake and how people can influence decision-making processes. Finally, we wanted a program that could promote critical thinking and the motivation to solve problems, particularly through the use of cooperative, collaborative, and experiential learning strategies. Our specific instructional objectives were drawn from the State of Ohio's curriculum guidelines for seventh grade students.

Beginning in the spring of 1994, this program, "Living at the Edge: Exploring Our North Coast Heritage" (or, informally, the Mather Project), was initiated at the Steamship William G. Mather Museum on the shores of Lake Erie. The program was a joint effort of John Carroll University, the Mather Museum staff, and Cleveland Public Schools. In the first year of the program, 48 seventh grade students from two Cleveland public schools participated. Students came to the Mather Museum one day per week for four consecutive weeks.

Course Description

Learning activities consisted of lectures, problem-solving simulations, specimen identification, videos, water sampling, and debates. The activities were conducted by John Carroll University faculty and undergraduate student volunteers and the Mather Museum staff. Preparation for the program and supporting classroom work was handled by teachers and staff from the public school system.

At the beginning of the course, the public school students were led on a tour of *The Mather,* an old ore boat permanently docked in Cleveland, which now serves as a museum. On the tour, they learned about life on the boat but also about the ship's earlier role in the development of the region. *The Mather* carried ore from the northern Great Lakes to Cleveland for use in industry. During their tour, the students were also asked to make visual observations about the lake as it appears today.

Following this introduction, and into the next week, the middle school students were introduced to basic issues of the ecology of Lake Erie. They tested water samples; they learned about predators and their prey; and they learned some of the basic taxonomic groups in the lake. They were also introduced to relevant social science issues. To help them understand the impact of human populations on the lakes, two simulations were employed. The first, "Are We a Crowd," divided the youngsters into groups on a large map of the lakes. They were concentrated around the lakes on both the American and the Canadian sides in proportion to the actual concentrations of population. Students were given pieces of candy in proportion to the amount of water used from each of the lakes, and were told to eat them and throw the wrappers on the floor. When they stood back, they could see a visual representation of the impact of population concentrations. Here we also discussed *why* certain lakes had larger concentrations of people.

The second simulation, "Use or Abuse," had the public school students take on roles of people around the lakes. These ranged from city government officials, to farmers, to individuals who have leaky septic systems. Each student had to resolve a value conflict in which he or she was forced to choose between stopping pollution of the lake or continuing to pollute while saving money. If they chose to pollute, they added food color or dirt to a tank of water with a Secchi disk at the bottom. They soon came to realize the cumulative impact of all of these seemingly harmless individual decisions.

Students were next introduced to the role that city governments play in decision making through a speech by a local mayor. He discussed the responsibilities of cities, but also made students understand the conflicts of interests that many politicians face. The program exposed the youngsters to the role of individuals in this process in a component dealing with the Remedial Action Plan (RAP) established by the International Joint Commission. The head of the Cuyahoga RAP taught the students about the identification of special "areas of concern" around all of the Great Lakes and discussed the role that citizens have played in identifying solutions to the serious pollution in these areas.

The heart of the course, however, was a debate about possibilities for future development near the lake. Here we attempted to incorporate principles of collaborative learning by having students work together in groups to prepare for the debate.

In this first year, the organizing issue for the debate was the hypothetical development of an oil refinery on the lakefront. The public school students were divided into groups representing six different special interests: the oil company, the city, the Ohio EPA, Greenpeace, recreation, and Canadian fisheries. We divided up the students from the two schools so that an equal number of students from each school was placed into each of these interest groups.

Service and Learning in the Mather Project

In order to meet all of the goals of this program, we decided from the very beginning that we would use undergraduate volunteers from John Carroll University to work with the public school students. The selection of volunteers during the first few years was very informal. In the first year, we worked with about six volunteers. Several were recruited from the Introduction to Community Service course. Others were recruited from an Environmental Politics and Policy course, as well as from the Biology Department. Prior to the start of the course, these volunteers made site visits to the schools that would be participating in the program. This accomplished two things: By meeting the John Carroll volunteers, the public school students could feel more at ease when they came to the Mather Museum. But for most of the volunteers, this visit was an eye-opener, in that it was the first time they had ever been to an inner-city school.

The John Carroll volunteers participated in the program in a variety of ways. During the first two days, biology majors who were pursuing an environmental studies concentration worked with Dr. Edwin Skoch, of the Biology Department, to introduce the middle school students to the ecology of Lake Erie. Here the volunteers were often forced to brush up on topics they had already covered in aquatic ecology and other courses. More important, they had to learn to organize and present material, a skill many had had little chance to practice.

The most critical dimension of the involvement of the John Carroll University volunteers, however, occurred in their work with the middle school students in the debate on future lake development. In the first year, one volunteer was assigned to each interest group to act as a debate coach. He or she was responsible for researching a particular interest group (the city, Ohio EPA, etc.) prior to the beginning of the program. The volunteers used this information in two ways. First, they gave information to the public school teachers in order to provide them with background material for their classes. Second, they used this information to help prepare the public school students for the debate.

On the first day dealing with social science issues, the seventh graders, randomly assigned to interest groups, rotated among the volunteers, and each of the volunteers gave a general overview of his or her interest group. Thus, each group of seventh graders was introduced to the perspectives of all the interest groups. Subsequently, each volunteer spent additional time with one particular group of students (e.g., the Canadian fisheries group). The John Carroll volunteers helped their groups to gain a more in-depth understanding of their interests and to prepare for the final debate. This occurred at the end of the four weeks, and in it each of the interest groups attempted to present an argument that supported its views while anticipating the arguments of other groups.

Evolution of the Program

After this first year, the staff recognized a few shortcomings and some difficulties, which we have since attempted to remedy. One of the first things we decided to change was the length of the program. Visiting *The Mather* for four weeks meant that schools incurred additional costs, especially for transportation and substitutes. It was also difficult to recruit college volunteers because the time commitment interfered with their other classes.

Beginning in the second year of the program (1995), we shortened the course to three weeks. We also decided to expand the number of schools that could participate to include two Cleveland public schools and one suburban school. Since some rivalries had developed between the students from the different schools during the first year, we only had one school participate on each day. (That is, one school would come on Tuesday, one on Wednesday, and one on Thursday for three consecutive weeks.) We also limited the number of students on any given day to 24. These students were divided up into four interest groups for the debate.

We also decided that we would accommodate the John Carroll volunteers by running the program after finals. From one perspective, this was beneficial — the volunteers had no other constraints on their time. On the other hand, volunteers could no longer be recruited from courses. This, we believe, weakened the learning dimension for the John Carroll students. This did not mean that our volunteers were not learning at all; it simply reflected our assumption that students learn best when they can reflect upon their experiences, as they did in the Introduction to Community Service papers. Such reflection is facilitated by a course connection.

In the third and fourth years (1996, 1997), we returned to our original idea of running the program during the John Carroll University semester, while retaining the three-week format. The program had become very popular and had a very good reputation among the John Carroll students, so we decided we would accommodate more volunteers by having two debate coaches for each of the four interest groups. We also accommodated more volunteers by having each work for only one day per week. Of course, they worked with the same school for all three weeks, so that they would develop rapport with the public school students.

All of this meant that we had to coordinate nearly two-dozen volunteers. This was difficult, because we wanted them to be at *The Mather* on days when they had no classes (or at least on those days when they had the fewest classes). While other faculty were generally supportive of their students' involvement in the program, we did not want to interfere with the volunteers' academic responsibilities.

The biggest change, however, occurred with regard to the focus of the debate. We wanted the problem debated to have a more realistic basis. Hence, in the spring of 1996, we decided to examine issues related to development of the site of the old Cleveland Municipal Stadium.

Following the departure of the Cleveland Browns for Baltimore, Cleveland officials negotiated a commitment from the National Football League for a new team, on the condition that Cleveland would build a new stadium. While we were planning the third year's program, there was significant public debate about where to locate the new stadium. For the purposes of this course, we focused on what would be the best use of the old stadium site. We organized the public school students around three broad ideas: to use the old site for a park, the new stadium, or a high-rise complex with marina. A fourth group represented regulatory interests. Those who represented the three proposals had to look at the potential environmental, economic, and social impacts of their plan. The regulatory group had to decide which of the three proposals it would back.

In this third year (1996), we also began to exercise more oversight over the volunteers. We asked them to pull together their research earlier in the semester so that we could give a packet to the public school teachers during an orientation that we held several weeks before the beginning of the program. This would enable the teachers to begin to incorporate materials into their lesson plans.

The volunteers now had a chance to explore their interests in much more detail. There read articles in local papers about some of the development issues, but they also began to explore the experience of other cities with waterfront projects: Boston, Baltimore (ironically), San Diego, etc. They could also explore how well different types of developments had worked in other cities. For example, the volunteers who represented the park plan thought at first that they would have the most trouble convincing people of their viewpoint. As they explored the issue, however, they found that parks in large cities could also have a positive economic impact. Restaurants and other businesses often grow up on the fringes of such parks. This sort of information broadened everyone's understanding of the complexities involved in development decisions, and it illustrates how the John Carroll volunteers were learning while they served.

In year four (1997), we broadened our approach to development issues, to focus on suburban sprawl versus urban renewal. We took a real-world proposal for a Wal-Mart complex in an outlying town and juxtaposed it with a hypothetical proposal for a similar development on the lakefront in downtown Cleveland. We worked closely with the county planning commission. Again, we required the college students to have their materials together very early in the semester. This permitted us to work with the schoolteachers to integrate the program into their curriculum. In addition to the work the public school students did at *The Mather,* they did much more work in their classes. Water testing was conducted at the stream closest to each of the schools. This allowed us to compare the pollution of the lake from suburban as well as downtown sources.

Beginning in year four, we also initiated more follow-up in the schools. Students there now have a homework assignment — visiting a parking lot at a large mall in their area following a rainstorm in order to observe the lot's impact on runoff. In addition, the youngsters work with a member of the local Cuyahoga Remedial Action Plan on a stormdrain stenciling program. All of these activities advance their understanding of their connection to the lake.

Proposals for the Future

Our pedagogical goals have become more ambitious as the program has matured. In addition to promoting a sense of caring about the environment, we want to develop a greater sense among all of the students, both from the public schools and from John Carroll, of their interconnectedness with other people in the area. We also want to instill in them a greater sense of their responsibility for the overall environmental health of the region.

This necessitates that we work more closely with the schoolteachers to have them incorporate this project even more specifically into the curriculum of the participating schools. Toward this end, our Spring 1998 volunteers worked primarily on helping the teachers to incorporate this program into their curriculum. Part of the work for volunteers drawn from our Applied Environmental Sociology course was to research one of the interest groups for the 1998 program in order to gather information for the teachers to use in their classroom. Volunteers also visited the schools and carried out some specific activities with the school students. The most important of these activities was water quality testing, which was conducted several times throughout the semester.

One final change is the development of an internship that we hope to implement in year six. We would like to use one of our senior environmental studies students to coordinate the volunteers, assist in their training and research, and lead the program at *The Mather,* including running the simulations, and so on. We believe that this would be an excellent opportunity for a student to develop valuable skills that complement the academic component of our environmental studies concentration.

Concluding Remarks

Service and learning are both essential aspects of this program. They are essential for several reasons: First, the John Carroll volunteers can impart basic knowledge about environmental issues that they have learned through their coursework in our environmental studies program. In addition, the way in which our volunteers coach the public school students for the debate helps these seventh graders to develop their own critical abilities. Finally, the participation of John Carroll volunteers allows us to pursue a cooperative, collaborative pedagogy by making it possible for us to have the seventh graders work in small groups. At the same time, the college students benefit from brushing up on basic environmental knowledge they may have gained earlier in their college careers. For those interested in pursuing environmental education — and there are many of these — the program introduces techniques and skills they can employ in working with younger students. Volunteers also learn a wide variety of other skills: organizing and presenting information, interpersonal skills, and the like. Thus, participation in this program clearly enhances the education of the John Carroll student participants.

We have found this to be such a valuable experience for everyone concerned that we hope to develop other, similar programs in the near future. We have been talking with the local Audubon Society chapter about the possibility of new programs focused on wetlands. We have also had preliminary discussions with the Chagrin River Watershed Project about a similar program focusing on a different watershed. Our students may also begin to work more closely with SEED Ohio and the Ohio Energy Project on energy education in the public schools. We believe that opportunities such as these serve to enhance the education of the students in our concentration.

References

Diffenderfer, M., and J. Earle. (1996). "The Role of Bioregional Education in Fostering Water Quality Awareness: A Case Study of the Mather Project." In *Our Natural Environment: Concepts and Solutions, Proceedings of the Second International Interdisciplinary Conference on the Environment,* Newport, RI, June 15-19, edited by Kevin Hickey and Demetri Katarelif, pp. 115-122. Worcester, MA: Assumption College.

Diffenderfer, M., and J. Earle. (Forthcoming). "Fostering a Sense of Place: Bioregional Education in Theory and Practice." *International Journal of Environmental Education and Information.*

International Joint Commission. (1991). *Great Lakes Environmental Education.* Special Report. Detroit, MI: International Joint Commission.

Afterword

by Peter Blaze Corcoran

> *A society is a number of people held together because they are working along common lines, in a common spirit, and with reference to common aims. The common needs and aims demand a growing interchange of thought and growing unity of sympathetic feeling. The radical reason that the present school cannot organize itself as a natural social unit is because just this element of common and productive activity is absent.*
>
> — John Dewey (1899: 39)

The "common and productive activity" that builds society is best learned in school, Dewey believed. One hundred years ago he wrote, "the tragic weakness of the present school is that it endeavors to prepare future members of the social order in a medium in which the conditions of the social spirit are eminently wanting" (1899: 39).

He concluded the first of his famed three lectures on "The School and Society" by saying

> *When the school introduces and trains each child of society into membership within such a little community, saturating him with the spirit of service, and providing him with the instruments of effective self-direction, we shall have the deepest and best guarantee of a larger society which is worthy, lovely, and harmonious.* (49)

This social spirit, this "spirit of service," learned in community and applied in the academy, is alive and well in the recrudescence of Deweyan philosophy seen in today's service-learning.

The kind of discipline-based service-learning discussed in this volume represents a commitment to common, productive activity and is an expression of social spirit so much needed if we are to reconstruct community on campus and reconnect with the torn communities surrounding campus. Just as important, these programs are pedagogically sound. This volume provides a much-needed explication of service-learning as it is defined in practice at certain colleges. The opportunity to see various definitions play out in descriptive narratives of the academic and experiential goals of those college programs provides a way to view their educational value. These nar-

---

Peter Blaze Corcoran is former president of the North American Association for Environmental Education (NAAEE) and professor of environmental studies and environment education at Florida Gulf Coast University.

ratives allow us to see the various definitions of service-learning as related to active student research.

In 1929, Alfred North Whitehead said in his great essay "The Rhythmic Claims of Freedom and Discipline" that we need to apply such learning:

> [E]ducation should begin in research and end in research. After all, the whole affair is merely a preparation for battling with the immediate experiences of life, a preparation by which to qualify each immediate moment with relevant ideas and appropriate actions. An education which does not begin by evoking initiative and end by encouraging it must be wrong. For its whole aim is the production of active wisdom. (37)

Such "active wisdom" in the form of service-learning is no stranger to environmental studies. Since the founding of the first program, at Antioch College in 1968, application of environmental understanding to practical problems has been the rule rather than the exception.

This is consistent with the definition of environmental education that holds that awareness and knowledge are necessary but not sufficient for informed citizenship. In order to achieve effectiveness, education about the environment must be brought into the realm of values and action — into Dewey's "community," into Whitehead's "research." Service-learning in environmental studies fulfills a long-standing definition of environmental education much hailed, but little achieved, in higher education.

The most widely accepted definition of environmental education, adopted at the world's first Intergovernmental Conference on Environmental Education, convened in 1977 at Tbilisi, Georgia, also includes the attitudes, skills, and participation to provide social groups and individuals with an opportunity to be involved actively in identifying and solving environmental problems. The work of students and professors portrayed in this volume is entirely consistent with a three-decades-long effort to move higher education to action on behalf of the environmental concerns of scientists and students. Further, it is essential that we have models of a diversity of ways to accomplish this — both direct and indirect ways, as Harold Ward calls them, and case studies, field studies, action research.

The programs in this volume represent best practice in environmental education and a hope that higher education can equip its graduates with the awareness, knowledge, values, attitudes, and skills to effect the resolution of environmental problems through community action research. The work described is also a step in the direction of the significant new reinterpretation of environmental education as education for sustainability. Indeed, perhaps the most encouraging aspect of this volume is its embodiment of institutional responsibility-taking toward a sustainable environment.

An enormous problem for society is created by the failure of American higher education to accept moral responsibility for the relationship between people and the environment. The need to develop effective education for sustainability in the liberal studies remains largely unmet. The urgency to develop action research capable of resolving ecosystem-threatening environmental problems is increasing. The questions for us in the academy are: Can we change education and research about the human relationship to environments, particularly the natural systems upon which life depends, so that such efforts can become a priority? Can we learn a "spirit of service" to the environment? Can we educate for "active wisdom" in service to sustainability?

Tony Cortese, in an essay entitled "The Role of Higher Education in Achieving a Sustainable Society" (1995), wrote:

> Society has conveyed a special charter on institutions of higher learning. Within the United States, they are allowed academic freedom and tax-free status to receive public and private resources in exchange for their contribution to the health and well-being of society through the creation and dissemination of knowledge and values. Higher education institutions bear a profound moral responsibility to increase the awareness, knowledge, skills, and values needed to create a just and sustainable future. These institutions have the mandate and potential to develop intellectual and conceptual framework for achieving this goal. They must play a strong role in education, research, policy development, information exchange and community outreach and support. The 3,500 institutions of higher education in the United States are significant but largely overlooked leverage points in the transition to a sustainable world — they influence future leaders through their students and current leaders through their alumni. They have the unique freedom to develop new ideas, comment on society, and engage in bold experimentation, as well as contribute to the creation of new knowledge. (5)

Do institutions of higher education exercise this freedom and accept this responsibility? In a recent paper given at the symposium "Academic Planning in College and University Environmental Programs," on the campus of Florida Gulf Coast University, David Orr (1998) said:

> [R]elative to the magnitude of the challenges ahead, the inescapable fact is that 20-25 years of dedicated and often visionary work to build environment into the curriculum have not dented the problem. Higher education goes on much as it has for a century or more but now with computers. In the face of impending problems and potential catastrophes, the response of colleges and universities is generally lethargic. As a result, despite the growth in numbers of environmental studies programs, most college and university graduates are fundamentally ignorant about ecology, global

environmental change, and why these things ought to matter to them. Why have institutions of higher education — of all organizations — been so complacent in the face of mounting evidence that humanity is in real jeopardy of mutilating its earthly home? This is not, on the surface at least, what one might expect of institutions dedicated to advancing knowledge and presumably to the health of the world their students will inherit. (2)

Within this context of peculiar resistance to what might be the great problem of our age, the community and the active wisdom of service-learning become all the more significant. The work presented here in its breadth and in its commonality is the first collection to my knowledge demonstrating service-learning as practiced in light of this great need to put the disciplines in service to the resolution of environmental problems. In this volume, we see the making of ecologically literate citizens committed to the resolution of community environmental problems. Environmental studies in general and service-learning in environmental studies in particular offer the hopeful possibility of showing higher education a path to engaged ecological literacy, of showing a way to accept responsibility for our earthly community.

References

Cortese, Tony. (1995). "The Role of Higher Education in Achieving a Sustainable Society." Washington, DC: President's Council on Sustainable Development.

Dewey, John. (1899). "The School and Society." Chicago, IL: University of Chicago Press.

Orr, David. (1998). "Transformation or Irrelevance: The Challenge of Academic Planning for Environmental Education in the 21st Century." Address given at "Academic Planning in College and University Environmental Programs" Symposium, March 4-8, 1998. Florida Gulf Coast University, Fort Myers, FL.

Whitehead, Alfred North. (1929). *The Aims of Education*. New York, NY: Free Press.

Appendix

Annotated Bibliography

Alliance for Service-Learning in Education Reform. (1993). "Standards of Quality for School-Based Service-Learning." *Equity and Excellence in Education* 26(2): 71-73.

Ten clearly stated standards for evaluating a service-learning course.

Barber, B.R., and R. Battistoni. (1993). "A Season of Service: Introducing Service-Learning Into the Liberal Arts Curriculum." *PS: Political Science and Politics* 16(2): 235-240.

This article explores the choices that need to be made when a school considers developing a service-learning program. The authors address 10 questions, including choices of making the program mandatory or not, credit or not, single- or multi-course, individual or team-based, whether students should be part of the planning process, and whether the community should be "client" or "partner in education."

Batchelder, T.H., and S. Root. (1994). "Effects of an Undergraduate Program to Integrate Academic Learning and Service: Cognitive, Prosocial Cognitive, and Identity Outcomes." *Journal of Adolescence* 17: 341-355.

The research done tested the effects of the service-learning experience on the students. Responses were made before and after the experience, and journals were kept along with self-evaluations. Students had significant gains, particularly in areas such as an awareness of multidimensionality. Gains were significantly higher than in students only in the classroom.

Bringle, R.G., and J.A Hatcher. (1996). "Implementing Service-Learning in Higher Education." *Journal of Higher Education* 67(2): 221-239.

A helpful statement of the goals of a service-learning course.

Dillon, P.W., and R. Van Riper. (1993). "Students Teaching Students: A Model for Service and Study." *Equity and Excellence in Education* 26(2): 48-52.

This article is built on an example of service-learning, that of the Berkshire Energy Project at Williams College. The focus is on the students doing the planning of the project and teaching one another the necessary information and skills. The article focuses on the benefits to both students and the community of the service-learning approach.

Galura, Joseph, and Rachael Meiland. (1993). *PRAXIS II: Service-Learning Resources for University Students, Staff, and Faculty*. Ann Arbor, MI: OCSL Press.

This book is part of a two-part series funded by a grant from the Kellogg Foundation. It was written by 18 faculty members in 14 different disciplines at the University of Michigan. Part two of the series features the work of selected University of Michigan students and staff, who describe ways to incorporate community service into an academic institution as a way to enhance academic learning. Examples include coordinating student site work with seminar opportunities for reflection, as well as relevant readings, use of journals, discussions, and integrative papers combining the service in the community with a combination of intentional and varied opportunities for reflection. The authors offer guiding principles for those in the roles of coordinator, trainer, and supervisor and for evaluation. This volume serves to inform, add credibility to, and strengthen academic valuing of community service-learning within the academic culture. It describes how to develop a successful task force to promote these efforts on campuses, and vital public relations and human resources to develop and support community service-learning opportunities. It offers clear rationale for integrating opportunities into a curriculum and details, including course outlines, demonstrating how to incorporate service-learning into the class, with examples from case studies drawing from after-school tutoring programs in education and county jail involvement in criminal justice courses.

Harkavy, Ira, and John Puckett. (Summer 1995). "Lessons From Hull-House for the Contemporary Urban University." *Service* 1:9-20.

This excellent article documents the historical basis for the service part of the traditional research/teaching/service triad on which U.S. institutions of higher education are based. It is useful to distribute to administrators who have come to believe that service is no more than membership on a university committee.

Hem, John D. (1985). "Study and Interpretation of the Chemical Characteristics of Natural Water." U.S. Geological Survey, Water-Supply Paper 2254. 3d ed. Washington, DC: U.S. Government Printing Office.

A guide to the "normal" concentrations of chemicals in natural waters in the United States. Can be used at all levels, to compare local chemistry with that elsewhere, or to help understand geochemical reactions and controls in aqueous systems.

Hubbard, A., and C. Fong. (1995). *Community Energy Workbook: A Guide to Building a Sustainable Economy.* Snowmass, CO: Rocky Mountain Institute.

The energy handbook is one of several "how-to" books prepared by the Rocky Mountain Institute. It is a good guide for doing community service-learning and can been used successfully as a kind of textbook. Its pages of tables and activities are ideal for students because they provide clear directions for seeking information, in this case for the purpose of developing a town energy plan.

Land Trust Alliance. (1997). *The Standards and Practices Guidebook: An Operating Manual for Land Trusts.* Washington, DC: The Land Trust Alliance.

Presents the standard operating procedure for land trusts, with types of data of interest and other pertinent information.

Lempert, David C. (1996). *Escape From the Ivory Tower.* San Francisco, CA: Jossey-Bass Publishers.

This book describes programs that take students out of the classroom to connect what they learn with issues of community. It details an experiential education approach that combines discussion and interaction, field learning and laboratory work, community involvement and service, democratic citizenship, and skills training as well as student-initiated learning — in projects, courses, and clinical programs from across the disciplines. Offered are pragmatic solutions to problems and implementation strategies, along with detailed descriptions of courses at different universities.

Meadows, Dennis L., and Amy Seif. (1996). "Creating High-Performance Teams for Sustainable Development — 58 Initiatives." Durham, NH: Laboratory for Interactive Learning, University of New Hampshire.

This text provides detailed instructions and overhead slide originals for introducing, conducting, and debriefing 58 initiatives and games that help team members learn the skills required for more-effective collaboration. The exercises are classified by the team attribute they address: trust, vision, problem solving, conflict resolution, and related dimensions.

Mitchell, M.K., and William B. Stapp. (1996). *Field Manual for Water Quality Monitoring: An Environmental Education Program for Schools.* 10th ed. Dubuque, IA: Kendall/Hunt Publishing.

A guide to standard protocols for water sampling and analysis. Primarily intended for use at the 9-12 level, and with a focus on water quality in rivers and streams.

National Research Council. (1992). *Restoration of Aquatic Ecosystems: Science, Technology, and Public Policy.* Washington, DC: National Academy Press.
General information on restoration of aquatic ecosystems, including lakes, streams, rivers, and wetlands. Includes case studies and discussion.

Pallant, E. (1996). "Assessment and Evaluation of Environmental Problems: Teaching Students to Think for Themselves." *Journal of College Science Teaching* 26:167-171.
This article describes a course required of all sophomore environmental science and studies majors at Allegheny College. The course lies between the introductory survey and the junior seminar in service-learning. It is taught with equal success by social scientists and natural scientists and is essential to teaching our students the fundamental techniques of critical analysis they need to be successful in research and when working in communities beyond the classroom.

Phillips, Steven L., and Robin L. Elledge. (1989). *The Team Building Source Book.* San Francisco, CA: Jossey-Bass/Pfeiffer.
The sourcebook is designed for those who conduct training sessions with teams that wish to become more successful. It includes materials for 11 complete mini-courses related to clarifying roles, conflict management, problem solving, and other basic skills.

Potvin, J., and L. Bacon. (1996). "Standard Field Methods for Lake Water Quality Monitoring." Maine Department of Environmental Protection, Publication number DEPLW-4-A96. Augusta, ME.
A guide of standard methodology for lake water quality monitoring written for volunteers. This presents simple and inexpensive (for the most part) techniques for getting the necessary data.

Appendix
Contributors to This Volume

Janice Alexander
Chemistry Instructor
Flathead Valley Community College
Department of Chemistry and Environmental Science,
777 Grandview Drive, Kalispell, MT 59901
406/756-3948
jalexand@fvcc.cc.mt.us
www.fvcc.cc.mt.us/~jalexand.html

Peter Bloch
Professor of Radiation Physics
University of Pennsylvania School of Medicine

Curtis Bohlen
Assistant Professor
Bates College
Environmental Studies Program, Carnegie Science Hall, Rm. 214,
44 Campus Avenue, Lewiston, ME 04240
207/786-8315
cbohlen@bates.edu

F. Russell Cole
Oak Professor of Biological Science
Colby College
5728 Mayflower Hill Drive, Department of Biology, Waterville, ME 04901
207/872-3324
frcole@colby.edu

Walter Cressler
Student, Graduate Arts & Sciences
University of Pennsylvania
Department of Geology, Hayden Hall, Philadelphia, PA 19104
215/898-5630
cressler@sas.upenn.edu

Mark Diffenderfer
Associate Professor of Sociology and Codirector,
Environmental Studies Concentration
John Carroll University
Department of Sociology, University Heights, OH 44118
mdiff@jcu.edu
www1.jcu.edu/SOCIO/diffend/envst/envsthom.htm

John Elder
Stewart Professor of English and Environmental Studies
Middlebury College
Middlebury, VT 05753
802/443-5281
elder@middlebury.edu
www.middlebury.edu/~es/

Calvin Fred Exoo
Professor and Chair, Government Department, and
Director of Service-Learning
St. Lawrence University
Government Department, Hepburn Hall, Canton, NY 13617
315/229-5219
fexo@ccmaillink.stlawu.edu
www.stlawu.edu

David H. Firmage
Piper Professor of Environmental Studies
Colby College
Department of Biology, Waterville, ME 04901
207/872-3319
dhfirmag@COLBY.EDU
www.colby.edu/biology/BI493/BI493.html

Alanah Fitch
Professor of Chemistry and Director of Environmental Studies/Sciences
Loyola University of Chicago
Flanner Hall 402 E, 6525 N. Sheridan Road, Chicago, IL 60626
773/508-3119
afitch@luc.edu
www.luc.edu/depts/chem/fitchgroup/drfitchs.html

Orin G. Gelderloos
Professor of Biological Sciences, Professor of Environmental Studies,
and Director of Natural Areas
University of Michigan-Dearborn
Department of Natural Sciences, Dearborn, MI 48128-1491
313/593-5339
ogg@umd.umich.edu

Robert Giegengack
Professor of Geology and Director, Institute for Environmental Studies
University of Pennsylvania
Department of Earth and Environmental Science, 240 S. 33rd Street,
Philadelphia, PA 19104-6316
215/573-3164; (215) 898-5191
rgiegeng@sas.upenn.edu
www.sas.upenn.edu/geology/

James F. Hornig
Professor of Chemistry and Environmental Studies, Emeritus
Dartmouth College
6182 Steele Hall, Hanover, NH 03755
(603) 646-2033
James.F.Hornig@dartmouth.edu
www.dartmouth.edu/
www.dartmouth.edu//projects_envs50.html

Thomas R. Hudspeth
Associate Professor, Environmental Interpretation/Education
University of Vermont
Environmental Program and School of Natural Resources,
153 S. Prospect, Burlington, VT 05401
802/656-4055
thudspet@nature.snr.uvm.edu

Nan Jenks-Jay
(previously Hedco Professor of Environmental Studies at
University of Redlands)
Director of Environmental Affairs and Planning
Middlebury College
Farrell House, Middlebury, VT 05753
802/443-5090
jenksjay@middlebury.edu

Katrina Smith Korfmacher
Assistant Professor of Environmental Studies
Denison University
Environmental Studies Program, Granville, OH 43023
740/587-5707
korfmacher@denison.edu
www.denison.edu/enviro

Christopher McGrory Klyza
Associate Professor of Political Science and
Program in Environmental Studies
Middlebury College
Middlebury, VT 05753
802/443-5309
klyza@middlebury.edu

Alison S. Lathrop
Assistant Professor of Earth Sciences
Millersville University of Pennsylvania
717/872-3288
alathrop@maraudev.millerv.edu
www.millerv.edu/~esci/

Jim Northrup
Part-Time Lecturer in Environmental Studies and
Principal, Ad Hoc Associates
Middlebury College
Middlebury, VT 05753
802/223-3216
jnorthrup@together.net

Lois K. Ongley
Assistant Professor
Bates College
Department of Geology and Environmental Studies Program,
Carnegie Science Hall, Rm. 214, 44 Campus Avenue, Lewiston, ME 04240
207/786-6154
longley@bates.edu
www.bates.edu/acad/depts/geology

Eric Pallant
Associate Professor of Environmental Science and Codirector,
Center for Economic and Environmental Development
Allegheny College
Box E, Meadville, PA 16335
814/332-2870
epallant@alleg.edu
webpub.alleg.edu/employee/e/epallant

Joanne Piesieski
Student, College of Arts & Sciences
c/o University of Pennsylvania
Philadelphia, PA 19104
215/222-0753
piesiesk@sas.upenn.edu

Aron Reppmann
Assistant Professor of Philosophy
Trinity Christian College
6601 West College Drive, Palos Heights, IL 60463
708/239-4750
aron.reppmann@trnty.edu

John Schmidt
Executive Director
Chicago Do Something
1650 W. Foster, Chicago, IL 60640
773/728-7150
jonadine@mindspring.com

Stephen Trombulak
Professor of Biology and Director, Program in Environmental Studies
Middlebury College
Middlebury, VT 05753
802/443-5439
trombulak@middlebury.edu

Harold R. Ward
Lindemann Professor of Environmental Studies and Professor of Chemistry
Brown University
Box 1943, Providence, RI 02912
401/863-3449
Harold_Ward@brown.edu
www.brown.edu/Departments/Environmental_Studies/

Candie C. Wilderman
Associate Professor of Environmental Science
Dickinson College
Carlisle, PA 17013
717/245-1573
wilderma@dickinson.edu
www.dickinson.edu/departments/envsc
www.dickinson.edu/storg/allarm